The Clip Art Image Library™

The Clip Art Image Library™
Published by Walnut Creek CDROM
Suite 260, 1547 Palos Verdes Mall,
Walnut Creek CA 94596, USA
• sales +1-800-786-9907 • technical support +1-800-731-7177
• Fax +1-510-674-0821 • info@cdrom.com • http://www.cdrom.com/

Cover Design: Greg Long

Printed in the United States of America

0 9 8 7 6 5 4 3 2

ISBN 1-57176-083-0

Related Titles

If you like this CDROM, you'll enjoy these too!

Clipart Cornucopia™
000 Clipart images to use in your newsletters, greeting cards, and more.

Raytrace! The Official POV-RAY CDROM
A beautiful collection of POV-Ray images, plus programs to create your own images.

Visions Series
0 royalty free stock photographs from the Preferred Stock Photo Agency. Each disc includes a full color booklet. 10 Categories and growing.

Travel Adventure
95 royalty free photographs from around the world, color booklet included.

Fractal Frenzy
000s of fractals including examples of all the major types of Mandlebrot.

Fractal Frenzy II
A collection of 2127 images by eight renowned fractal artists.

000 True Type Fonts
000 True Type Fonts and 5000 Clipart Images in PCX format.

Font Garden
00 Professional quality fonts in both Truetype and Type 1 PostScript. Huge book with each font printed included.

INTRODUCTION

This disc contains public domain and shareware files and programs collected, compiled and catalogued by the Public Domain and Shareware Library (PDSL), Winscombe House, Beacon Road, Crowborough, Sussex TN6 1UL, United Kingdom. Tel +441 892 663 298, Fax +441 892 667 473. This CDROM is produced by Walnut Creek CDROM, 1547 Palos Verdes Mall, Suite 260, Walnut Creek, CA 94596 USA, Tel +1 800-786-9907, Fax +1 510-674-0821.

IMPORTANT

To help you gain the greatest benefit from the programs on this disk PLEASE READ the files READ.ME and MANUAL.TXT which can be found in the root of the CDROM. These contain information on how to use this CDROM and on installing and using shareware programs.

COPYRIGHT

The copyright of all programs on this disk are retained by their original authors. In general, you are encouraged to pass on copies of shareware programs to friends and colleagues but check authors distribution requirements first.

The disk (file) numbering system program and disk descriptions, hardware requirements codes, file descriptions, and material anthology are copyright © 1992/3/4/5 PDSL, whether in printed or machine readable form, and may not be reproduced in any way without written permission from PDSL. PDSL also acknowledges copyright names and trademarks which may be incidentally mentioned in this material.

SHAREWARE

Many of the programs on this CDROM are shareware. This can be considered a “try before you buy” system where you are expected to pay the program author a registration fee if you find his/her program useful. Any payment you have made for this CDROM is entirely separate and does NOT go to program authors and does not reduce your duty to register programs you find useful.

WARNING/DISCLAIMER

Before testing any software, make sure that you have adequate backups of any valuable data or programs that may be on your system. It is possible through inexperience, mistakes, undetected program errors or other causes that you may accidentally delete or corrupt valuable data or programs. Please make sure you have good backups so you won’t be in trouble if something goes wrong. Neither Walnut Creek CDROM or PDSL makes any guarantee as to the suitability of any software of data on this CDROM for any purpose. All software is provided in good faith on an “as-is” basis and no charge has been made for it. Any charges made for this CDROM relate to compilation, copying. general costs and making the material available only. However, the CDROM disk itself is covered by the Walnut Creek unconditional guarantee.

USING THE CDROM

QUICK-START

If you have previous experience and do not require additional instruction, from DOS just log into the root of the CDROM and type **VIEW** Otherwise read on!

CONTENT & DIRECTORY STRUCTURE

The images on this CDROM are organized into categories, each having its own directory. For the most part, categories are subject based, but others are groups of images from a particular author. The registration information for these images will be found in text files in relevant subdirectories. Note that author collections often include a wide variety of subjects.

MONO & COLOR

This CDROM contains a total of some 7000 images, of which 1000 are in color. For some mono DTP uses, these color images may not print well so we have also provided mono grey scale versions. Where color images are available, they are contained in a separate subdirectory. For example, the directory ANIMAL1 has beneath it the subdirectory ANIM1COL which contains the color images. For example, the first image file in ANIMAL1 is C0000083.TIF this is a mono version of the color image in the ANIM1COL subdirectory. A filename beginning with "C" tells you there is a color version available, the filenames beginning with "M" are only available in mono.

IMAGE VIEWING

This CDROM comes with a front end program called VIEW. This will provide you with an easy way to view, copy, and unpack files.

MSDOS:

Change to your CDROM drive and type **VIEW**.

Example:

C:\> **D:**

D:\> **view**

WINDOWS:

1) Start up Windows
2) Choose RUN from the Program Manager File menu to see the RUN dialog box.
3) In the command line box:

If you're running Windows 3.1 or Windows for Workgroups, type:

D:\setup.exe

If you're running Windows NT or Windows 95, type:

D:\setup95.exe

(If the D: drive is not your CDROM drive, change it to the appropriate drive letter.)

4) Click OK to start the installation.

GRAPHICS UTILITIES

2296.ZIP PICLAB is a command-driven image processing system operating on grayscale, color-mapped and true-color images regardless of the display capabilities of the hardware on which it is running.

2307A.ZIP ALCHEMY MINDWORKS GRAPHICS TOOLKIT includes GRAFCAT v3.0d, a graphics cataloguing program producing 16-to-a page printouts (needs Laserjet or Postscript printer). *New version is a complete rewrite, with file selector screen, portrait or landscape printing, and Postscript halftone printing for color or grayscale files*; CINEMA v1.0, a slide show program supporting all image types and graphics displays handled by Graphic Workshop (see vol. 2865); VENTURA FONT MANAGER v1.4 is a menu-driven front end to create width tables for Laserjet soft fonts used with Ventura Publisher; CROPGIF v1.1 allows you to crop fragments from large GIF files to make smaller ones, using a cut & paste type interface; STORYTELLER v1.0 is a mouse-driven hypertext system which includes pictures, proportional serif and sanserif fonts, symbols, special characters, boldface etc.; FILE INVESTIGATOR v1.1 will identify mystery image files, including formats handled by GWS, GEM Metafiles, Coreldraw CDR files etc.; GIFINFO v1.0 is an on-disk GIF cataloguing program which keeps reduced versions of GIF files with relevant data appended; STRTSC v1.0 creates self-displaying COM files from PCX files.

2307B.ZIP Alchemy Graphics Toolkit CropGIF, GIFInfo, StartSc, VFM

2672.ZIP IMAGE ACCESS is a simple database program that associates a graphics image file with each text record, resulting in a database of pictures. Graphics files may be in PCX, MSP or TIFF format. Normal database functions such as sort, search etc. are included. Also prints to Epson LQ family 24-pin, IBM Proprinter X24 series or HP Laserjet printers.

2699.ZIP GRAPHICS UTILITIES MVGAVU, PCXUT, GIF2BMP etc. GRAFIXBUSTERS include ART2IMG convert Fleet Street Publisher/First Publisher .ART to GEM IMG format; READST view Atari Degas, Tiny, Small, & Spectrum 512 format files & convert to GIF format (needs VGA card); MVGAVU v4.1 Targa 16/24/32 viewer & GIF 87a/89a decoder/slideshow (EGA, MCGA, VGA, SVGA); GIF2BMP converts GIF to BMP format; PCX2LASR prints PCX files on HP Laserjet II; RON9VW v1.05 Picture Librarian for PCX format files; PCXUT contains PCX ScreenView & PCXCAP screen capture utilities.

2708.ZIP TURBO PAINT is a paint

program that works in CGA 4-color, EGA 16-color, and MCGA 256-color modes and features the ability to read and write in PCX, LBM, and GIF format graphics files and also make use of standard GEM fonts for text entry.

2880.ZIP ANIMATE creates and displays animated movies.

2929.ZIP DOTS accepts a file of triples of numbers (X, Y, and Z coordinates of points) and displays a perspective projection of them as points or connected by lines.

3005.ZIP GRAFIXBUSTERS 2 includes PCX VIEW v2.1, a UK screen show & presentation program with timed sequences, fades, horizontal and vertical merges. Allows enlarging, positioning and coloring of PCX files prior to display; VCGM v1.41 allows viewing of CGM vector graphics files on EGA/VGA.

3036.ZIP FINGER VGA is a color image processing, painting and animation program using 320x200 256-color VGA graphics mode for all operations. Reads and writes ZSoft's PC Paintbrush .PCX format bitmapped graphics files, and will print at 300dpi on HP Laserjets.

3351.ZIP MERGEIT utility for merging scanner images in PCX format. MERGEIT is a utility for merging black & white (not grayscale) scanned images together, either horizontally or vertically. Automatic merging will do a good job of joining scanned image sections.

3305.ZIP IMPROCES is a SVGA image processor supporting Ahead, ATI, Chips & Tech, Everex, Paradise, Trident Tseng 3000 & 4000, Video7 and VESA cards in modes from 320x200x256 to 1024x768x256. Features image contrast enhancement, histograms, sharpening by convolution, custom filters, full palette control, clipboard, five fonts in five sizes, FAT BIT editor, many drawing tools, flips, mirror, color cycling, plasma and terrain fractals, SVGA modes, undo, XMS/EMS support, save images to GIF, PCX or PRF format, virtual video etc.

3412.ZIP GRAFIXBUSTERS 3 includes GIFPRT v5.0 which displays GIF bitmap graphics files on any graphics monitor and will print on Epson 9 or 24-pin, Epson-compatible color printers, HP Laserjets, Toshiba/Qume 24-pin and Deskjet 500C color printers; GIFDXF convert GIF format files to DXF format as used by Autodesk 3D Studio; PCXALBUM PCX display program for VGA can show pictures either randomly or as a slide show. Also allows accompanying sound file if you have a Covox sound board; SCR2GIF v3.4 capture EGA and VGA (up to 256 color) screens to GIF files; PICEM v2.7 general purpose graphics viewer for any monitor handles PCX, GIF, and PC Paint PIC; NEWPRINT v1.0 prints PCX files on

Epson 24-pin or Laserjet; TEXTSHOT v2.1 dump text screens to 2-color PCX files; LJVGA v1.71 VGA/SVGA to Laserjet print screen utility allowing printing of any VGA or SVGA screen to HP Laserjet or compatible printer in 785 or 300 dpi.

3481.ZIP OCRSHARE is a complete shareware version of the Advantex Optical Character Recognition package.

3484.ZIP IMAGE PRO is a fast image processor for GIF, PCX, PIC, Tiff and Targa format bitmap graphics files, allowing them to be viewed, scaled clipped, dithered, printed to dot matrix or laser printer, have the brightness or contrast altered and changed between formats.

3514.ZIP FLICBOOK is a program that captures the fun of animation.

3550.ZIP DESKTOP PAINT is a monochrome paint package for EGA, VGA and Hercules graphics designed for use with desktop publishing applications. Supports MAC, IMG, PCX, GIF, TIFF, WPG, MSP, IFF/LBM, ART, BMP, PIC, TGA, and DR Halo CUT bitmap graphics, allowing the creation and editing of pictures in any of these formats; EMS support will allow handling of files up to the size of available memory. Features a gallery of image fragments, online help, gradient and fill tools, rotation scaling and flip functions, a complete set of drawing tools, cut copy and paste, left center and right text justification.

3551.ZIP IMAGE GALLERY visual database for bitmapped image files.

3580.ZIP COLOR VIEW for Windows high speed JPEG viewer/converter

3583.ZIP DESKTOP PAINT 16 is a 16-color VGA resolution paint program. Supports MAC, IMG, PCX, GIF, TIFF, WPG, MSP, IFF/LBM, BMP, PIC, TGA and DR Halo CUT bitmap graphics, allowing the creation and editing of pictures in any of these formats; EMS support will allow handling of files up to the size of available memory. Features a gallery of image fragments, online help, gradient and fill tools, rotation scaling and flip functions, a complete set of drawing tools, cut, copy and paste, left, center and right text justification. Although some fonts are included, registered users get a font toolkit that will import fonts from GEM/Ventura, Mac FONT and Windows 3 FON files and the ability to edit self-displaying EXE files.

3605.ZIP PC-DRAFT II is a high resolution pixel-oriented drawing and graphing utility designed to facilitate a variety of drawing and drafting needs. Features include drawings up to 1280x700 using CGA high resolution mode (640x200 per screen), built-in functions allow you to draw circles, lines, boxes, arcs and curves; draw bar, line and pie graphs; create patterns with which to fill areas; cut and paste objects and save objects to files for later use, load and edit fonts, support for Epson & IBM dot matrix, HP Laserjet Plus and HP Deskjet printers, portions of the screen or full drawings can be saved as GEM .IMG files which can be imported into DTP applications such as Ventura, graphics presentation language called PIX allows you to perform all PC-Draft II commands from a script file without displaying any cursor or menu information (allows slide show facility), screen capture utility (CAPTURE.COM) allowing capture of screen images from other programs to be loaded into PC-Draft II for enhancement printing. Also GEMCAP v4.01 screen capture utility which saves screen images in GEM .IMG format. Supports mono text, CGA, EGA and VGA 640x480 116-color nodes. FANTASY v5.0 is a program allowing the creation of flowing graphic images as you move the mouse around the screen.

3650.ZIP DESKTOP PAINT 256 is a powerful SuperVGA paint program allowing you to create and edit full color pictures. It can load and save to MacPaint, GEM IMG, PC, GIF, TIFF, WPG, MSP, IFF/LBM, BMP, Halo CUT, and Targa formats making it suitable for a wide variety of applications. Features a full range of drawing tools and effects including rectangle and ellipse, zoom, freehand brush, cut & paste, undo function, rotate/flip/invert image areas, stain, smudge, posterize and soften image areas and also allows text to be added. Needs one of the following Super VGA cards (or genuine compatible): Paradise, ATI VGA Wonder, headland Video 7, Tseng Labs 4000 series, Trident 8900 series and OAK TECHNOLOGIES cards.

3730.ZIP COLORVIEW is a color image viewer, converter and editor which supports JPEG (JFIF subset), GIF87, GIF89, and BMP (4, 8 and 24-bit including 8-bit RLE) formats.

3716.ZIP VPIC is a file viewer for EGA/MCGA/VGA/SVGA allowing viewing of files in the following formats -DR Halo .CUT (with PAL if present), GIF 87a and 89a, Deluxe Paint LBM or IFF regular and enhanced, MAC, Pictor/PC Paint PIC, ZSoft PCX (include 256 color), Viewpoint PIC, ColorRIX/EGA Paint SCx files, Targa 16 or 24 TGA files, Windows 3 BMP or BIF binary image files. Will convert to any of these except MAC, BIF or Viewpoint PIC and will convert to GIF 89a format in regular, interlaced, inverted, mirrored or rotated 90 degrees CW or CCW. Slide show facility with animation. Also GIFDESK v4.5 allows multiple GIF files to be displayed on a single screen.

3837.ZIP TECHVIEW is a memory-resident program allowing bitmap graphics files in GIF format to be linked into a program that displays text.

3838.ZIP DISP is a utility to read, write and display bitmap images with different formats and can perform some special effects such as rotation and dithering on them. There is no limit on image size, and the program currently supports 8, 15, 16 and 24-bit displays. It will read bitmap files in GIF, Japan MAC/PIC/MKI, Sun RAS, JPEG, XBM, Utah RLE, PBM, PGM PPM, PM, PCX, TIFF, Targa, XPM, MAC, GEM/IMG, IFF/LBM, BMP, QRT ray tracer, Mac PCT, VIS, PDS, Viking VIK and VICAR VIC formats and will print on HP Laserjet and convert to GIF, SUN, JPG, XBM, PBM, PGM, PPM, PM, TIFF, Targa, XPM, MAC, IFF/LBM, BMP, PCT GEM/IMG, PCX and VIS. Directly supports a wide range of SVGA cards plus any VESA compatible.

3870.ZIP VISAGE LITE is a document image management system.

3895.ZIP TOGETHER! is a TSR that will allow you to add .PCX image files to text based applications.

3898.ZIP MVP-PAINT a VGA based paint program with many advanced features, such as animation, sunbursting, interpolation, trending and palette manipulation (permits use of over 200,000 colors). File formats supported are PCX, GIF and several peculiar to MVP-Paint. The program is menu/icon driven and has full online help.

3913.ZIP OPTIKS is a graphics utility allowing graphics files in various formats to be viewed, edited, cropped, squeezed, have text & lines added etc. Graphics may also be merged with other graphics images. Can read files in Lotus PIC, Postscript, Autocad SLD, BLOAD, MAC, PCX, EFS Image, WIPS, RLE, DR Halo II & III CUT, Fontasy, Microsoft Paint, Ricoh IS30 PIG, RAS, TIFF, IMG, IBM ISF, Atari ST Degas, First Publisher .ART, PC Paint v1, Palantir PDA, IFF GIF, Printshop, Newsmaster and Newsmaster Pro, and outputs in ACAD DXB/DXF/SLD, ART, BLOAD, IMG/GEM, CUT, MSP, TIFF, WPG, PCX, MAC and its own PC Rockland format, in addition to producing self scrolling COM files. Also useful as a display and printing utility many printers are supported.

3944.ZIP ROTOR is a graphic design program with animation facilities.

3949.ZIP WINOCR is an Optical Character Recognition system for Windows.

3964.ZIP IMGFUN image enhancement and compression utility for gray and color-mapped GIF, PCX, BMP and JPEG images. Features instant zoom and scroll images onscreen, adjust colors, brightness, contrast and cut area of images. Enable fast JPEG compression to reduce GIF images to a fraction of their original size. Also includes CHIARO SUITE V1.0 of utilities for image formats information, GIF image checking and excess character removal.

3989.ZIP DAUB FOR WINDOWS is an object based general purpose vector graphics drawing program.

4039.ZIP MULTIMEDIA WORKSHOP LITE FOR WINDOWS is an easy to use browser program for Windows WAV wave files, MIDI sequence files and AVI video for Windows movies.

4071.ZIP THE COMPLETE IMAGE is a command-line bitmap conversion and image processing utility. Reads, writes and converts between TGA, IMG, BMP, GIF, and IPI format files.

4152.ZIP LVIEW is an image file editor for Windows 3.1 able to handle files in JPEG, JFIF, GIF 87a / 89a, Truevision Targa, Windows and OS/2 BMP formats. Features include cut / copy / paste to clipboard, resize, redimension, crop, add text, flip, rotate, retouch (grayscale, HSV adjust, color balance, contrast enhance, gamma correction, smooth filter, interactive RGB, palette entry) plus many printer options, slideshow facility, contact sheet options and much more.

4155.ZIP WINJPEG is an image viewer with image processing and conversion capabilities for Windows 3.x able to display JPEG, TIFF, Targa, GIF, PCX or Windows BMP images.

4176.ZIP BMP TOOLKIT is a Windows 8 & 24 bit BMP and GIF (read only) color bitmap viewer, image processor and printer.

H036.ZIP SURF-MODL surface modeling package.

H063.ZIP IRIT solid modeling system

H064.ZIP ESSENTIAL VIDEO UTILS for PAL encoder/genlock users

H144.ZIP IMAGE ALCHEMY is a command-line operated utility supporting JPEG compression and converts between 60 different graphics files formats including GIF, TIFF, Amiga IFF / LBM, PCX (including 24-bit), Macintosh PICT, Sun RAS and RLE, HP PCL, Encapuslated Postscript, BMP, SGI, PBM / PPM / PGM, GIF 89a plus Group III, Group IV, PICIO and SGI RLE, Vivid, MTV, DCX, QDV, Erdas, QRT, GEM Utah RLE, ADEX, RTL, WPG, Pictor, Autologic, q0, BIF Stork, XWD, Scodl, AVHRR, CALS, Cubicomp and IBM Picture Maker, DR Halo CUT, First Publisher ART, GOES, PDS, RIX, SPOT Image, XPM, XBM and TIFF compression types and Targa 8-32 bit images are supported. Shareware version is restricted to 640x480 and lower resolutions. Also PRO-CR v2.12 an Optical Character Recognition program which reads several common fonts in a range of point sizes, with no font selection required by the user. Runs at 200 and 300dpi and allows image preview and online correction of processed text. Supports the HP ScanJet directly and other scanners via TIFF and PCX files.

H164.ZIP GRAPHIC WORKSHOP FOR WINDOWS is a utility for working with bitmapped graphics files, allowing you to view them, convert between any two formats (with a few restrictions), print them, produce composite catalogue images of multiple files, dither color images to black and white, reverse them, rotate and flip them, scale them, reduce the number of colors and do color dithering, crop them down to smaller files, plus other effects. Currently handles Mac, PCX up to 24-bit, GEM IMG up to 24-bit, Compuserve's GIF, TIFF (gray scale and color), WordPerfect WPG, MS-Paint, Deluxe Paint IFF / LBM, Windows 3. BMP, PC Paint PIC, PFS: First Publisher ART, Targa, DR Halo CUT, Kodak Photo-CD, JPEG compression, Windows WMF (read only), ICO, CLP plus AVI, FLI and FLC animation formats.

H196.ZIP PIXFOLIO (ex-SHOWGIF) is a utility that allows viewing and cataloging of bitmapped graphics images. The program handles IFF, TIFF, PCX, TGA, GIF, BMP, RLE and a number of other formats. FONT PREVIEW v1.3 is a program that displays a list of all the typefaces supported by the current printer. The required typeface and point size can be selected from within the current application at any time.

H203.ZIP THE TIFF TOOLKIT specs for v5.0 +TACS, TFTOOL etc. THE TIFF TOOLKIT includes a full v5.0 specification in ASCII format. Also DTIFF v2.0 which displays TIFF files on CGA, EGA, VGA MCGA, Hercules, IBM 8514/A or AT&T cards and includes C source code; TIFF-DUMP utility to dump a TIFF file with C source code fragments for PackBits and UnpackBits routines; TIFFTOOLS includes source and executables for dumping TIFF headers and a byte-swapping utility to reverse the order of bytes between Intel & Motorola formats. Also includes a specification of TIFF FAX format with example.

H233.ZIP NEOPAINT graphics package for Herc / EGA / VGA / SVGA.

H237.ZIP GRAPHIC WORKSHOP is a graphics file utility allowing you to view files, convert between different formats, print to dot matrix, Laserjet Plus or Postscript laser printers and dither color files to black and white. File formats handled are Mac, PCX (with up to 256 colors, GEM / IMG files of the sort used with Ventura Publisher, GIF files of any size and up to 256 colors, TIFF (grayscale, color, LZW, Huffman, Group 3 & 4), Word Perfect WPG, MS-Paint, Deluxe Paint IFF / LBM, Windows 3 .BMP and RLE, Pictor / PC Paint PIC, Targa, DR Halo CUT and PFS: First Publisher ART, handles JPEG image compression and can also output encapsulated PostScript files. Will use XMS / EMS / LIM memory, and features image rotation, flipping, scaling and non-dither halftoning, cropping, scanning and interactive color adjustment. Image cataloging function produces composite bitmaps of multiple thumbnail images with titles.

H253.ZIP JPEG bitmapped graphics compression system with source.

H344.ZIP PAINT SHOP PRO is a Windows program that will display, convert, alter and print bitmapped graphic images in 23 formats including BMP, DIB, GIF, IMG, JAS, MAC, MSP, PIC, PCX, RAS, RLE, TGA, TIFF, WPG, CLP, CUT, EPS, IFF / LBM, JIF, JPEG, PCD (Kodak Photo CD) and WMF formats.

H418.ZIP TOP DRAW is a paint program for Windows 3.1 able to read and write Windows WMF, BMP or PCX format files.

H429.ZIP WINWALL PLUS Windows wallpaper management utility.

H447.ZIP PICTURE MAN true color image process for Windows.

H461.ZIP Russell's Animation Machine animated graphics system.

H463.ZIP GRAPHIC TOOLBOX convert obscure graphics formats.

H464.ZIP ELECTRONIC SCRIMSHAW graphic design program.

H524.ZIP TICO utility to make self-displaying graphic files.

H593.ZIP THUMBS PLUS is a graphic file previewer, locator and organizer which simplifies the process of finding and maintaining graphics and clip art files. It displays a small image (thumbnail) of each file. Allows you to browse, view, crop, launch editors, copy images to the clipboard, and to browse, view, crop, launch editors, copy images to the clipboard, and organize graphics files by moving them to the appropriate directories. Can create a slideshow from selected graphics, and install bitmap files as Windows wallpaper. Can print individual graphics files, or thumbnails themselves as a catalogue. Currently handles BMF, BMP, CDR, CGM, EPS, GEM, GIF, ICO, IFF / LBM, IMG, JPG, MND, PCD, PCX, RAW, RAS, TGA, TTF, TIF, and WMF files.

H638.ZIP IMAGE'N'BITS image package for Windows 3.1.

Table of Contents

The Clip Art Image Library™

C0000005.TIF

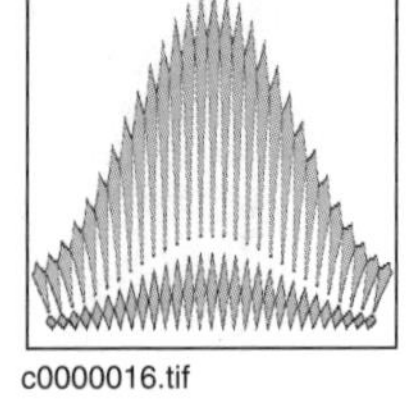
c0000016.tif

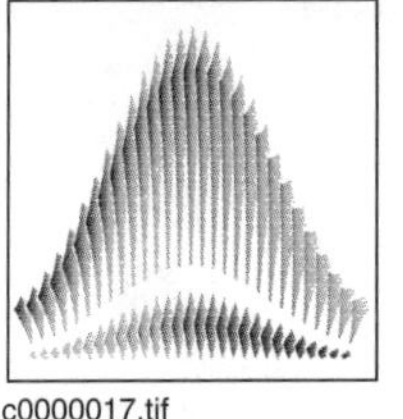
c0000017.tif

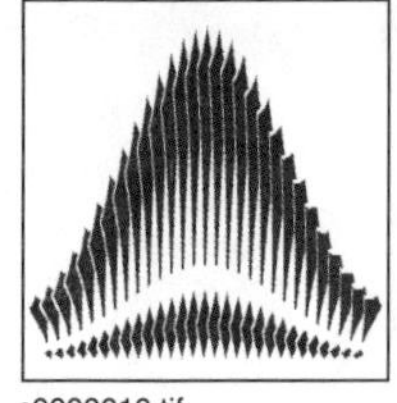
c0000018.tif

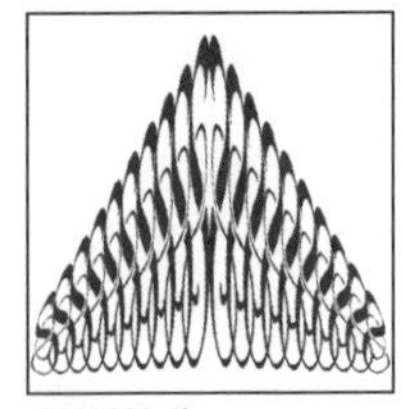
c0000022.tif

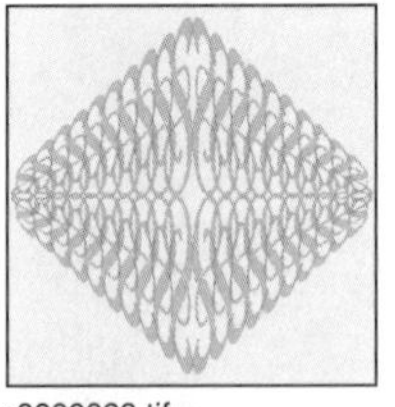
c0000023.tif

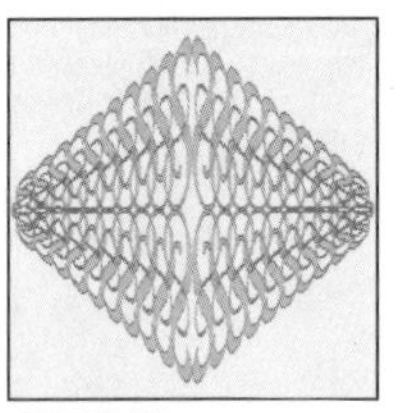
c0000024.tif

c0000025.tif

c0000026.tif

c0000028.tif

c0000029.tif

c0000034.tif

c0000038.tif

c0000040.tif

c0000041.tif

c0000044.tif

m0000002.tif

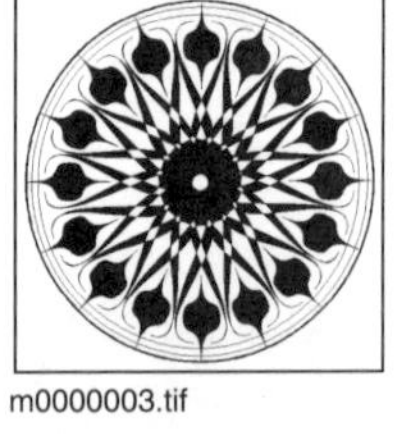
m0000003.tif

m0000004.tif

m0000006.tif

m0000007.tif

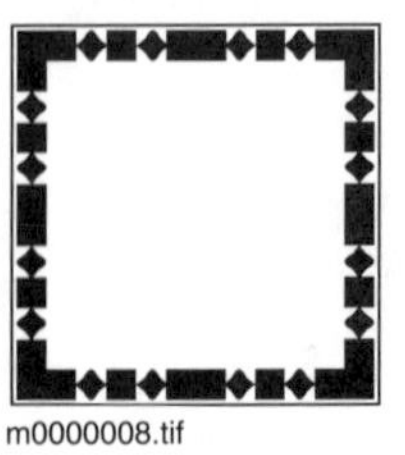
m0000008.tif

m0000009.tif

m0000010.tif

d:\images\abc

m0000011.tif

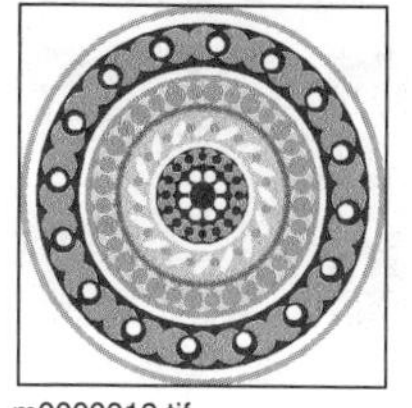
m0000012.tif

m0000013.tif

m0000014.tif

m0000015.tif

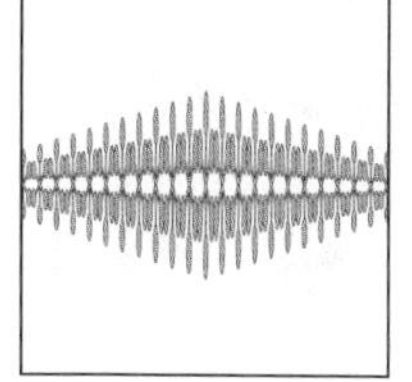
m0000019.tif

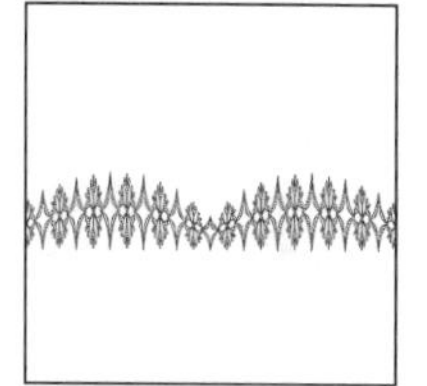
m0000020.tif

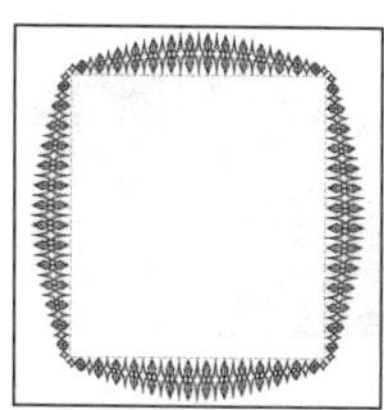
m0000021.tif

m0000027.tif

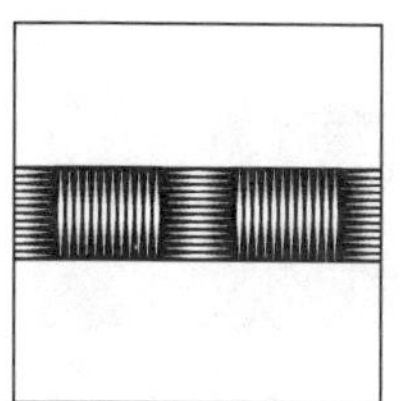
m0000030.tif

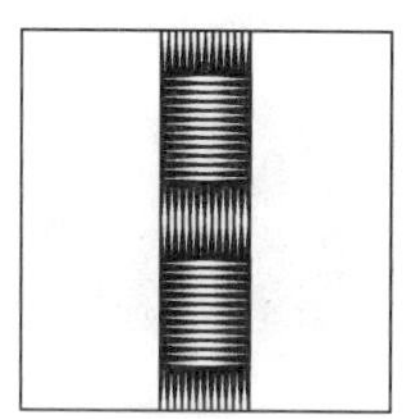
m0000031.tif

m0000032.tif

m0000033.tif

m0000035.tif

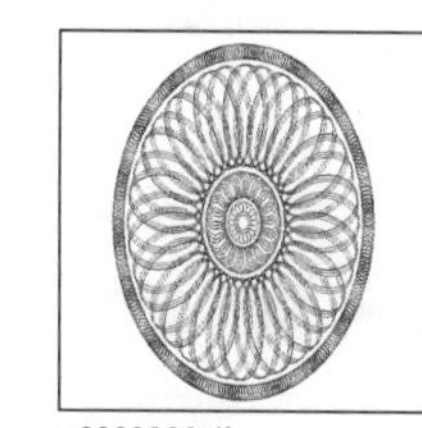
m0000036.tif

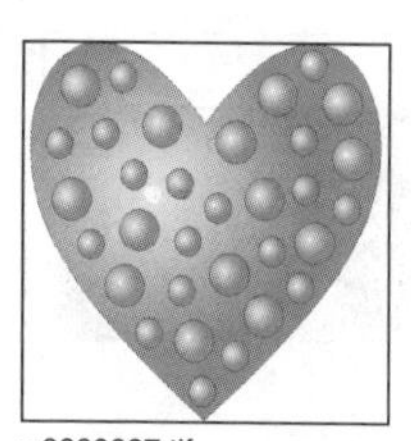
m0000037.tif

m0000039.tif

m0000042.tif

m0000043.tif

d:\images\abc

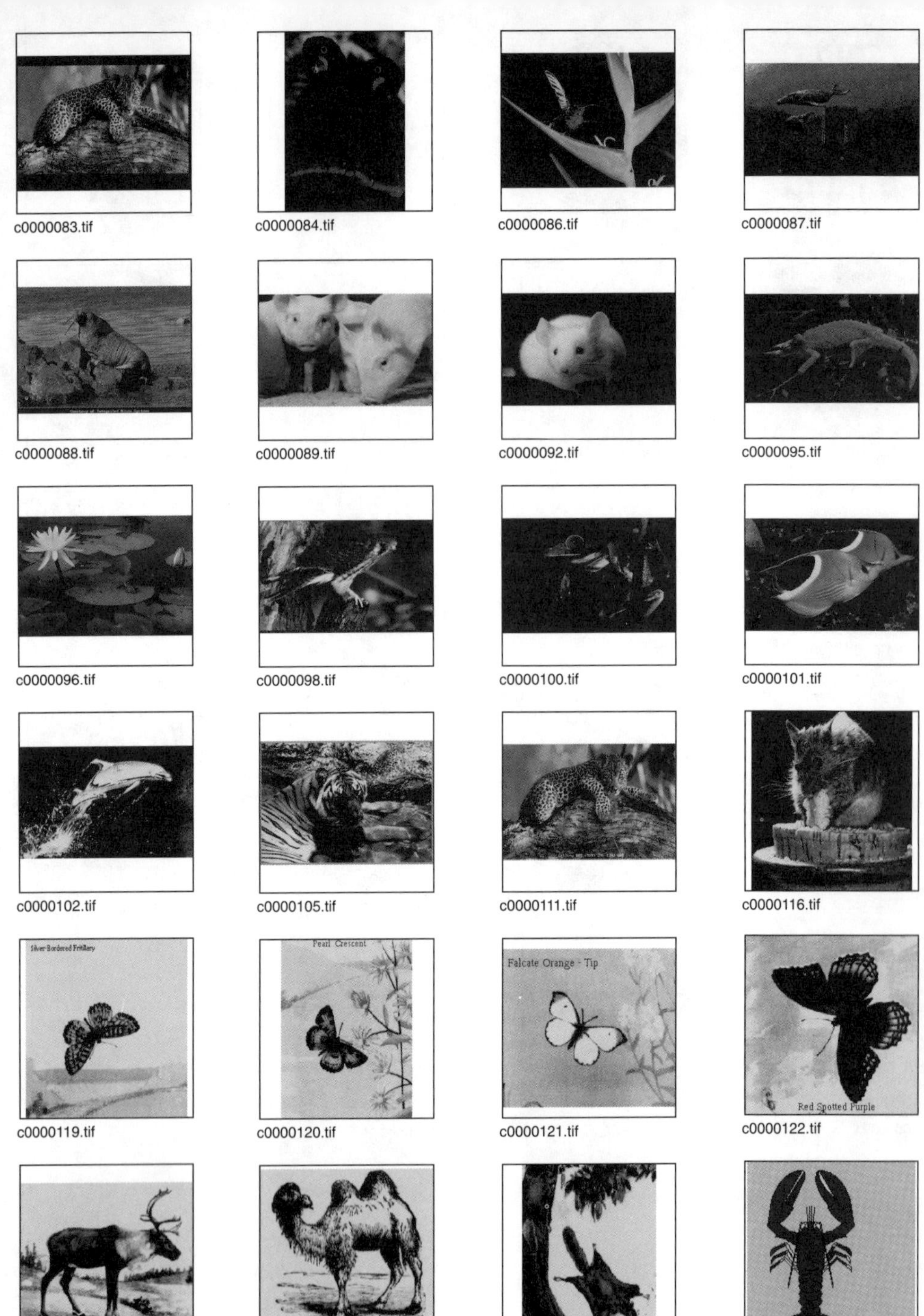

d:\images\animal1

c0000169.tif

c0000176.tif

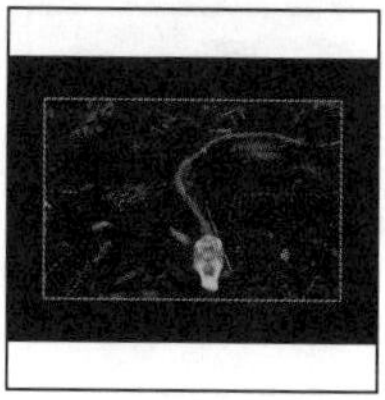

c0000179.tif

c0000185.tif

c0000186.tif

m0000045.tif

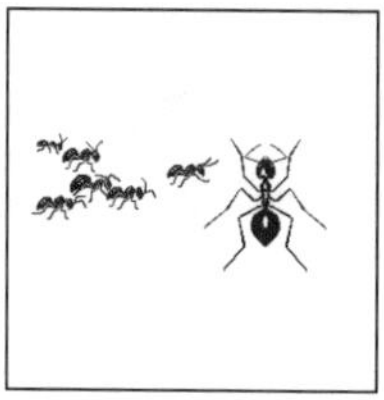

m0000046.tif

m0000047.tif

m0000048.tif

m0000049.tif

m0000050.tif

m0000051.tif

m0000052.tif

m0000053.tif

m0000054.tif

m0000055.tif

m0000056.tif

m0000057.tif

m0000058.tif

m0000059.tif

m0000060.tif

m0000061.tif

m0000062.tif

m0000063.tif

d:\images\animal1

m0000064.tif

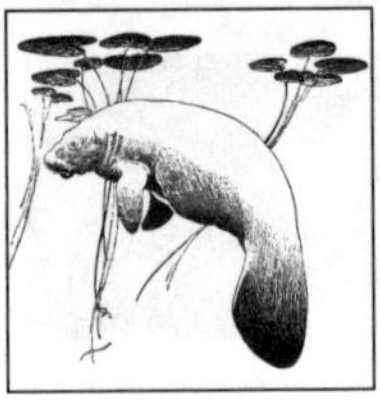

m0000065.tif

m0000066.tif

m0000067.tif

m0000068.tif

m0000069.tif

m0000070.tif

m0000071.tif

m0000072.tif

m0000073.tif

m0000074.tif

m0000075.tif

m0000076.tif

m0000077.tif

m0000078.tif

m0000079.tif

m0000080.tif

m0000081.tif

m0000082.tif

m0000117.tif

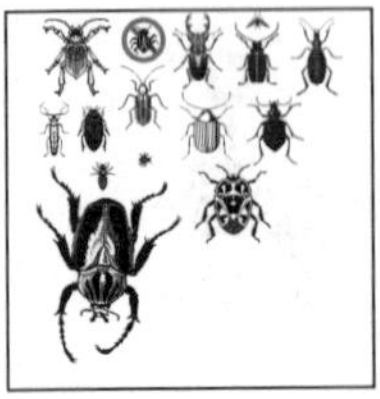

m0000118.tif

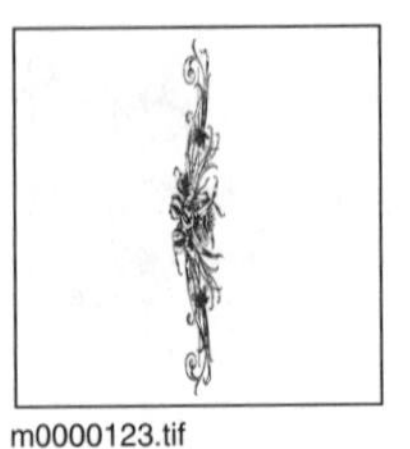

m0000123.tif

m0000124.tif

m0000125.tif

d:\images\animal1

m0000130.tif

m0000131.tif

m0000132.tif

m0000134.tif

m0000135.tif

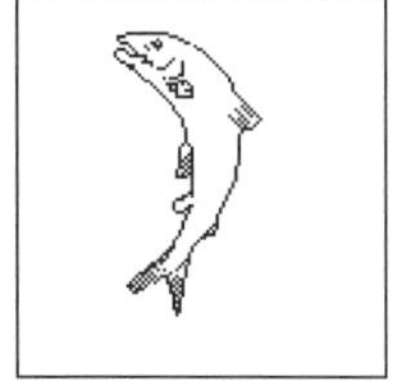
m0000136.tif

m0000137.tif

m0000139.tif

m0000140.tif

m0000141.tif

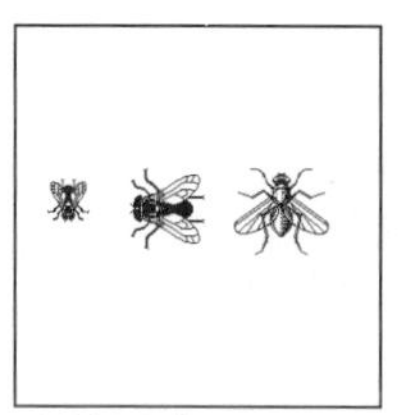
m0000142.tif

m0000144.tif

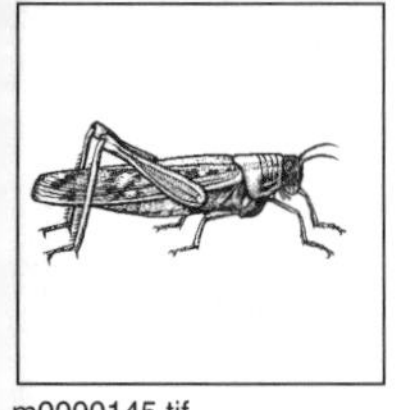
m0000145.tif

m0000147.tif

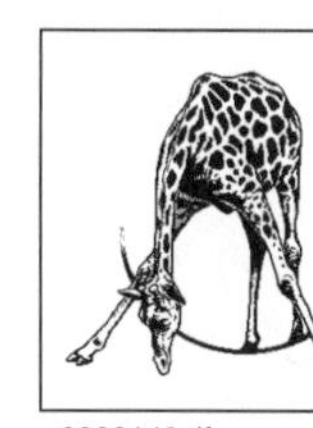
m0000148.tif

m0000149.tif

m0000151.tif

m0000153.tif

m0000156.tif

m0000157.tif

m0000158.tif

m0000161.tif

m0000162.tif

m0000163.tif

d:\images\animal1

m0000164.tif

m0000165.tif

m0000167.tif

m0000168.tif

m0000170.tif

m0000172.tif

m0000173.tif

m0000174.tif

m0000175.tif

m0000177.tif

m0000178.tif

m0000180.tif

m0000181.tif

m0000183.tif

m0000184.tif

c0000188.tif c0000190.tif c0000191.tif c0000192.tif

c0000196.tif c0000197.tif c0000200.tif c0000203.tif

c0000204.tif c0000205.tif c0000206.tif c0000207.tif

c0000208.tif c0000209.tif c0000210.tif c0000211.tif

c0000212.tif c0000213.tif c0000214.tif c0000215.tif

c0000216.tif c0000217.tif c0000218.tif c0000219.tif

d:\images\animal2

c0000220.tif c0000221.tif c0000222.tif c0000223.tif

c0000224.tif c0000226.tif c0000227.tif c0000228.tif

c0000229.tif c0000230.tif c0000231.tif c0000232.tif

c0000233.tif c0000234.tif c0000235.tif c0000236.tif

c0000237.tif c0000238.tif c0000239.tif c0000240.tif

c0000241.tif c0000242.tif c0000243.tif c0000244.tif

d:\images\animal2

c0000245.tif c0000246.tif c0000247.tif c0000248.tif

c0000249.tif c0000252.tif c0000253.tif c0000254.tif

c0000255.tif c0000256.tif c0000257.tif c0000258.tif

c0000259.tif c0000260.tif c0000262.tif c0000264.tif

c0000266.tif c0000267.tif c0000270.tif c0000271.tif

c0000273.tif c0000274.tif c0000275.tif c0000276.tif

d:\images\animal2

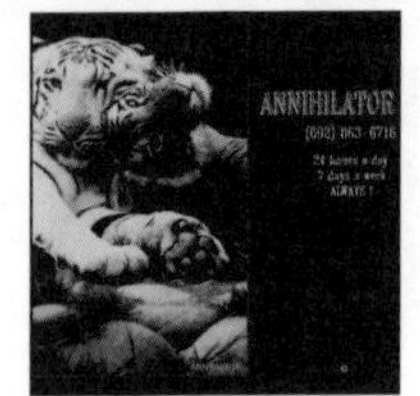

c0000277.tif

c0000278.tif

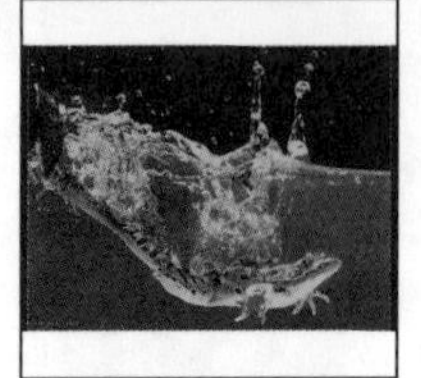
c0000279.tif

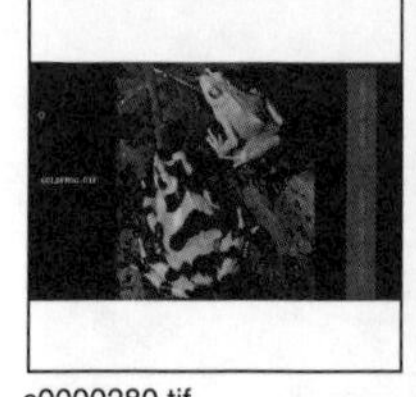
c0000280.tif

c0000282.tif

c0000284.tif

c0000286.tif

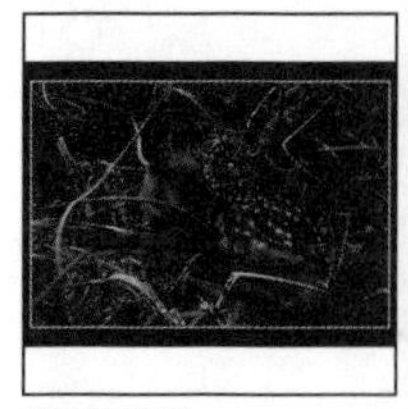
c0000290.tif

c0000292.tif

m0000250.tif

m0000265.tif

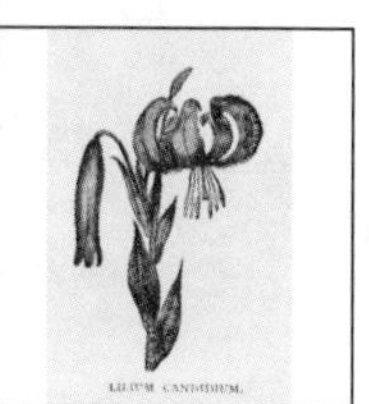

0000296.tif

c0000297.tif

c0000298.tif

c0000299.tif

0000300.tif

c0000301.tif

c0000302.tif

c0000303.tif

0000304.tif

c0000305.tif

c0000306.tif

c0000307.tif

0000308.tif

c0000309.tif

c0000310.tif

c0000311.tif

0000312.tif

c0000313.tif

c0000314.tif

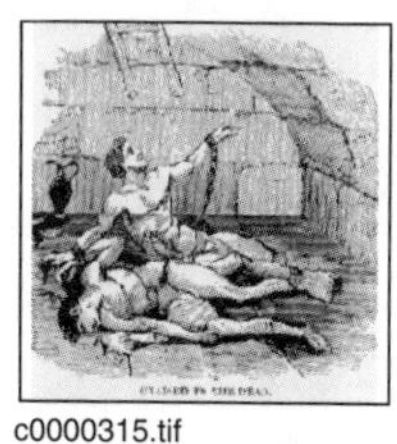

c0000315.tif

0000316.tif

c0000317.tif

c0000318.tif

c0000319.tif

:\images\asg

c0000320.tif

c0000321.tif

c0000322.tif

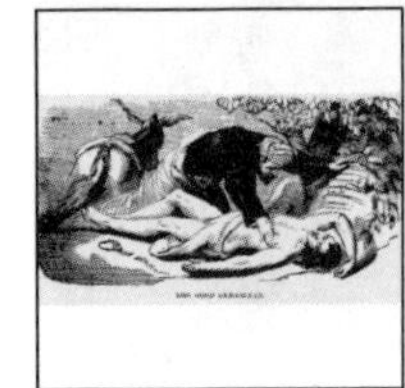
c0000323.tif

c0000324.tif

c0000325.tif

c0000326.tif

c0000327.tif

c0000328.tif

c0000329.tif

THE CZAR
c0000330.tif

THE MIKADO
c0000331.tif

TRAINING THE JAPANESE SOLDIER
c0000332.tif

c0000333.tif

c0000334.tif

c0000335.tif

c0000336.tif

c0000337.tif

c0000338.tif

c0000340.tif

c0000343.tif

c0000344.tif

c0000345.tif

c0000346.tif

d:\images\asg

c0000360.tif

c0000361.tif

c0000362.tif

c0000363.tif

c0000364.tif

c0000365.tif

c0000366.tif

c0000367.tif

c0000368.tif

c0000369.tif

c0000370.tif

c0000371.tif

c0000372.tif

c0000373.tif

c0000374.tif

c0000375.tif

c0000376.tif

c0000377.tif

c0000378.tif

c0000379.tif

c0000380.tif

c0000381.tif

c0000382.tif

c0000384.tif

d:\images\asg

c0000385.tif

c0000386.tif

c0000387.tif

c0000388.tif

c0000389.tif

c0000390.tif

c0000391.tif

c0000392.tif

c0000393.tif

c0000394.tif

m0000293.tif

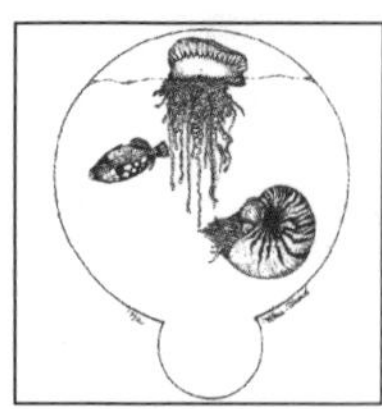
m0000339.tif

m0000341.tif

m0000342.tif

m0000347.tif

m0000348.tif

m0000349.tif

m0000350.tif

m0000351.tif

m0000352.tif

m0000353.tif

m0000354.tif

m0000355.tif

m0000356.tif

m0000357.tif

m0000358.tif

m0000359.tif

m0000383.tif

c0000395.tif

c0000396.tif

c0000397.tif

c0000398.tif

c0000399.tif

c0000400.tif

c0000401.tif

c0000402.tif

c0000403.tif

c0000404.tif

c0000405.tif

c0000406.tif

c0000407.tif

c0000408.tif

c0000409.tif

c0000410.tif

c0000411.tif

c0000412.tif

c0000413.tif

c0000414.tif

c0000415.tif

c0000416.tif

c0000417.tif

c0000418.tif

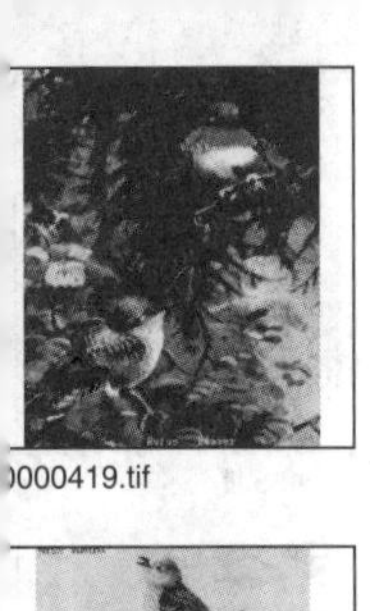
000419.tif

c0000420.tif

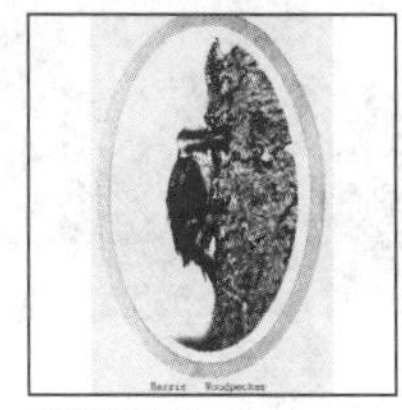
c0000421.tif

c0000426.tif

000427.tif

c0000428.tif

c0000429.tif

c0000430.tif

000431.tif

c0000432.tif

c0000433.tif

c0000434.tif

000437.tif

c0000438.tif

c0000441.tif

c0000442.tif

000443.tif

c0000444.tif

c0000445.tif

c0000446.tif

000452.tif

c0000453.tif

c0000454.tif

c0000455.tif

:\images\asg2

c0000456.tif

c0000457.tif

c0000458.tif

c0000463.tif

c0000484.tif

c0000485.tif

c0000486.tif

c0000497.tif

c0000498.tif

c0000499.tif

c0000500.tif

m0000422.tif

m0000423.tif

m0000424.tif

m0000425.tif

m0000435.tif

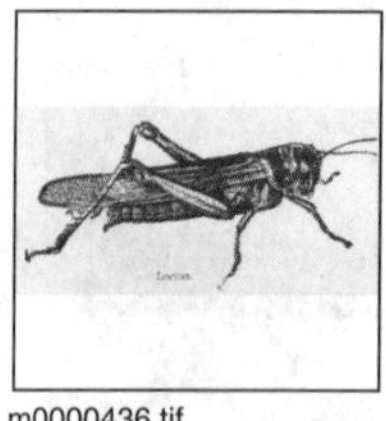
m0000436.tif

m0000439.tif

m0000440.tif

m0000447.tif

m0000448.tif

m0000449.tif

m0000450.tif

m0000451.tif

d:\images\asg2

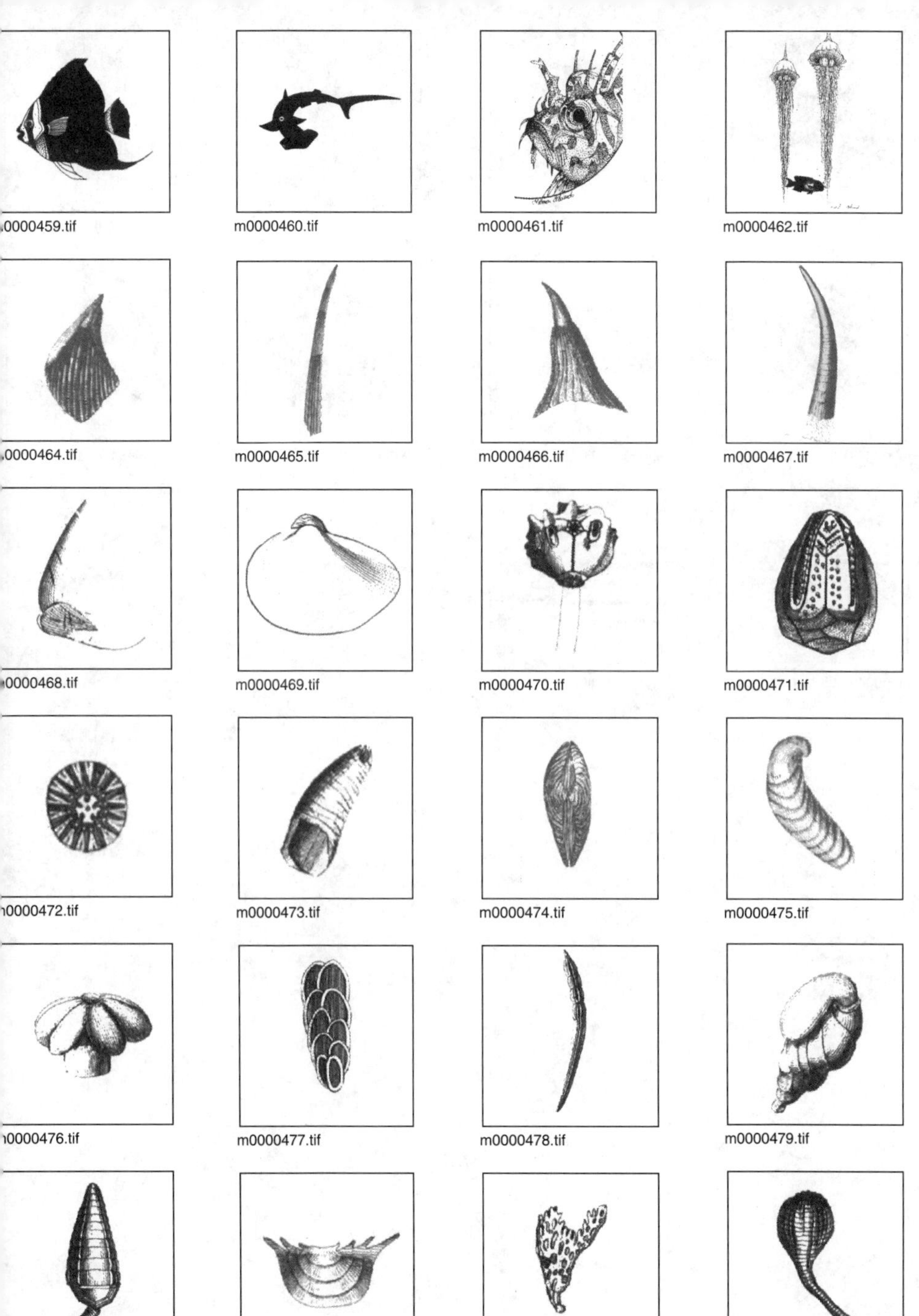

0000480.tif m0000481.tif m0000482.tif m0000483.tif

d:\images\asg2

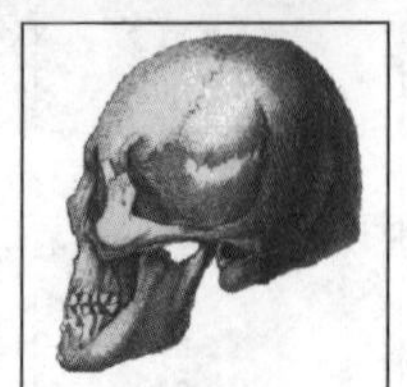
m0000487.tif

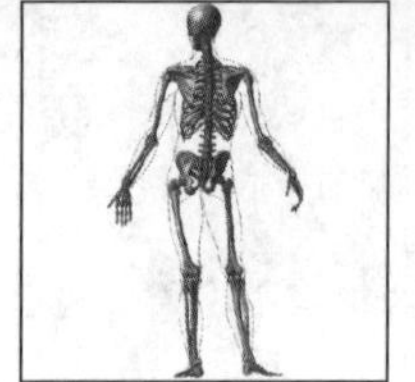
m0000488.tif

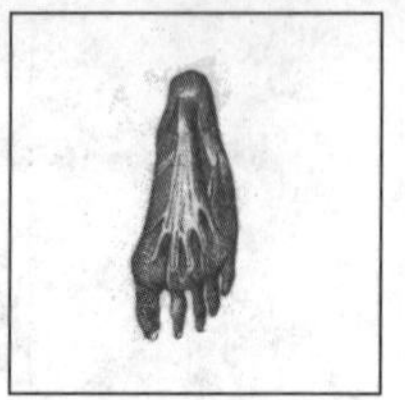
m0000489.tif

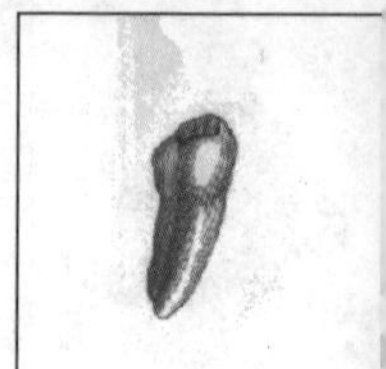
m0000490.tif

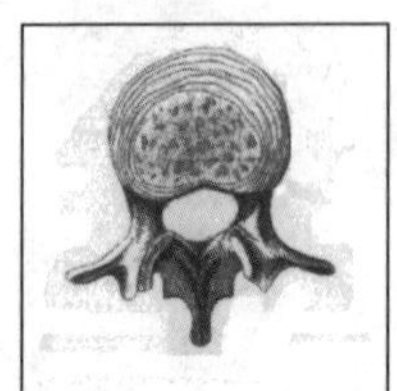
m0000491.tif

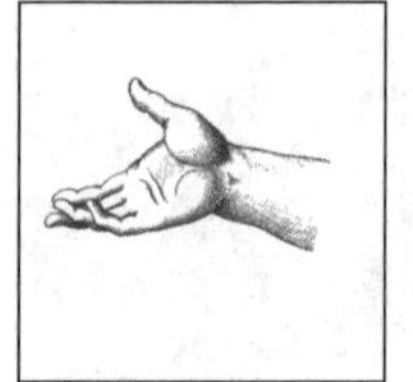
m0000492.tif

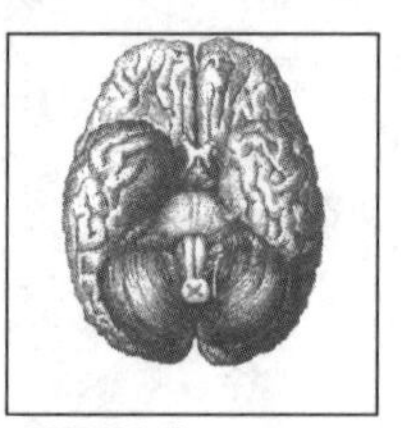
m0000493.tif

m0000494.tif

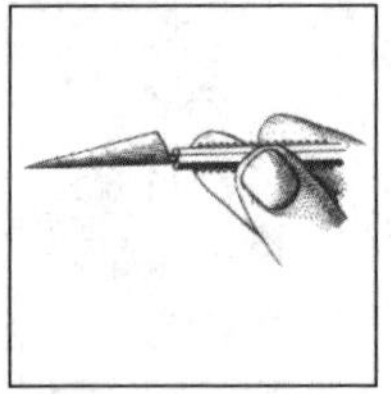
m0000495.tif

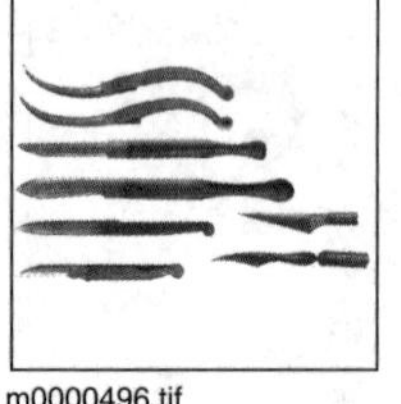
m0000496.tif

m0000501.tif

m0000502.tif

m0000503.tif

m0000504.tif

m0000505.tif

m0000506.tif

m0000507.tif

m0000508.tif

m0000509.tif

m0000510.tif

m0000511.tif

m0000512.tif

m0000513.tif

m0000514.tif

m0000515.tif

m0000516.tif

m0000517.tif

m0000518.tif

m0000519.tif

m0000520.tif

m0000521.tif

m0000522.tif

m0000523.tif

m0000524.tif

d:\images\bears

m0000525.tif

m0000526.tif

m0000527.tif

m0000528.tif

m0000529.tif

m0000530.tif

m0000531.tif

m0000532.tif

m0000533.tif

m0000534.tif

m0000535.tif

m0000536.tif

m0000537.tif

m0000538.tif

m0000539.tif

m0000540.tif

m0000541.tif

m0000542.tif

m0000543.tif

m0000544.tif

m0000545.tif

m0000546.tif

m0000547.tif

m0000548.tif

d:\images\bears

0000549.tif

m0000550.tif

m0000551.tif

d:\images\bears

c0000555.tif c0000556.tif c0000557.tif c0000558.tif

c0000559.tif c0000560.tif c0000561.tif c0000562.tif

c0000564.tif c0000565.tif c0000566.tif c0000567.tif

c0000568.tif c0000569.tif c0000570.tif c0000571.tif

c0000572.tif c0000573.tif c0000574.tif c0000575.tif

c0000578.tif c0000580.tif c0000584.tif c0000594.tif

d:\images\birc

0000596.tif

c0000600.tif

c0000614.tif

c0000622.tif

0000632.tif

c0000638.tif

c0000643.tif

c0000657.tif

:0000666.tif

m0000552.tif

m0000576.tif

m0000577.tif

n0000579.tif

m0000581.tif

m0000582.tif

m0000583.tif

n0000585.tif

m0000586.tif

m0000587.tif

m0000588.tif

n0000589.tif

m0000590.tif

m0000591.tif

m0000592.tif

d:\images\bird

m0000593.tif

m0000595.tif

m0000597.tif

m0000598.tif

m0000599.tif

m0000601.tif

m0000602.tif

m0000603.tif

m0000604.tif

m0000605.tif

m0000606.tif

m0000607.tif

m0000608.tif

m0000609.tif

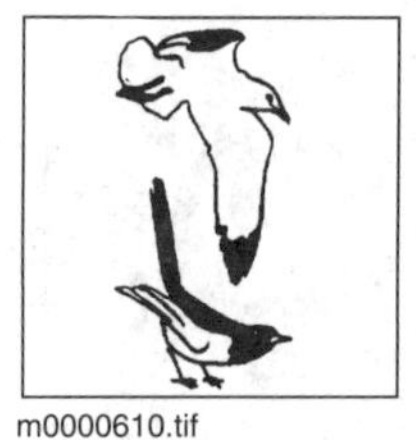
m0000610.tif

m0000611.tif

m0000612.tif

m0000613.tif

m0000615.tif

m0000616.tif

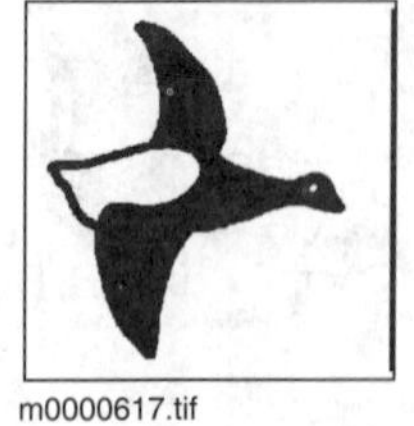
m0000617.tif

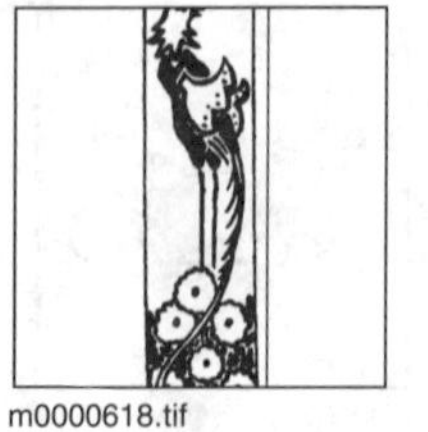
m0000618.tif

m0000619.tif

m0000620.tif

m0000621.tif

m0000623.tif

m0000624.tif

m0000625.tif

m0000626.tif

m0000627.tif

m0000628.tif

m0000629.tif

m0000630.tif

m0000631.tif

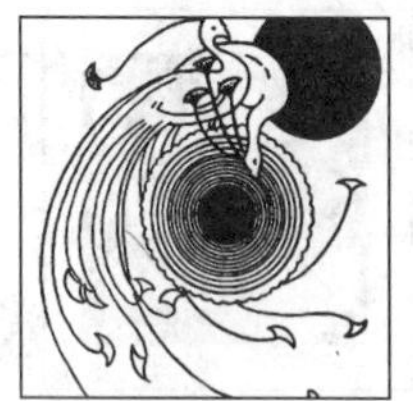
m0000633.tif

m0000634.tif

m0000635.tif

m0000636.tif

m0000637.tif

m0000639.tif

m0000640.tif

m0000641.tif

m0000642.tif

m0000644.tif

m0000645.tif

m0000646.tif

m0000647.tif

m0000648.tif

d:\images\bird

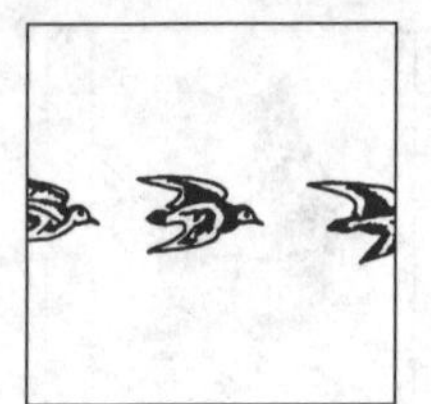
m0000649.tif

m0000650.tif

m0000651.tif

m0000652.tif

m0000653.tif

m0000654.tif

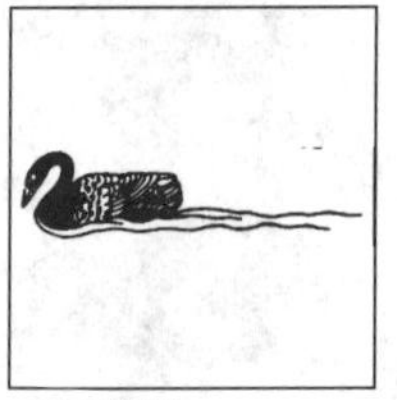
m0000655.tif

m0000658.tif

m0000659.tif

m0000660.tif

m0000661.tif

m0000662.tif

m0000663.tif

m0000664.tif

m0000665.tif

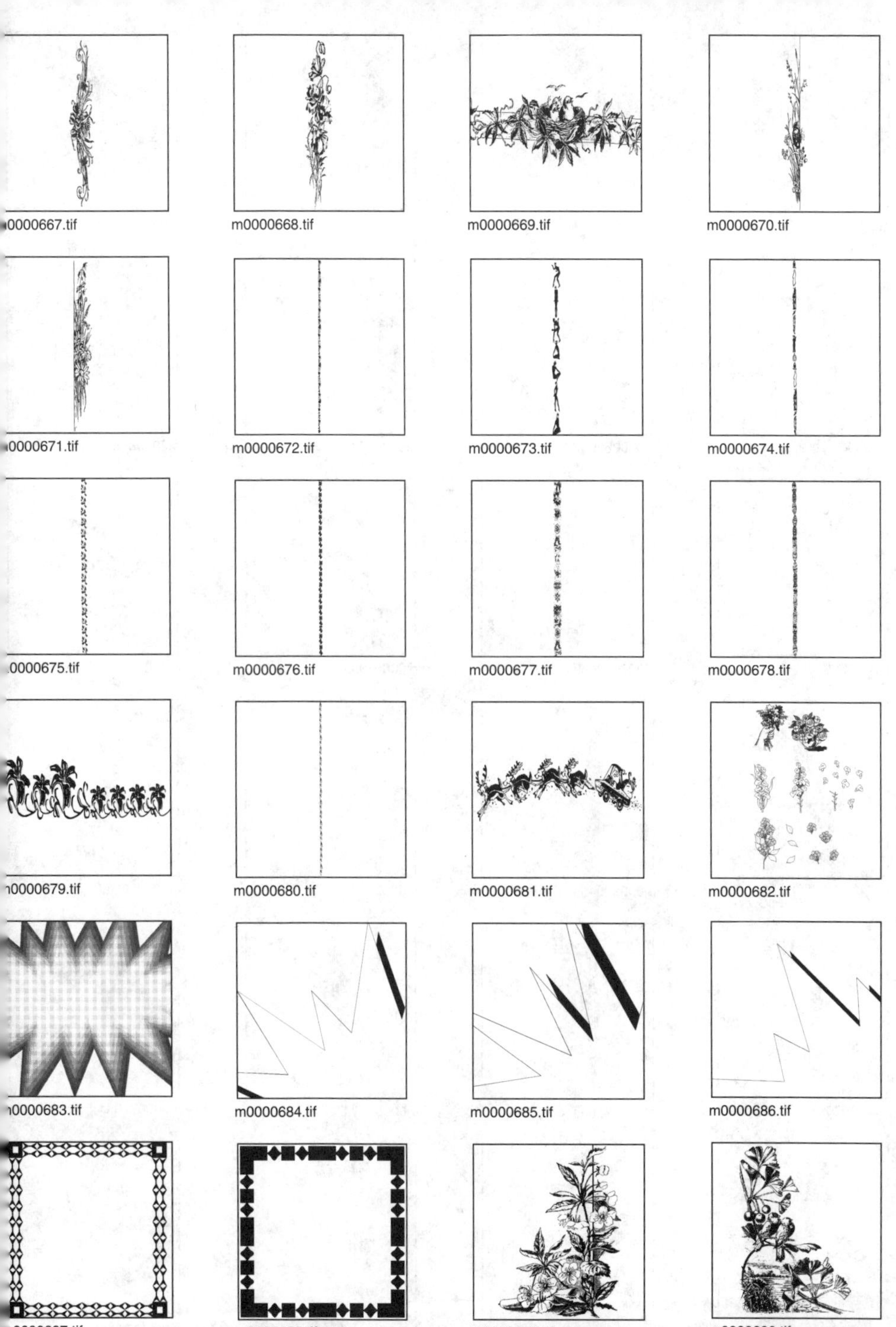

0000667.tif m0000668.tif m0000669.tif m0000670.tif

0000671.tif m0000672.tif m0000673.tif m0000674.tif

0000675.tif m0000676.tif m0000677.tif m0000678.tif

0000679.tif m0000680.tif m0000681.tif m0000682.tif

0000683.tif m0000684.tif m0000685.tif m0000686.tif

0000687.tif m0000688.tif m0000689.tif m0000690.tif

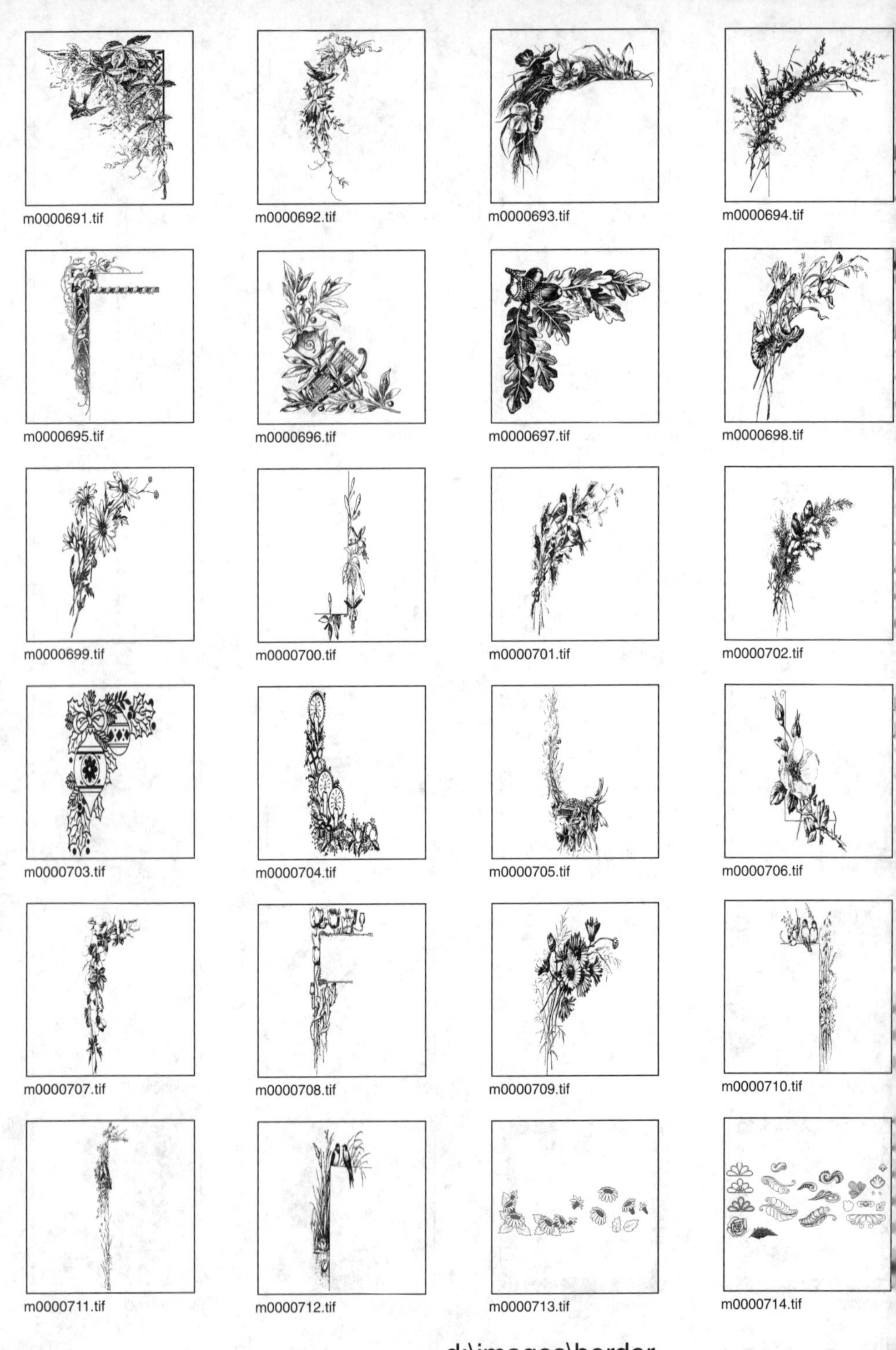
m0000691.tif
m0000692.tif
m0000693.tif
m0000694.tif
m0000695.tif
m0000696.tif
m0000697.tif
m0000698.tif
m0000699.tif
m0000700.tif
m0000701.tif
m0000702.tif
m0000703.tif
m0000704.tif
m0000705.tif
m0000706.tif
m0000707.tif
m0000708.tif
m0000709.tif
m0000710.tif
m0000711.tif
m0000712.tif
m0000713.tif
m0000714.tif

d:\images\border

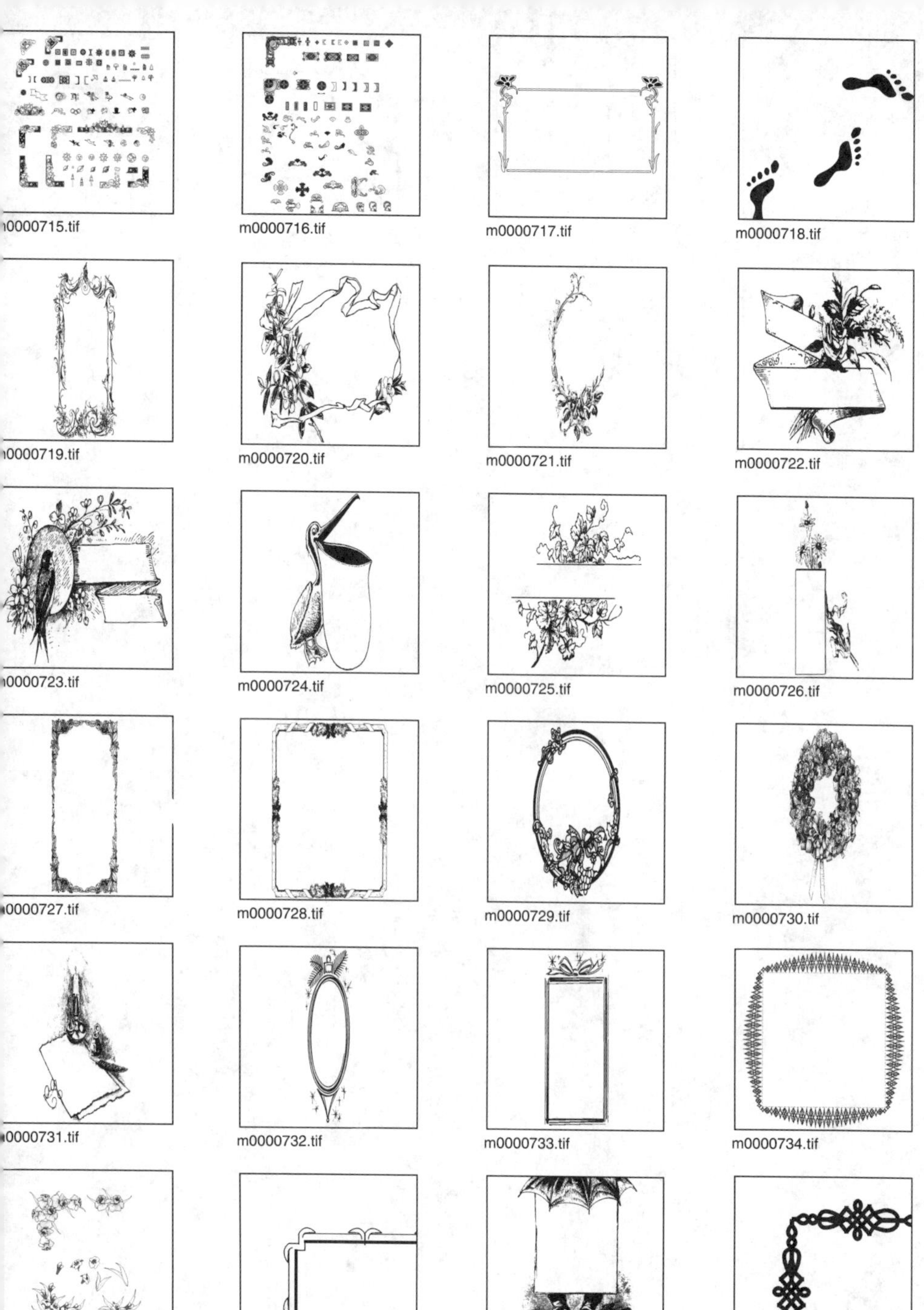

0000715.tif m0000716.tif m0000717.tif m0000718.tif

0000719.tif m0000720.tif m0000721.tif m0000722.tif

0000723.tif m0000724.tif m0000725.tif m0000726.tif

0000727.tif m0000728.tif m0000729.tif m0000730.tif

0000731.tif m0000732.tif m0000733.tif m0000734.tif

0000736.tif m0000737.tif m0000740.tif m0000741.tif

d:\images\border

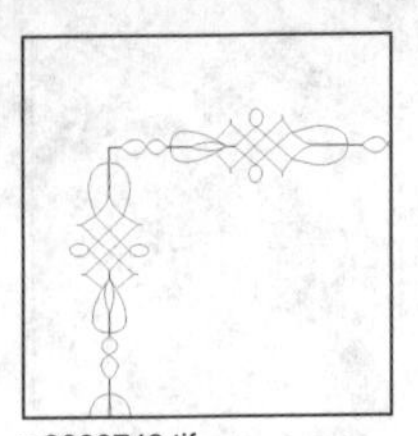

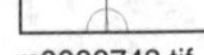

m0000742.tif

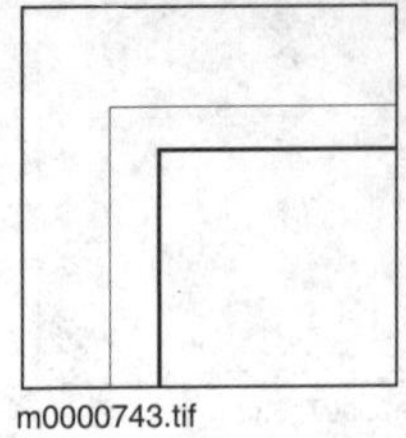

m0000743.tif

m0000744.tif

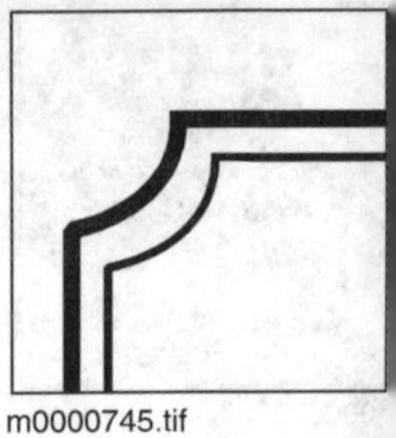

m0000745.tif

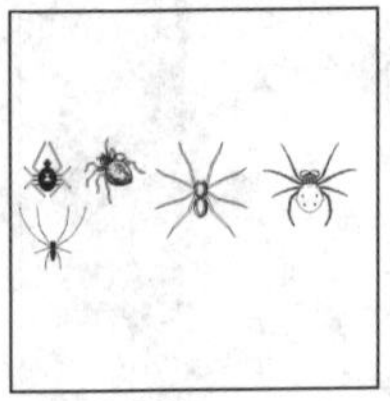

m0000746.tif

m0000747.tif

m0000748.tif

m0000749.tif

m0000750.tif

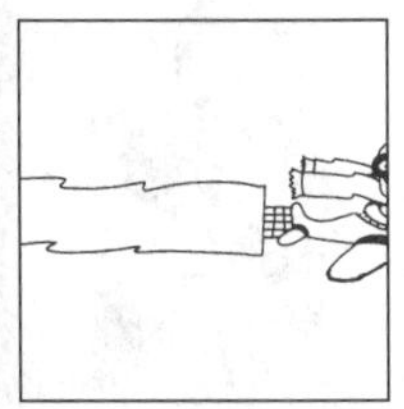
m0000751.tif

m0000752.tif

m0000753.tif

m0000754.tif

m0000755.tif

m0000756.tif

m0000757.tif

m0000758.tif

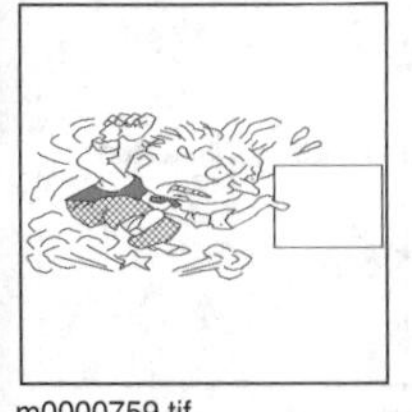
m0000759.tif

m0000760.tif

m0000761.tif

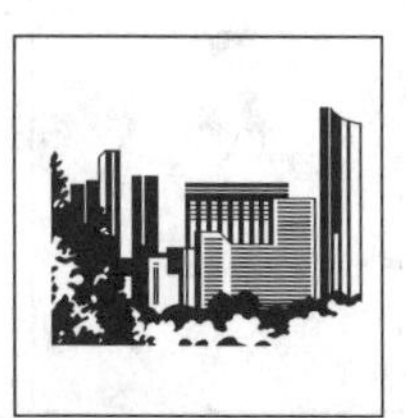
m0000762.tif

m0000763.tif

m0000764.tif

m0000765.tif

m0000766.tif

m0000767.tif

m0000768.tif

m0000769.tif

m0000770.tif

m0000771.tif m0000772.tif m0000773.tif m0000774.tif
m0000775.tif m0000776.tif m0000777.tif m0000778.tif
m0000779.tif m0000780.tif m0000781.tif m0000782.tif
m0000783.tif m0000784.tif m0000785.tif m0000786.tif
m0000787.tif m0000788.tif m0000789.tif m0000790.tif
m0000791.tif m0000792.tif m0000793.tif m0000794.tif

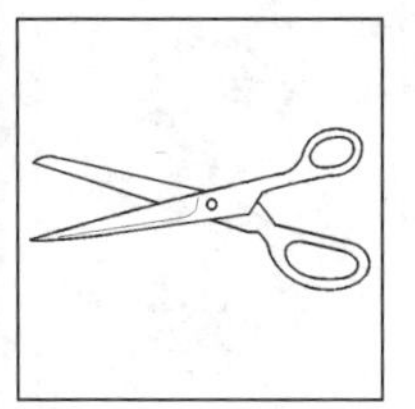
m0000795.tif

m0000796.tif

m0000797.tif

m0000798.tif

m0000799.tif

m0000800.tif

m0000801.tif

m0000802.tif

m0000803.tif

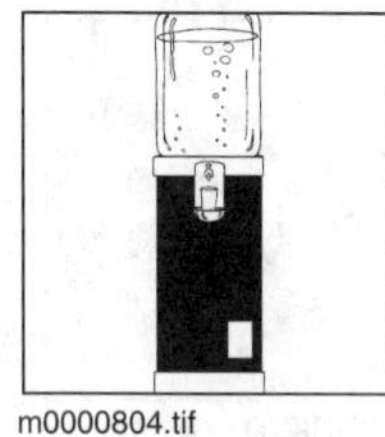
m0000804.tif

m0000805.tif

m0000826.tif m0000827.tif m0000828.tif m0000829.tif

m0000830.tif m0000831.tif m0000832.tif m0000833.tif

m0000834.tif m0000835.tif m0000836.tif m0000837.tif

m0000838.tif m0000839.tif m0000840.tif m0000841.tif

m0000842.tif m0000843.tif m0000844.tif m0000845.tif

m0000846.tif m0000847.tif m0000848.tif m0000849.tif

d:\images\cart

m0000850.tif

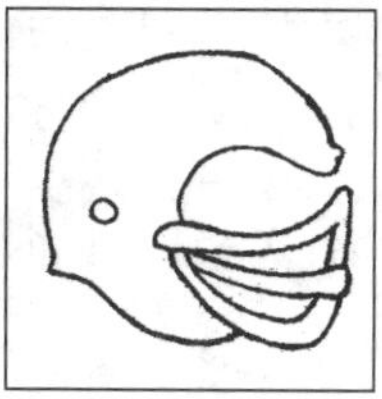

m0000851.tif

m0000852.tif

m0000853.tif

m0000854.tif

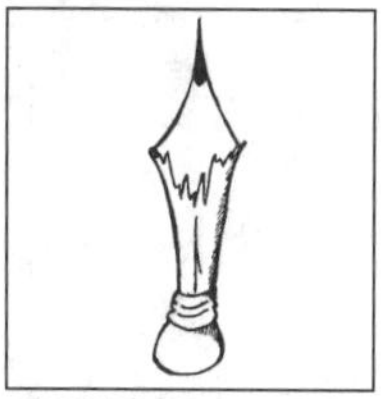

m0000855.tif

m0000856.tif

m0000857.tif

m0000858.tif

m0000859.tif

m0000860.tif

m0000861.tif

m0000862.tif

m0000863.tif

m0000864.tif

m0000865.tif

m0000866.tif

m0000867.tif

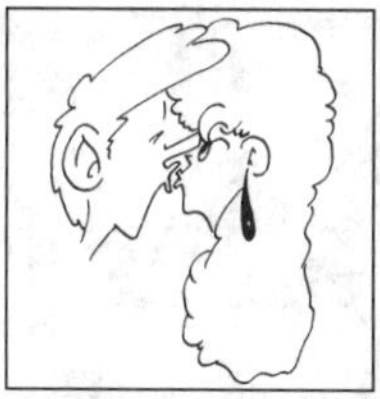

m0000868.tif

m0000869.tif

m0000870.tif

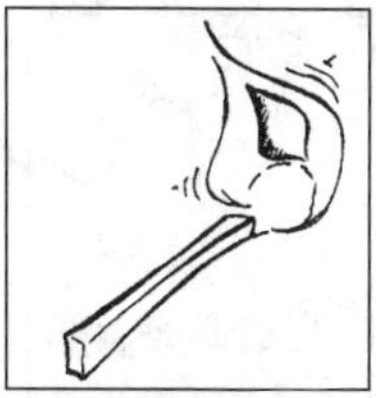

m0000871.tif

m0000872.tif

m0000873.tif

m0000874.tif m0000875.tif m0000876.tif m0000877.tif

m0000878.tif m0000879.tif m0000880.tif m0000881.tif

m0000882.tif m0000883.tif m0000884.tif m0000885.tif

m0000886.tif m0000887.tif m0000888.tif m0000889.tif

m0000890.tif m0000891.tif m0000892.tif m0000893.tif

m0000894.tif m0000895.tif m0000896.tif m0000897.tif

m0000898.tif
m0000899.tif
m0000900.tif
m0000901.tif
m0000902.tif
m0000903.tif
m0000904.tif
m0000905.tif
m0000906.tif
m0000907.tif
m0000908.tif
m0000910.tif
m0000911.tif
m0000912.tif
m0000913.tif
m0000914.tif
m0000915.tif
m0000916.tif
m0000917.tif
m0000918.tif
m0000919.tif
m0000920.tif
m0000921.tif
m0000922.tif

d:\images\cart

m0000923.tif

m0000924.tif

m0000925.tif

m0000926.tif

m0000927.tif

m0000928.tif

m0000929.tif

m0000930.tif

m0000931.tif

m0000932.tif

m0000933.tif

m0000934.tif

m0000935.tif

m0000936.tif

m0000937.tif

m0000938.tif

m0000939.tif

m0000940.tif

m0000941.tif

m0000942.tif

m0000943.tif

m0000944.tif

m0000945.tif

m0000946.tif

m0000947.tif

m0000948.tif

m0000949.tif

m0000950.tif

m0000951.tif

m0000952.tif

m0000953.tif

m0000954.tif

m0000955.tif

m0000956.tif

m0000957.tif

m0000958.tif

m0000959.tif

m0000960.tif

m0000961.tif

m0000962.tif

m0000963.tif

m0000964.tif

m0000965.tif

m0000966.tif

m0000967.tif

m0000973.tif

m0000974.tif

m0000977.tif

d:\images\cart

c0000979.tif c0000980.tif c0000981.tif c0000982.tif

c0000983.tif c0000985.tif c0000986.tif c0000988.tif

c0000989.tif c0000990.tif c0000992.tif c0000993.tif

c0000995.tif c0000996.tif c0001045.tif c0001047.tif

c0001049.tif c0001050.tif c0001052.tif c0001055.tif

c0001057.tif c0001063.tif m0000978.tif m0000997.tif

d:\images\cats

m0000998.tif m0000999.tif m0001000.tif m0001001.tif

m0001002.tif m0001003.tif m0001004.tif m0001005.tif

m0001006.tif m0001007.tif m0001008.tif m0001009.tif

m0001010.tif m0001011.tif m0001012.tif m0001013.tif

m0001014.tif m0001015.tif m0001016.tif m0001017.tif

m0001018.tif m0001019.tif m0001020.tif m0001021.tif

d:\images\cats

m0001022.tif

m0001023.tif

m0001024.tif

m0001025.tif

m0001026.tif

m0001027.tif

m0001028.tif

m0001029.tif

m0001030.tif

m0001031.tif

m0001032.tif

m0001033.tif

m0001034.tif

m0001035.tif

m0001036.tif

m0001037.tif

m0001038.tif

m0001039.tif

m0001040.tif

m0001041.tif

m0001042.tif

m0001043.tif

m0001044.tif

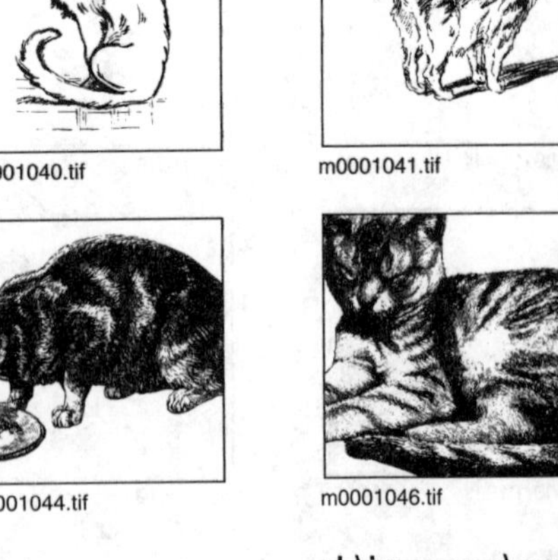

m0001046.tif

d:\images\cats

m0001048.tif

m0001051.tif

m0001053.tif

m0001054.tif

m0001056.tif

m0001058.tif

m0001059.tif

m0001060.tif

m0001061.tif

m0001062.tif

d:\images\cats

m0001064.tif

m0001065.tif

m0001066.tif

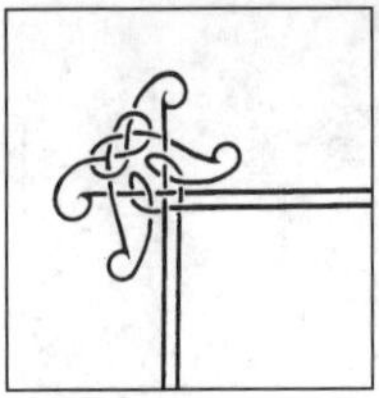

m0001067.tif

m0001068.tif

m0001069.tif

m0001070.tif

m0001071.tif

m0001072.tif

m0001073.tif

m0001074.tif

m0001075.tif

m0001076.tif

m0001077.tif

m0001078.tif

m0001079.tif

m0001080.tif

m0001081.tif

m0001082.tif

m0001083.tif

m0001084.tif

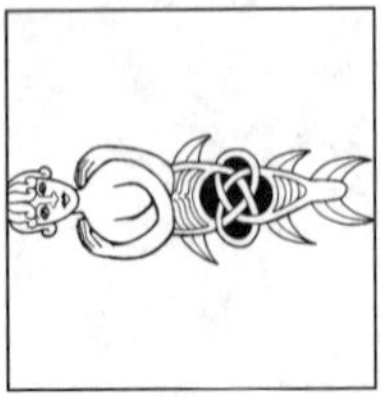

m0001085.tif

m0001086.tif

m0001087.tif

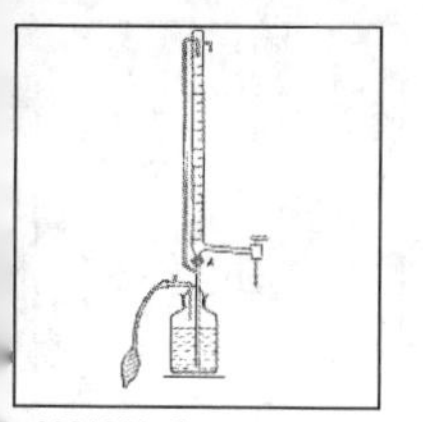
m0001088.tif

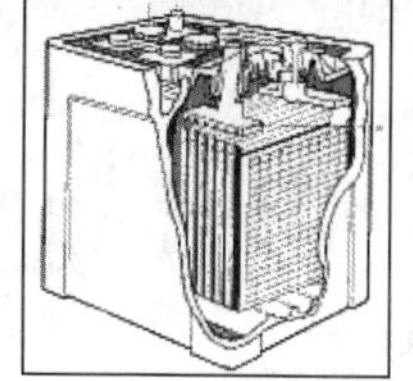
m0001089.tif

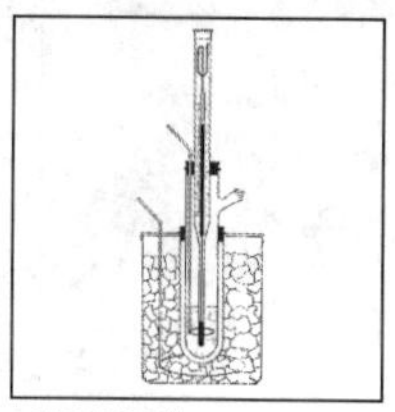
m0001090.tif

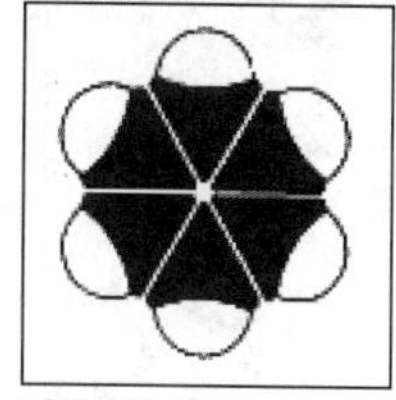
m0001091.tif

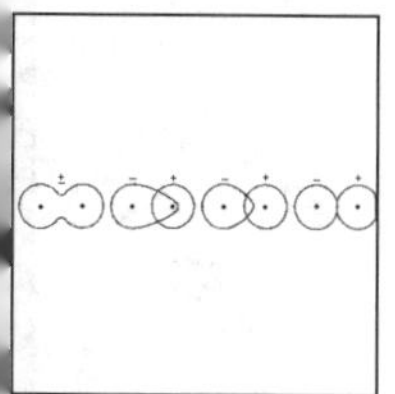
m0001092.tif

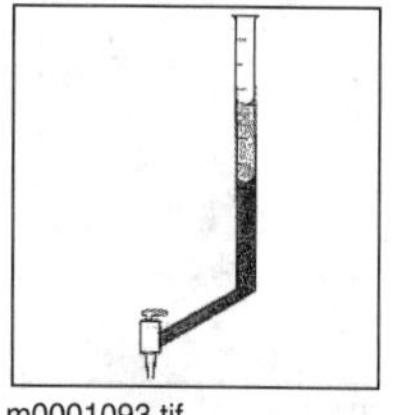
m0001093.tif

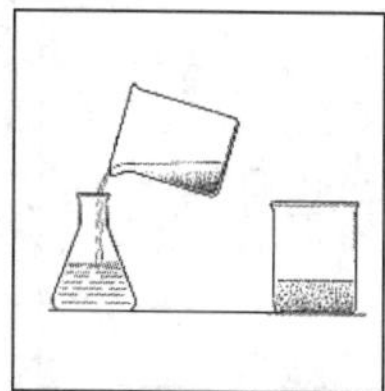
m0001094.tif

m0001095.tif

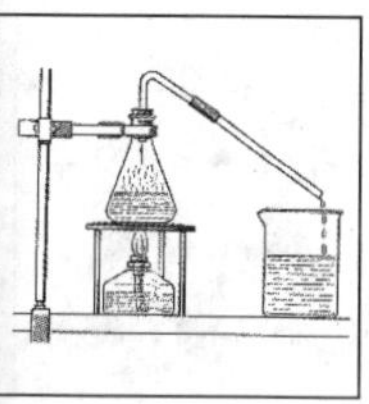
m0001096.tif

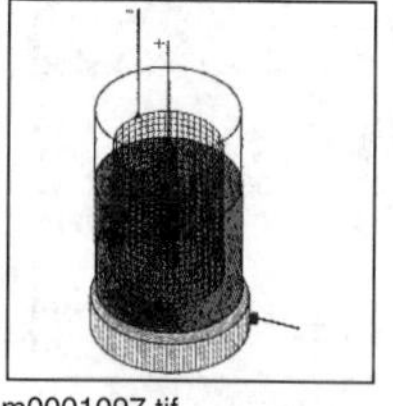
m0001097.tif

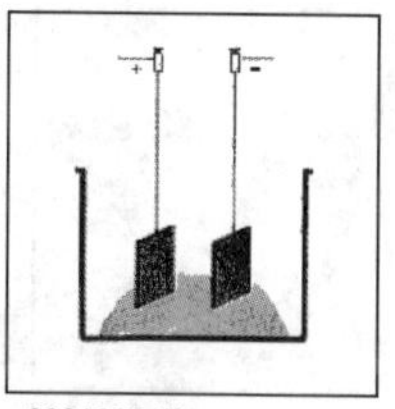
m0001098.tif

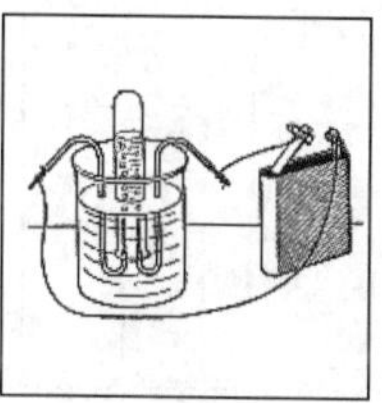
m0001099.tif

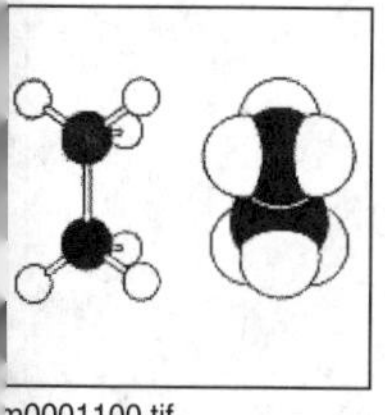
m0001100.tif

m0001101.tif

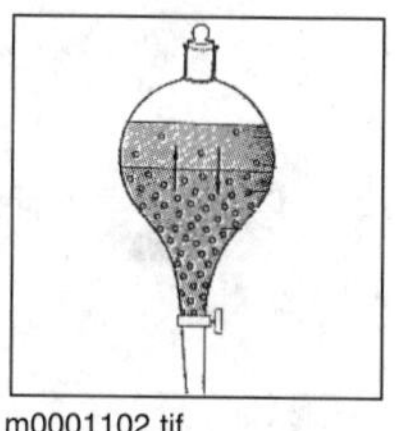
m0001102.tif

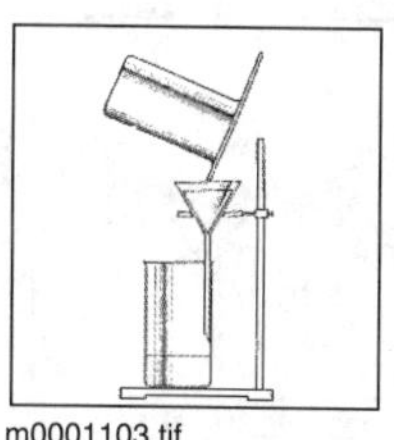
m0001103.tif

m0001104.tif

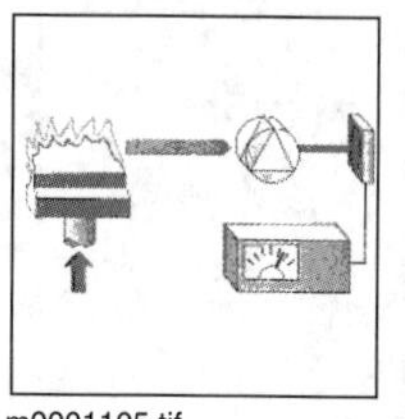
m0001105.tif

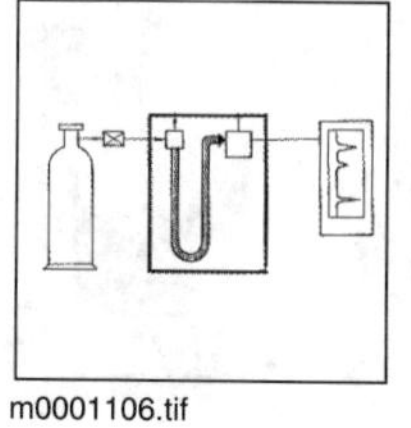
m0001106.tif

m0001107.tif

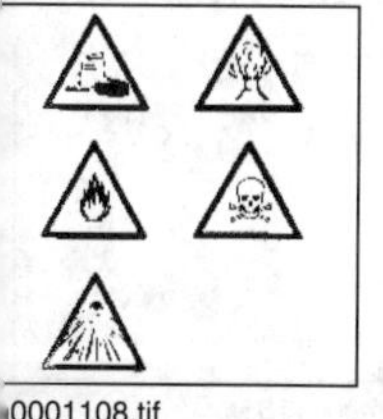
m0001108.tif

m0001109.tif

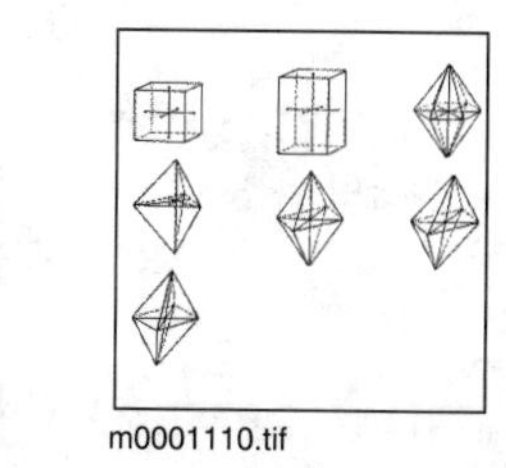
m0001110.tif

m0001111.tif

d:\images\chem

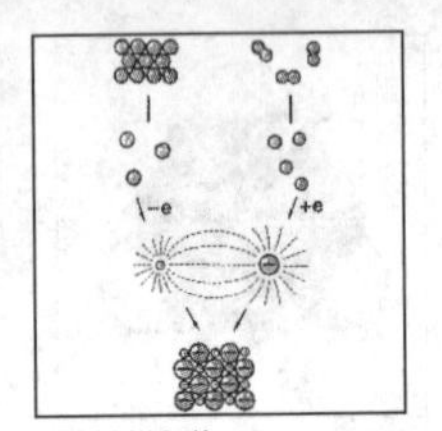
m0001112.tif

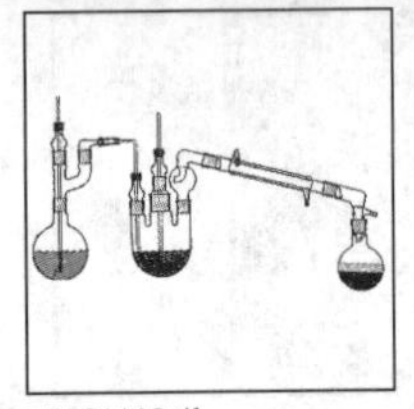
m0001113.tif

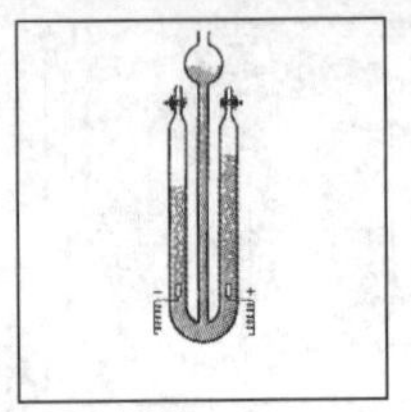
m0001114.tif

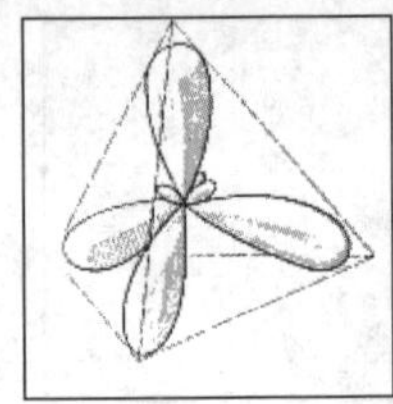
m0001115.tif

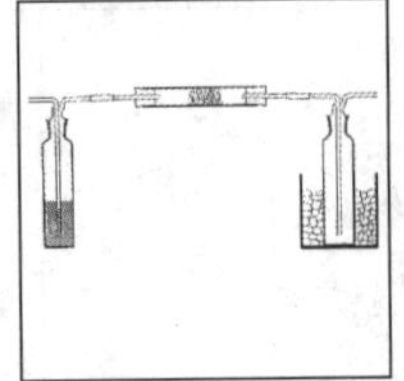
m0001116.tif

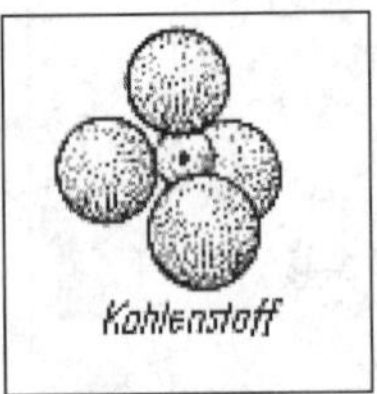

m0001117.tif

m0001118.tif

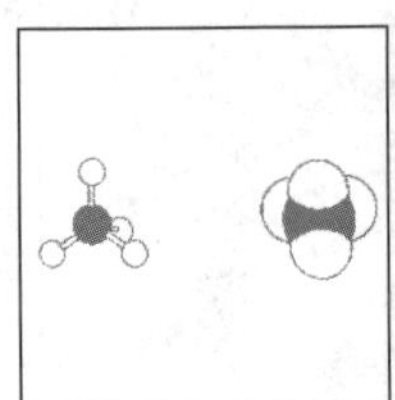
m0001119.tif

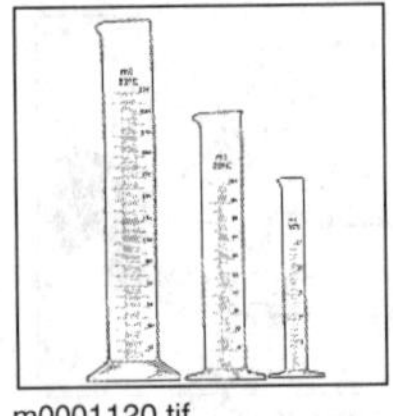
m0001120.tif

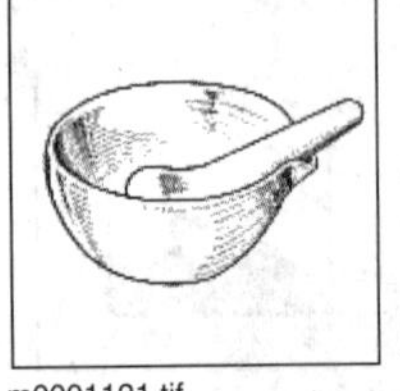
m0001121.tif

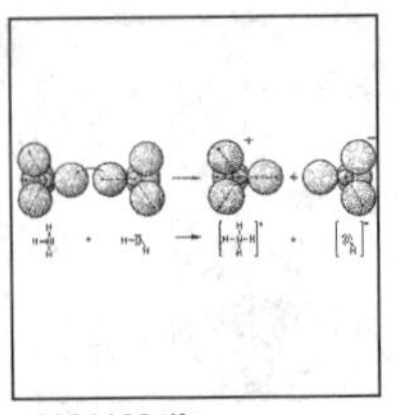
m0001122.tif

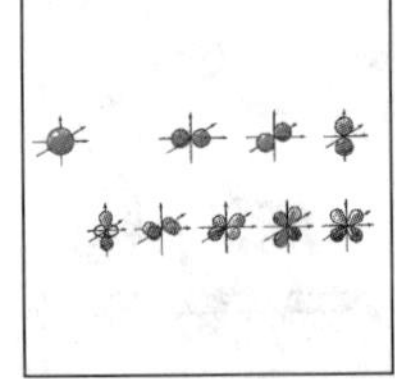
m0001123.tif

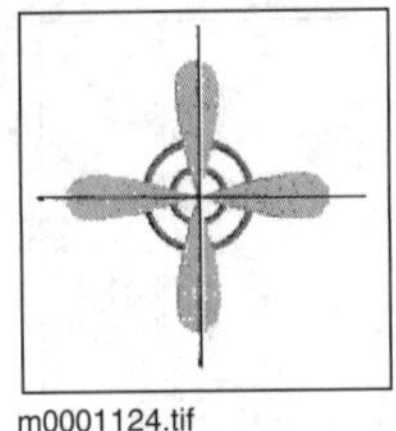
m0001124.tif

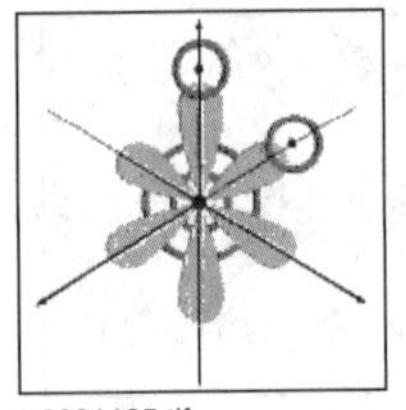
m0001125.tif

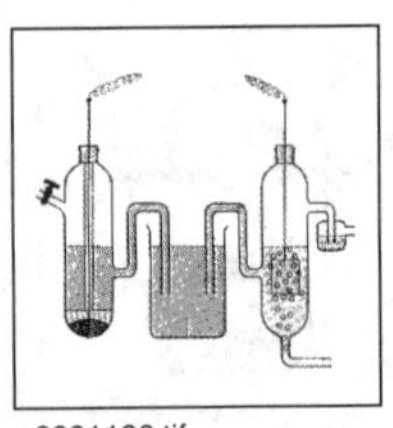
m0001126.tif

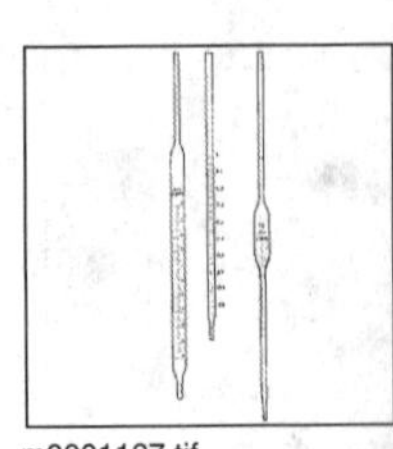
m0001127.tif

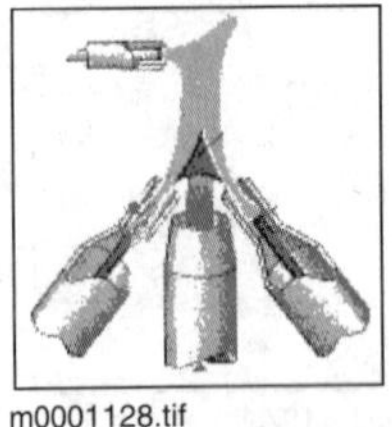
m0001128.tif

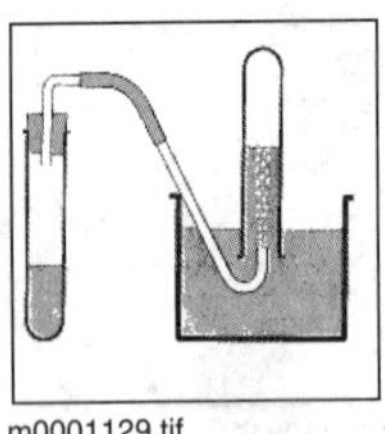
m0001129.tif

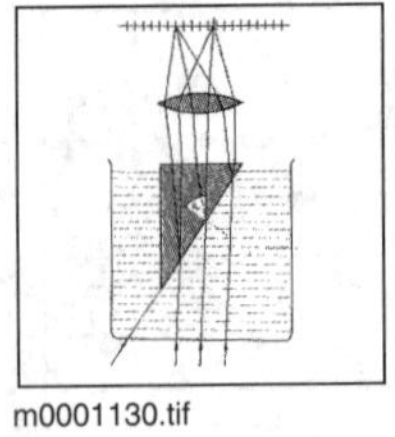
m0001130.tif

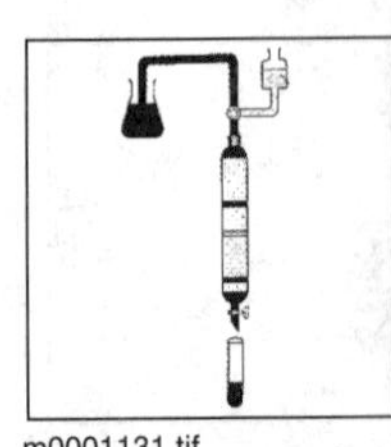
m0001131.tif

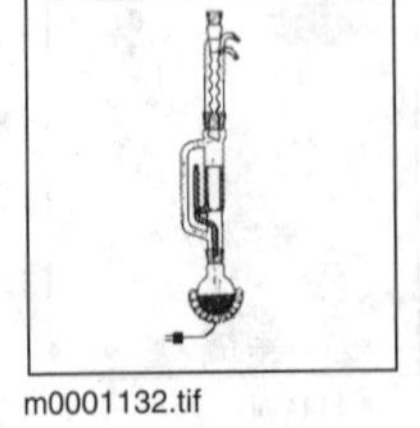
m0001132.tif

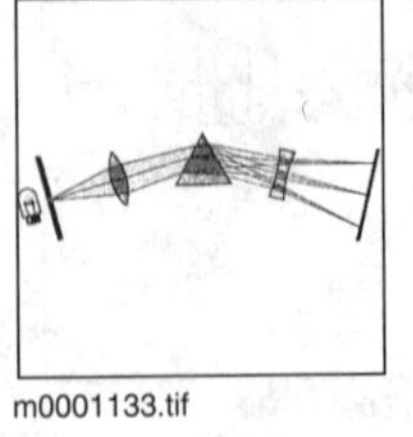
m0001133.tif

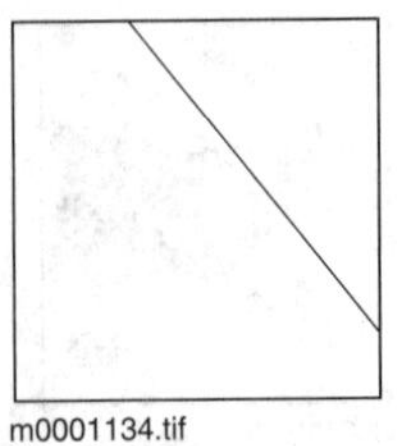
m0001134.tif

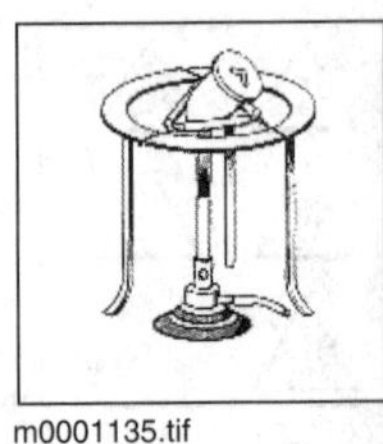
m0001135.tif

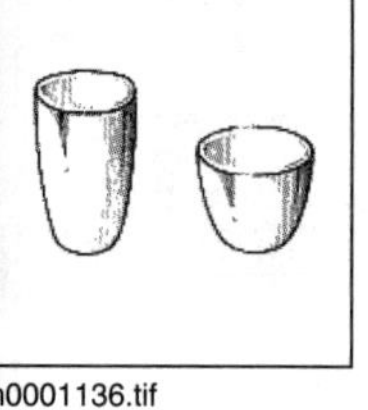
ı0001136.tif

ı:\images\chem

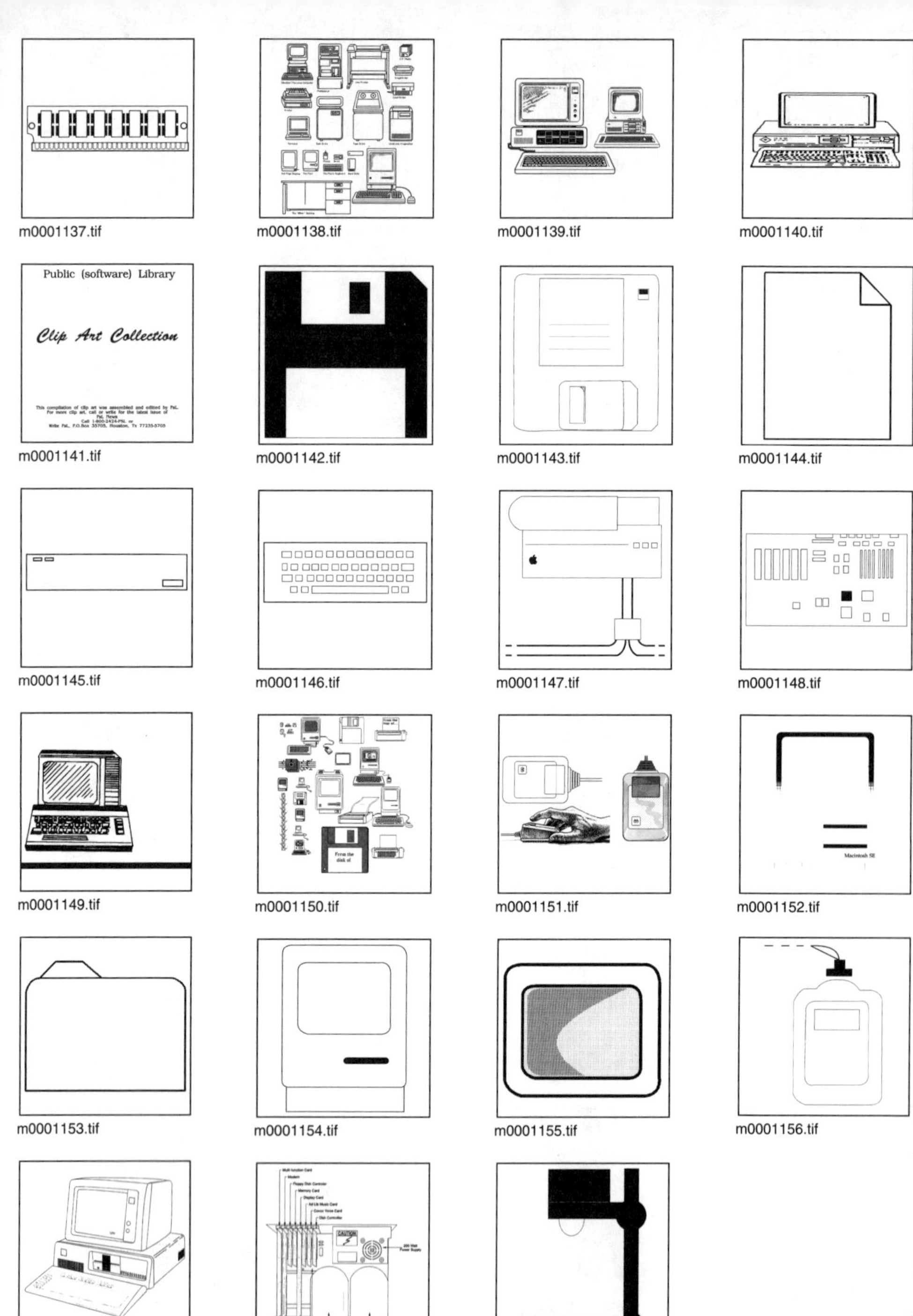

m0001137.tif m0001138.tif m0001139.tif m0001140.tif

m0001141.tif m0001142.tif m0001143.tif m0001144.tif

m0001145.tif m0001146.tif m0001147.tif m0001148.tif

m0001149.tif m0001150.tif m0001151.tif m0001152.tif

m0001153.tif m0001154.tif m0001155.tif m0001156.tif

m0001157.tif m0001158.tif m0001159.tif

m0001160.tif

m0001161.tif

m0001162.tif

m0001163.tif

m0001164.tif

m0001165.tif

m0001166.tif

m0001167.tif

m0001168.tif

m0001169.tif

m0001170.tif

m0001171.tif

m0001172.tif

m0001173.tif

m0001174.tif

m0001175.tif

m0001176.tif

m0001177.tif

m0001178.tif

m0001179.tif

m0001180.tif

m0001181.tif

m0001182.tif

m0001183.tif

d:\images\cooper1

m0001184.tif

m0001185.tif

m0001186.tif

m0001187.tif

m0001188.tif

m0001189.tif

m0001190.tif

m0001191.tif

m0001192.tif

m0001193.tif

m0001194.tif

m0001195.tif

m0001196.tif

m0001197.tif

m0001198.tif

m0001199.tif

m0001200.tif

m0001201.tif

m0001202.tif

m0001203.tif

m0001204.tif

m0001205.tif

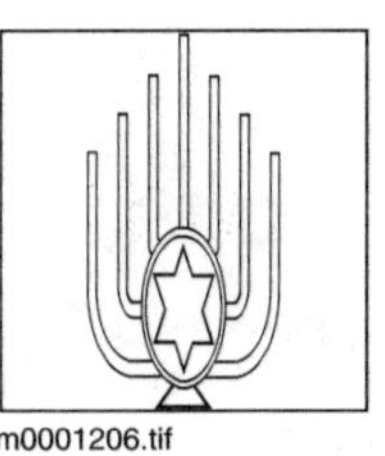
m0001206.tif

m0001207.tif

d:\images\cooper1

)001208.tif

m0001209.tif

m0001210.tif

m0001211.tif

)001212.tif

m0001213.tif

m0001214.tif

m0001215.tif

)001216.tif

m0001217.tif

m0001218.tif

m0001219.tif

)001220.tif

m0001221.tif

m0001222.tif

m0001223.tif

)001224.tif

m0001225.tif

m0001226.tif

m0001227.tif

)001228.tif

m0001229.tif

m0001230.tif

m0001231.tif

I:\images\cooper1

m0001232.tif

m0001233.tif

m0001234.tif

m0001235.tif

m0001236.tif

m0001237.tif

m0001238.tif

m0001239.tif

m0001240.tif

m0001241.tif

m0001242.tif

m0001243.tif

m0001244.tif

m0001245.tif

m0001246.tif

m0001247.tif

m0001248.tif

m0001249.tif

m0001250.tif

m0001251.tif

m0001252.tif

m0001253.tif

m0001254.tif

m0001255.tif

001256.tif

m0001257.tif

m0001258.tif

m0001259.tif

001260.tif

m0001262.tif

m0001263.tif

m0001264.tif

001265.tif

m0001266.tif

m0001268.tif

m0001270.tif

001271.tif

m0001272.tif

m0001273.tif

m0001274.tif

001275.tif

m0001276.tif

m0001277.tif

m0001278.tif

001279.tif

m0001281.tif

m0001282.tif

m0001283.tif

:\images\cooper1

m0001284.tif

m0001285.tif

m0001286.tif

m0001287.tif

m0001289.tif

m0001290.tif

m0001291.tif

m0001293.tif

m0001294.tif

m0001295.tif

m0001296.tif

m0001297.tif

m0001298.tif

m0001299.tif

m0001300.tif

m0001301.tif

m0001302.tif

m0001303.tif

m0001305.tif

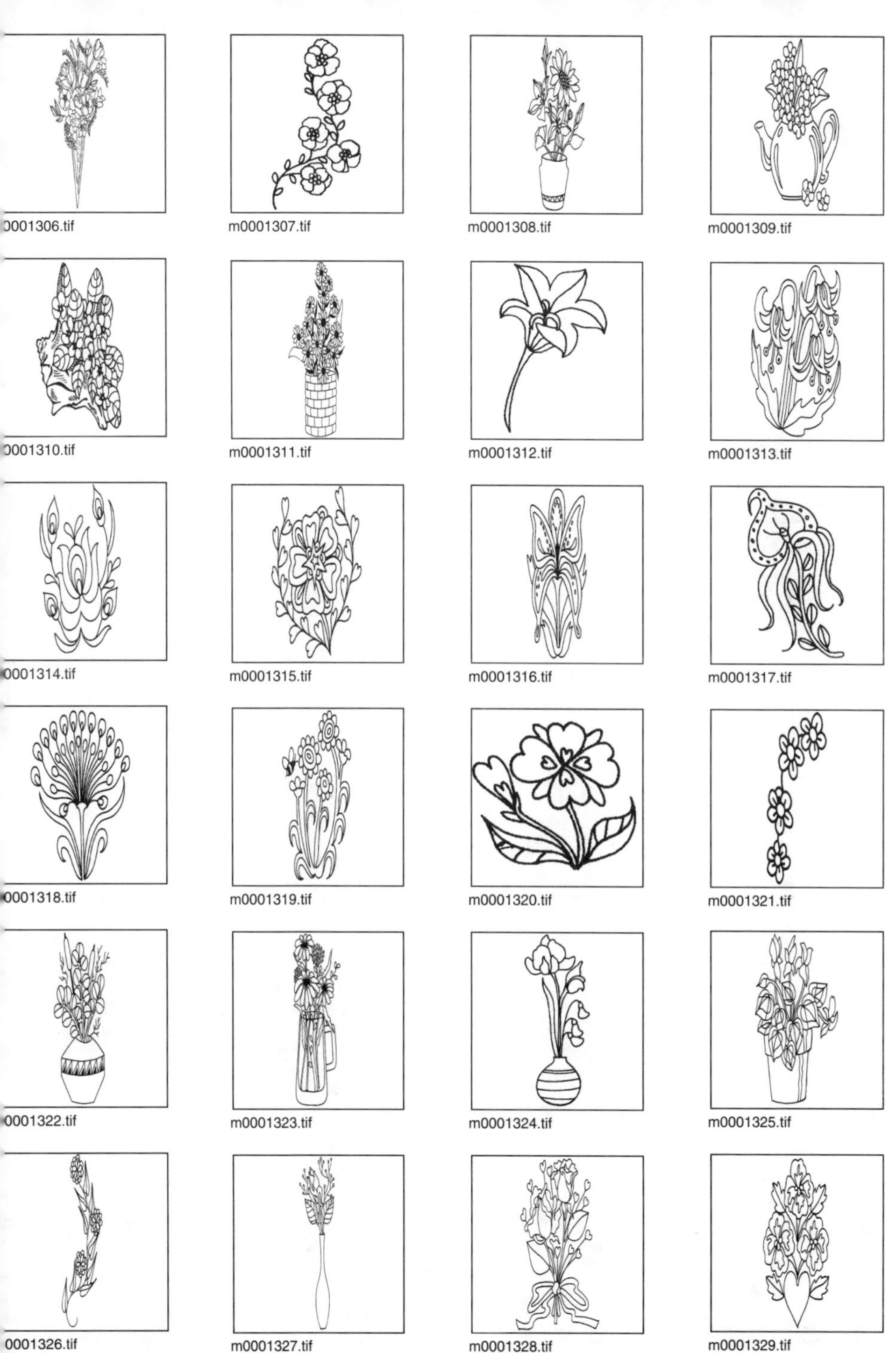

:\images\cooper2

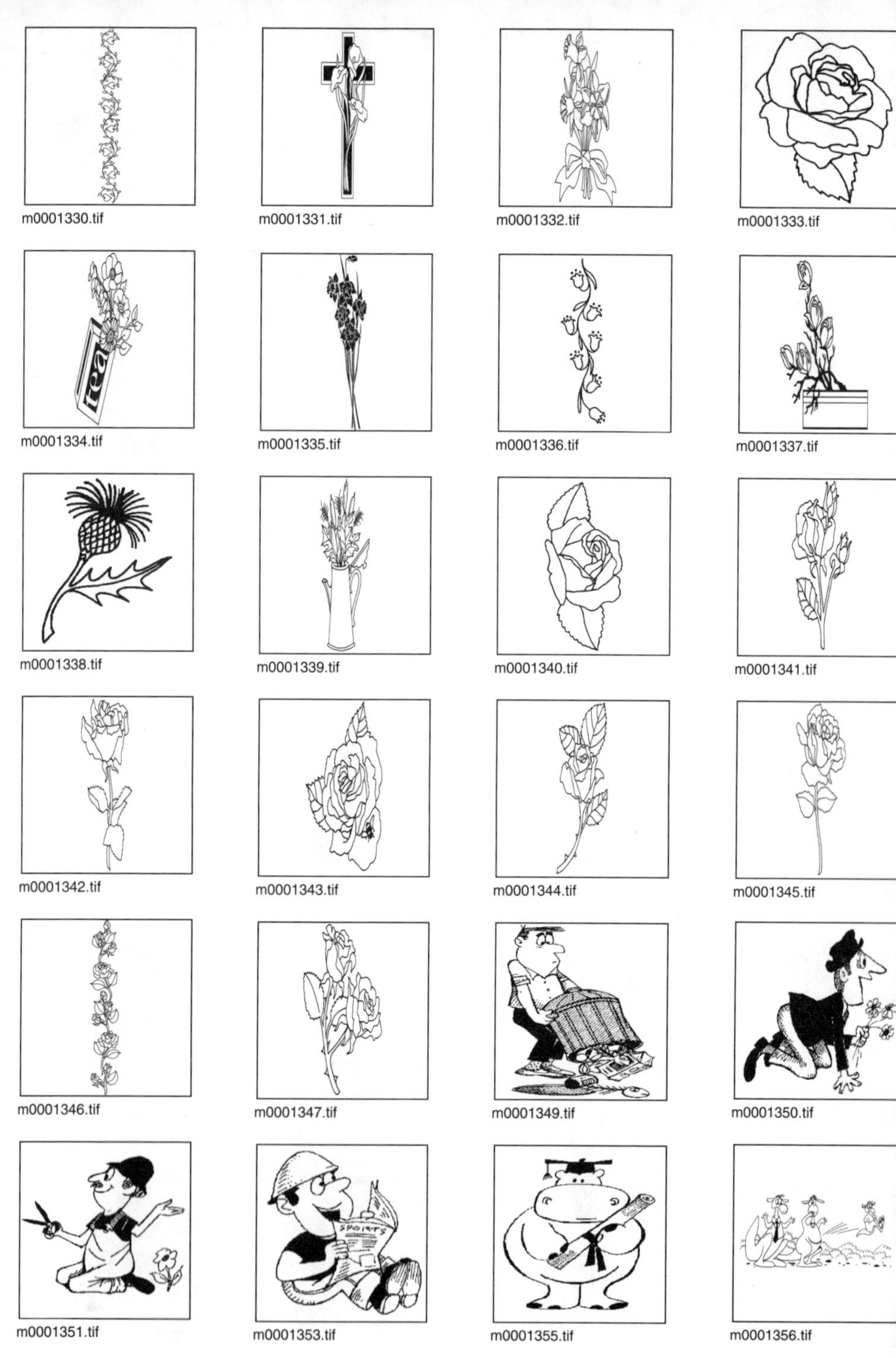

m0001330.tif m0001331.tif m0001332.tif m0001333.tif

m0001334.tif m0001335.tif m0001336.tif m0001337.tif

m0001338.tif m0001339.tif m0001340.tif m0001341.tif

m0001342.tif m0001343.tif m0001344.tif m0001345.tif

m0001346.tif m0001347.tif m0001349.tif m0001350.tif

m0001351.tif m0001353.tif m0001355.tif m0001356.tif

0001357.tif

m0001358.tif

m0001359.tif

m0001360.tif

0001361.tif

m0001362.tif

m0001363.tif

m0001364.tif

0001365.tif

m0001366.tif

m0001367.tif

m0001368.tif

0001369.tif

m0001370.tif

m0001371.tif

m0001372.tif

0001373.tif

m0001374.tif

m0001375.tif

m0001376.tif

0001377.tif

m0001378.tif

m0001379.tif

m0001380.tif

d:\images\cooper2

m0001381.tif

m0001382.tif

m0001383.tif

m0001384.tif

m0001385.tif

m0001386.tif

m0001387.tif

m0001388.tif

m0001389.tif

m0001390.tif

m0001391.tif

m0001392.tif

m0001393.tif

m0001394.tif

m0001395.tif

m0001396.tif

m0001397.tif

m0001398.tif

m0001399.tif

m0001401.tif

m0001402.tif

m0001403.tif

m0001405.tif

m0001406.tif

m0001407.tif

m0001408.tif

m0001409.tif

m0001410.tif

m0001411.tif

m0001412.tif

m0001413.tif

m0001414.tif

m0001415.tif

m0001416.tif

m0001417.tif

m0001418.tif

m0001419.tif

m0001421.tif

m0001422.tif

m0001423.tif

m0001424.tif

m0001425.tif

m0001426.tif

m0001427.tif

m0001428.tif

m0001429.tif

m0001430.tif

m0001431.tif

d:\images\coper2

m0001432.tif

m0001433.tif

m0001434.tif

m0001435.tif

m0001436.tif

m0001437.tif

m0001438.tif

m0001439.tif

m0001440.tif

m0001442.tif

m0001443.tif

m0001444.tif

m0001445.tif

m0001447.tif

m0001448.tif

m0001449.tif

m0001450.tif

m0001451.tif

m0001452.tif

m0001454.tif

m0001455.tif

m0001456.tif

m0001457.tif

m0001458.tif

m0001459.tif

m0001461.tif

m0001462.tif

m0001463.tif

m0001464.tif

m0001465.tif

m0001483.tif

m0001484.tif

m0001485.tif

d:\images\cooper3

m0001487.tif

m0001488.tif

m0001489.tif

m0001490.tif

m0001492.tif

m0001493.tif

m0001494.tif

m0001495.tif

m0001525.tif

m0001526.tif

m0001527.tif

m0001528.tif

m0001529.tif

m0001530.tif

m0001531.tif

m0001532.tif

m0001533.tif

m0001534.tif

m0001535.tif

m0001536.tif

m0001537.tif

m0001538.tif

m0001539.tif

m0001540.tif

d:\images\cooper3

m0001541.tif

m0001542.tif

m0001543.tif

m0001544.tif

m0001545.tif

m0001546.tif

m0001547.tif

m0001549.tif

m0001550.tif

m0001551.tif

m0001552.tif

m0001554.tif

m0001555.tif

m0001556.tif

d:\images\cooper3

m0001558.tif

m0001559.tif

m0001560.tif

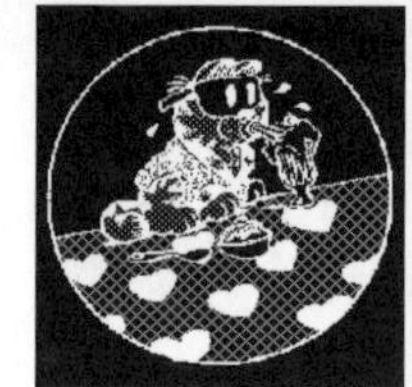
m0001561.tif

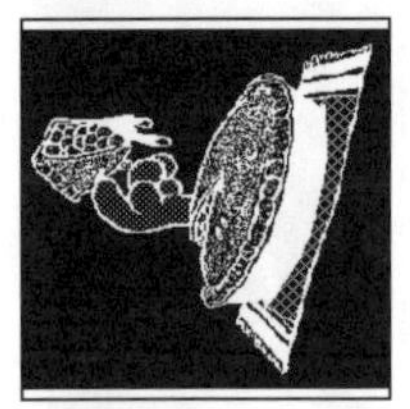
m0001562.tif

m0001563.tif

m0001564.tif

m0001565.tif

m0001566.tif

m0001567.tif

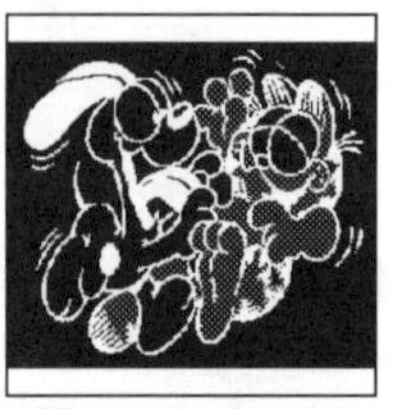
m0001568.tif

m0001569.tif

m0001570.tif

m0001571.tif

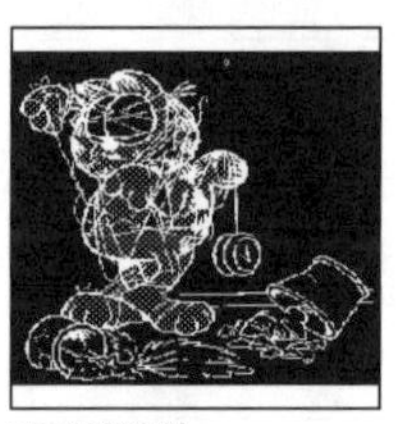
m0001572.tif

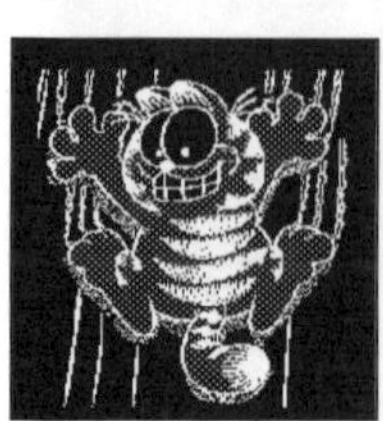
m0001573.tif

m0001574.tif

m0001575.tif

m0001576.tif

m0001577.tif

m0001578.tif

m0001579.tif

m0001580.tif

m0001581.tif

m0001582.tif

m0001583.tif

m0001584.tif

m0001585.tif

m0001586.tif

m0001587.tif

m0001588.tif

m0001589.tif

m0001591.tif

m0001593.tif

m0001594.tif

m0001595.tif

m0001596.tif

m0001597.tif

m0001598.tif

m0001599.tif

m0001600.tif

m0001601.tif

m0001602.tif

m0001603.tif

m0001604.tif

m0001605.tif

m0001606.tif

m0001607.tif

d:\images\cooper4

m0001608.tif

m0001609.tif

m0001610.tif

m0001612.tif

m0001614.tif

m0001615.tif

m0001616.tif

m0001617.tif

m0001618.tif

m0001619.tif

m0001620.tif

m0001621.tif

m0001623.tif

m0001624.tif

m0001625.tif

m0001626.tif

m0001627.tif

m0001630.tif

m0001631.tif

m0001632.tif

m0001633.tif

m0001634.tif

m0001636.tif

m0001637.tif

m0001638.tif

m0001639.tif

m0001640.tif

m0001641.tif

m0001643.tif

m0001644.tif

m0001645.tif

m0001646.tif

m0001647.tif

m0001648.tif

m0001649.tif

m0001650.tif

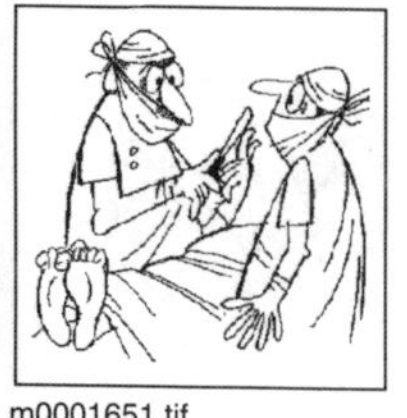
m0001651.tif

m0001652.tif

m0001653.tif

m0001654.tif

m0001655.tif

m0001656.tif

m0001657.tif

m0001658.tif

m0001659.tif

m0001660.tif

m0001661.tif

m0001662.tif

m0001663.tif

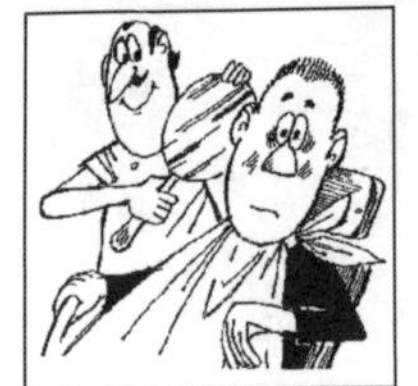
m0001664.tif

m0001665.tif

m0001666.tif

m0001667.tif

m0001668.tif

m0001669.tif

m0001670.tif

m0001671.tif

m0001672.tif

m0001673.tif

m0001674.tif

m0001675.tif

m0001676.tif

m0001677.tif

m0001678.tif

m0001680.tif

m0001681.tif

m0001682.tif

m0001683.tif

m0001684.tif

m0001685.tif

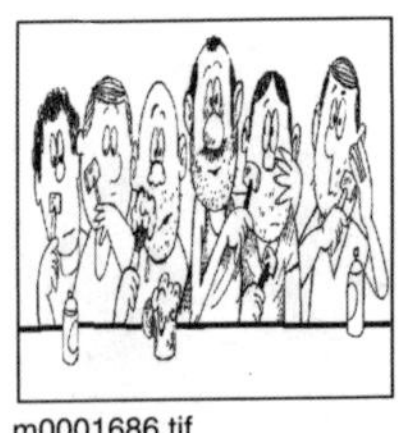
m0001686.tif

m0001687.tif

d:\images\cooper4

m0001688.tif

m0001689.tif

m0001691.tif

m0001692.tif

m0001693.tif

m0001694.tif

m0001695.tif

m0001696.tif

m0001697.tif

m0001698.tif

m0001699.tif

m0001700.tif

m0001701.tif

m0001702.tif

m0001703.tif

m0001704.tif

m0001705.tif

m0001706.tif

m0001707.tif

m0001708.tif

m0001709.tif

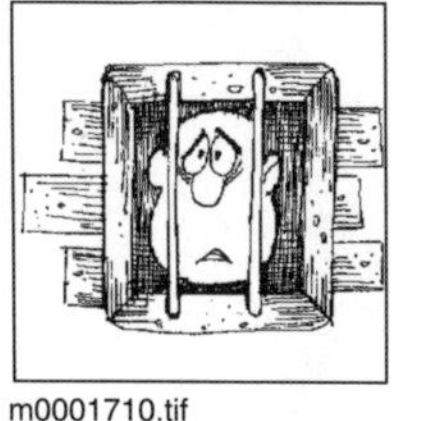
m0001710.tif

m0001711.tif

m0001712.tif

d:\images\cooper4

m0001713.tif

m0001714.tif

m0001715.tif

m0001716.tif

m0001717.tif

m0001718.tif

m0001719.tif

m0001720.tif

m0001721.tif

m0001722.tif

m0001723.tif

m0001724.tif

m0001725.tif

m0001726.tif

m0001727.tif

m0001728.tif

m0001729.tif

m0001730.tif

d:\images\cooper4

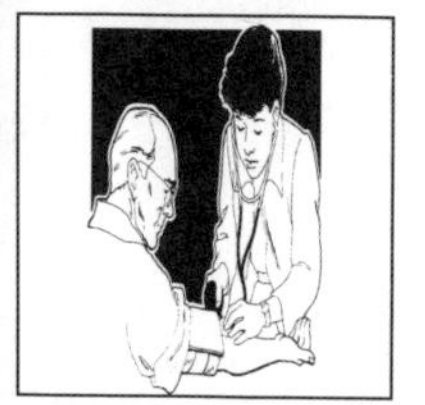
m0001731.tif

m0001732.tif

m0001733.tif

m0001734.tif

m0001735.tif

m0001736.tif

m0001737.tif

m0001738.tif

m0001739.tif

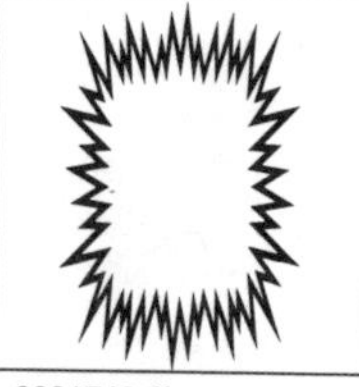
m0001740.tif

m0001741.tif

m0001742.tif

m0001743.tif

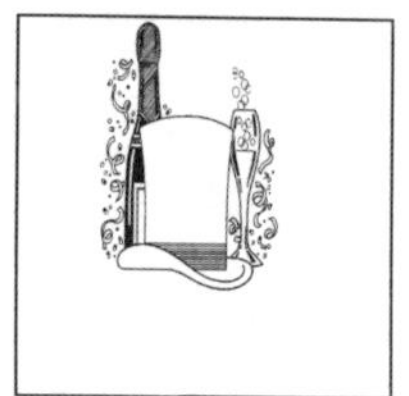
m0001744.tif

m0001745.tif

m0001746.tif

m0001748.tif

m0001749.tif

m0001750.tif

c0001752.tif m0001751.tif m0001758.tif m0001759.tif

m0001760.tif m0001762.tif m0001764.tif m0001765.tif

m0001766.tif m0001768.tif m0001769.tif m0001770.tif

m0001771.tif m0001772.tif m0001773.tif m0001774.tif

m0001775.tif m0001776.tif m0001777.tif m0001778.tif

m0001780.tif m0001784.tif m0001785.tif m0001788.tif

d:\images\dino

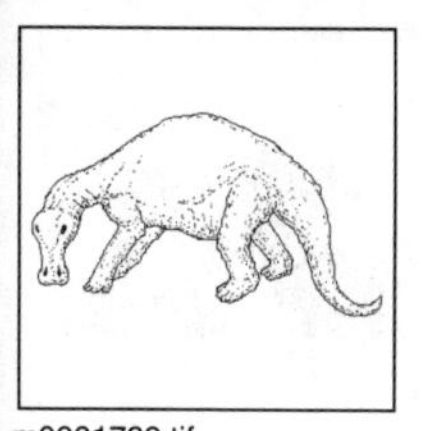

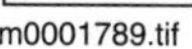

m0001789.tif

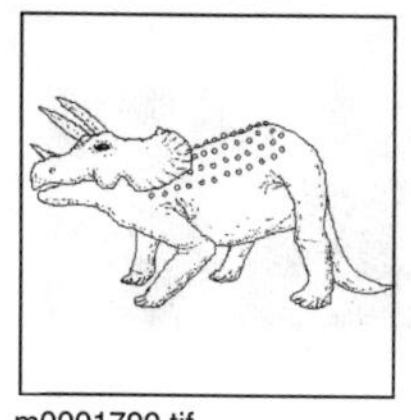

m0001790.tif

m0001793.tif

c0001856.tif

c0001859.tif

c0001860.tif

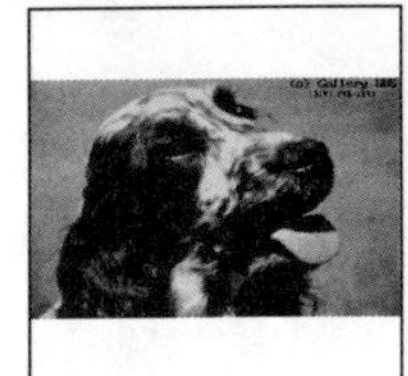
c0001861.tif

c0001862.tif

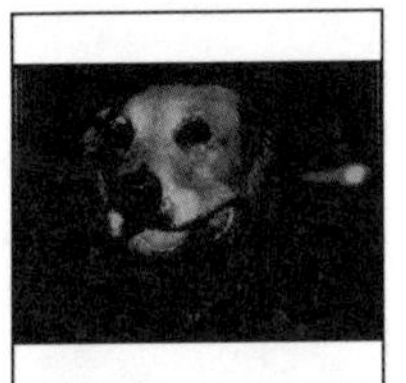
c0001863.tif

c0001864.tif

c0001867.tif

c0001868.tif

c0001869.tif

c0001871.tif

c0001872.tif

c0001875.tif

c0001876.tif

c0001877.tif

m0001795.tif

m0001796.tif

m0001797.tif

m0001798.tif

m0001799.tif

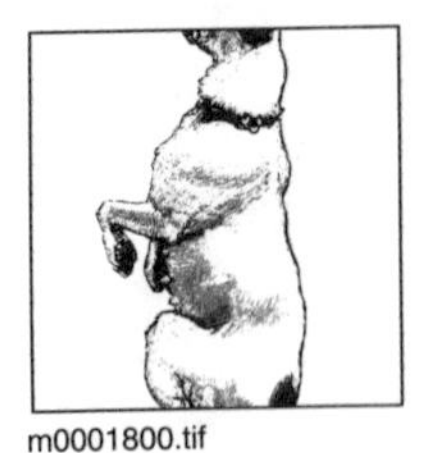
m0001800.tif

m0001801.tif

m0001802.tif

m0001803.tif

d:\images\dogs

m0001804.tif

m0001805.tif

m0001806.tif

m0001807.tif

m0001808.tif

m0001809.tif

m0001810.tif

m0001811.tif

m0001812.tif

m0001813.tif

m0001814.tif

m0001815.tif

m0001816.tif

m0001817.tif

m0001818.tif

m0001819.tif

m0001820.tif

m0001821.tif

m0001822.tif

m0001823.tif

m0001824.tif

m0001825.tif

m0001826.tif

m0001827.tif

d:\images\dogs

m0001828.tif

m0001829.tif

m0001830.tif

m0001831.tif

m0001832.tif

m0001833.tif

m0001834.tif

m0001835.tif

m0001836.tif

m0001837.tif

m0001838.tif

m0001839.tif

m0001840.tif

m0001841.tif

m0001842.tif

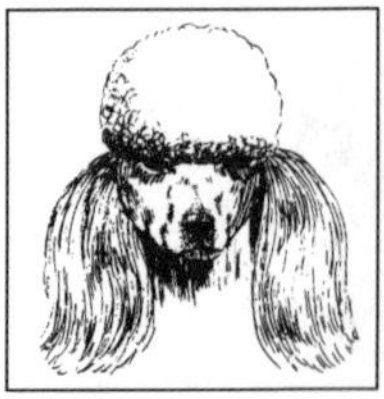

m0001843.tif

m0001844.tif

m0001845.tif

m0001846.tif

m0001847.tif

m0001848.tif

m0001849.tif

m0001850.tif

m0001851.tif

0001852.tif

m0001853.tif

m0001854.tif

m0001855.tif

0001857.tif

m0001858.tif

m0001865.tif

m0001866.tif

0001870.tif

m0001873.tif

m0001874.tif

m0001878.tif

m0001879.tif

m0001880.tif

m0001881.tif

m0001882.tif

m0001883.tif

m0001884.tif

m0001885.tif

m0001886.tif

m0001887.tif

m0001888.tif

m0001889.tif

m0001890.tif

m0001891.tif

m0001892.tif

m0001893.tif

m0001894.tif

m0001895.tif

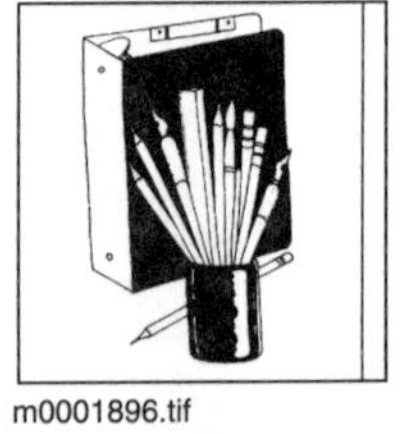
m0001896.tif

m0001897.tif

m0001898.tif

m0001899.tif

m0001900.tif

m0001901.tif

n0001902.tif

m0001903.tif

m0001904.tif

d:\images\educati

m0001905.eps

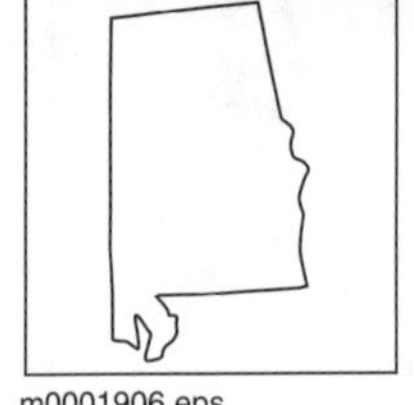
m0001906.eps

m0001907.eps

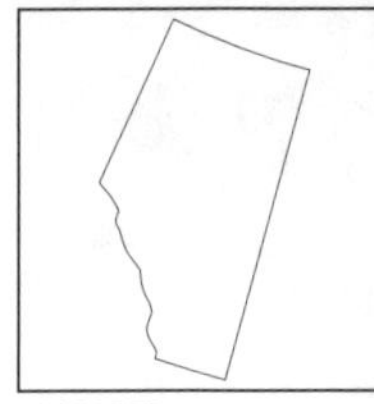
m0001908.eps

m0001909.eps

m0001911.eps

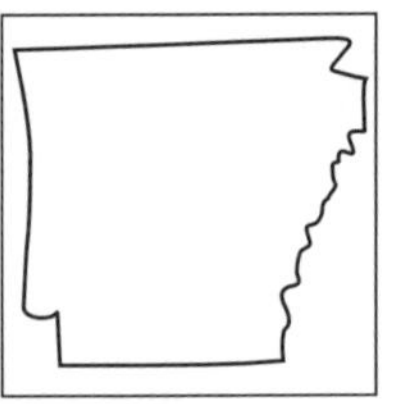
m0001912.eps

m0001913.eps

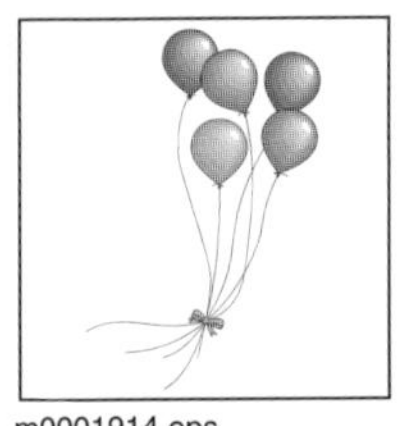
m0001914.eps

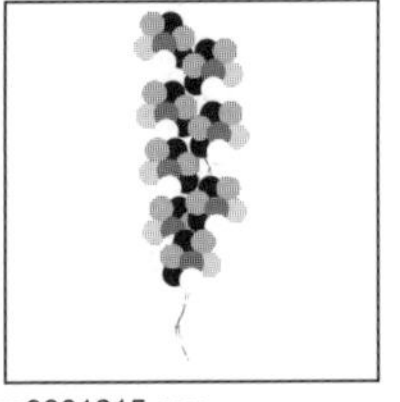
m0001915.eps

m0001916.eps

m0001917.eps

m0001918.eps

m0001919.eps

m0001920.eps

m0001921.eps

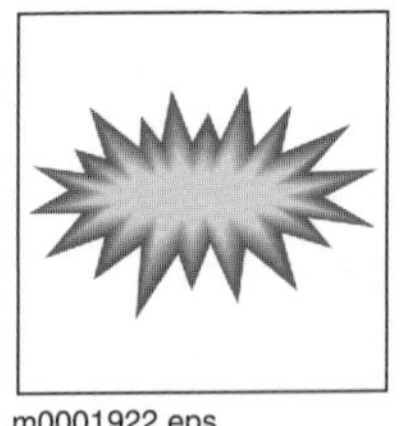
m0001922.eps

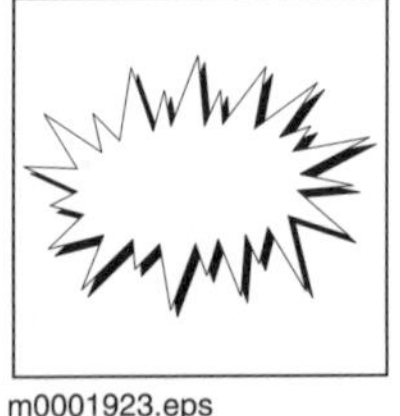
m0001923.eps

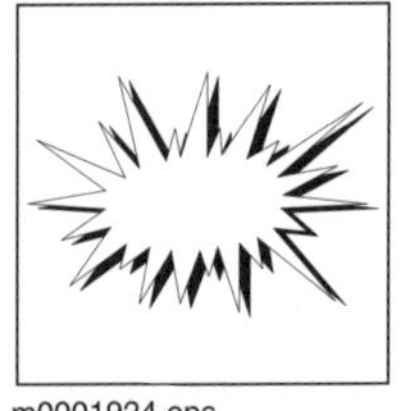
m0001924.eps

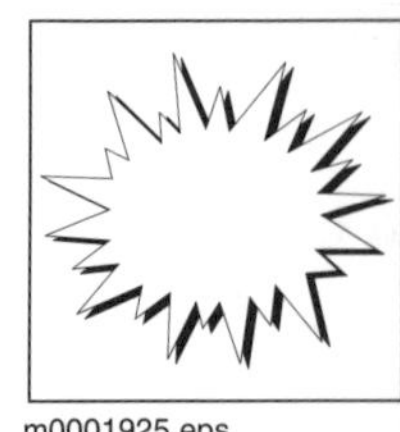
m0001925.eps

m0001926.eps

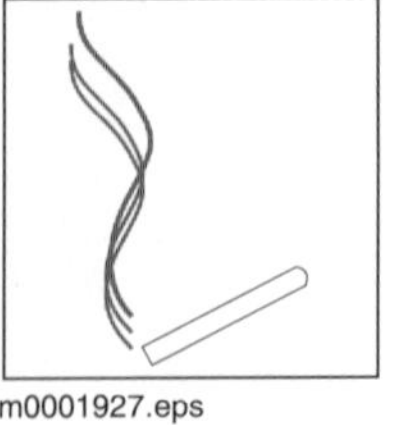
m0001927.eps

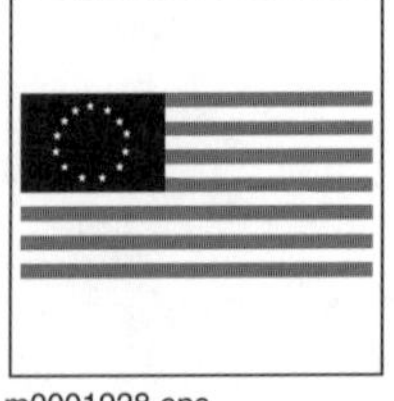
m0001928.eps

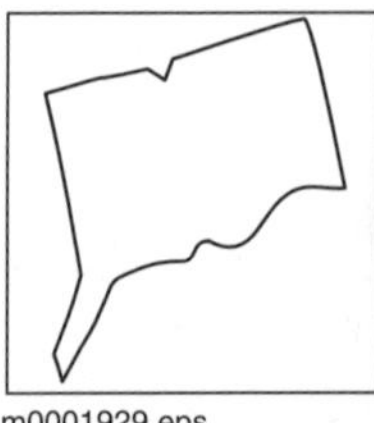
m0001929.eps

0001930.eps

m0001931.eps

m0001932.eps

m0001933.eps

0001934.eps

m0001935.eps

m0001936.eps

m0001937.eps

0001938.eps

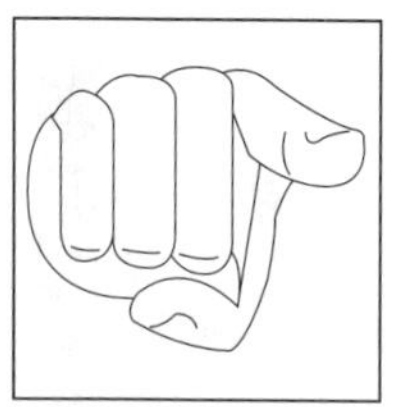
m0001939.eps

m0001940.eps

m0001941.eps

0001942.eps

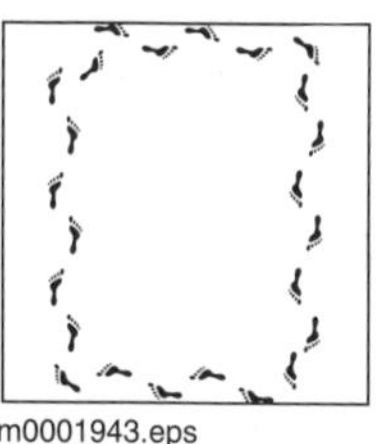
m0001943.eps

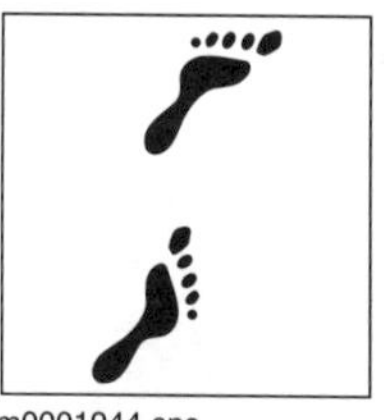
m0001944.eps

m0001945.eps

0001946.eps

m0001947.eps

m0001948.eps

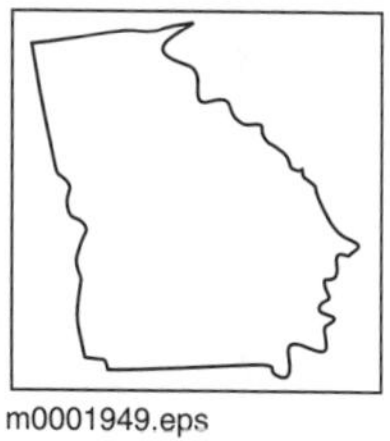
m0001949.eps

0001950.eps

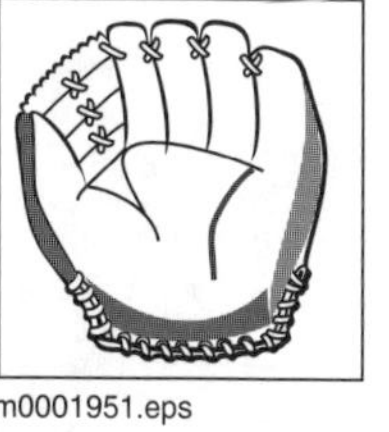
m0001951.eps

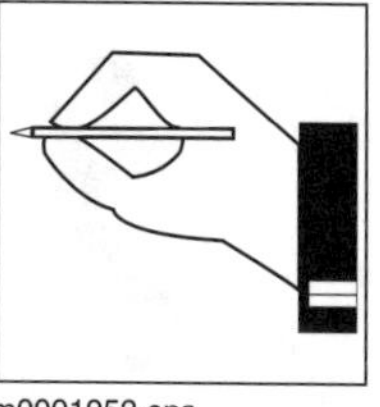
m0001952.eps

m0001953.eps

m0001954.eps

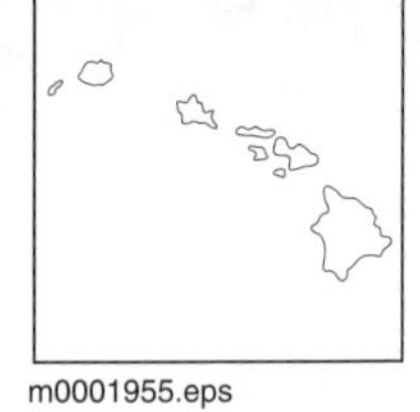
m0001955.eps

m0001956.eps

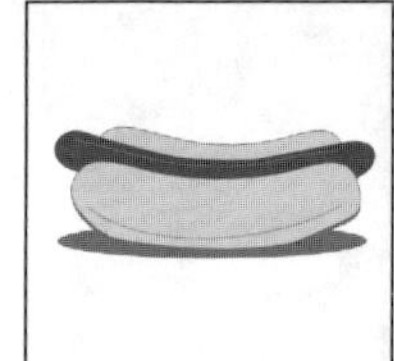
m0001957.eps

m0001958.eps

m0001959.eps

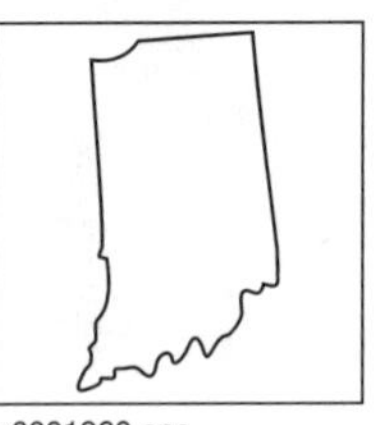
m0001960.eps

m0001961.eps

m0001962.eps

m0001963.eps

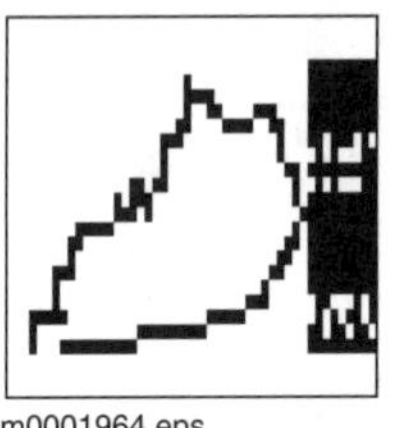
m0001964.eps

m0001965.eps

m0001966.eps

m0001967.eps

m0001968.eps

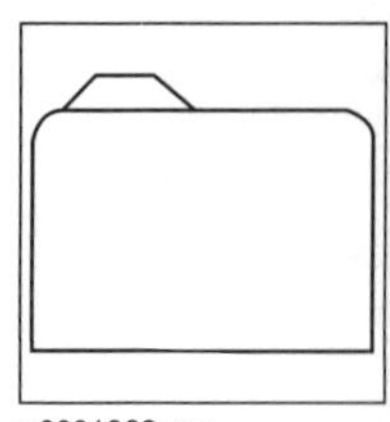
m0001969.eps

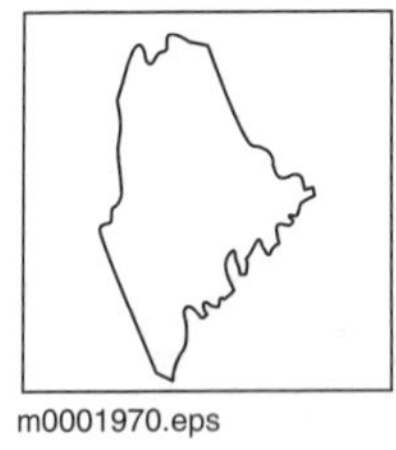
m0001970.eps

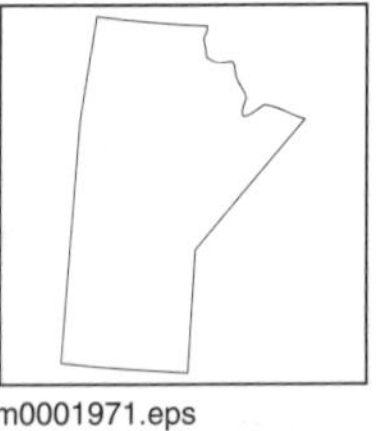
m0001971.eps

m0001972.eps

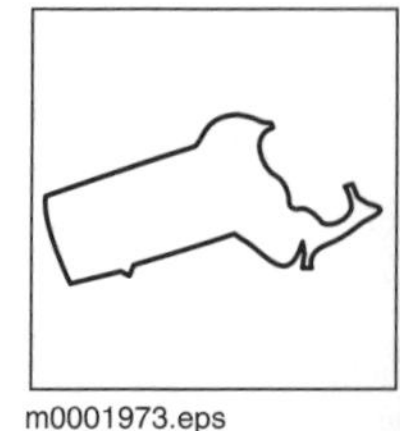
m0001973.eps

m0001974.eps

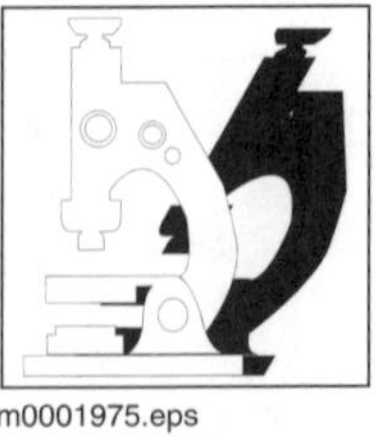
m0001975.eps

m0001976.eps

m0001977.eps

m0001978.eps m0001979.eps m0001980.eps m0001981.eps

m0001982.eps m0001983.eps m0001984.eps m0001985.eps

m0001986.eps m0001987.eps m0001989.eps m0001990.eps

m0001991.eps m0001992.eps m0001993.eps m0001994.eps

m0001995.eps m0001996.eps m0001997.eps m0001998.eps

m0001999.eps m0002000.eps m0002001.eps m0002002.eps

m0002003.eps

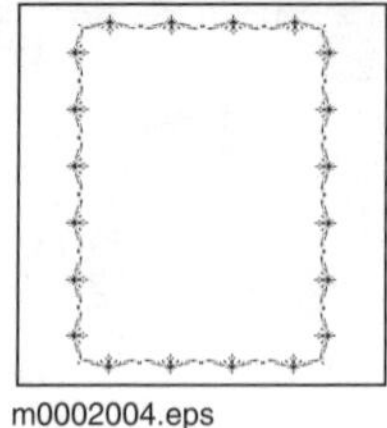
m0002004.eps

m0002005.eps

m0002006.eps

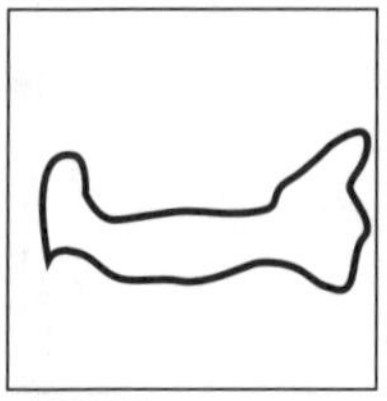
m0002007.eps

m0002008.eps

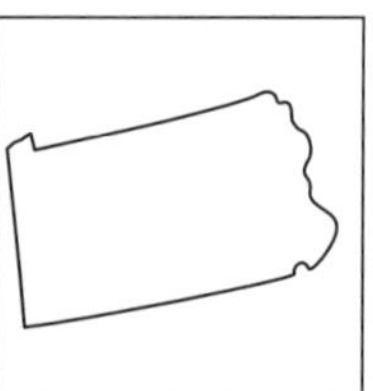
m0002009.eps

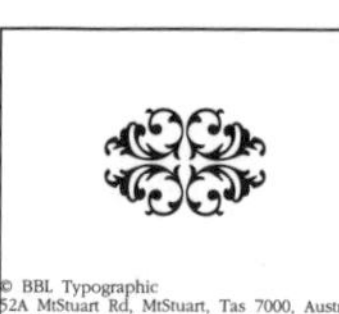

m0002010.eps

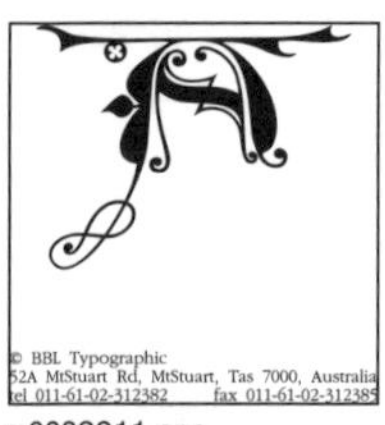

m0002011.eps

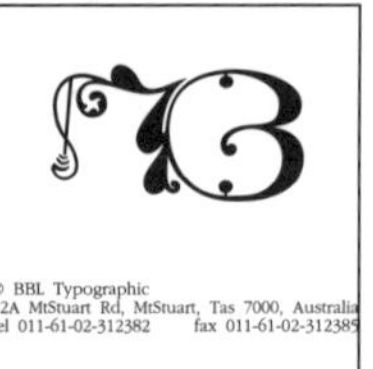

m0002012.eps

m0002013.eps

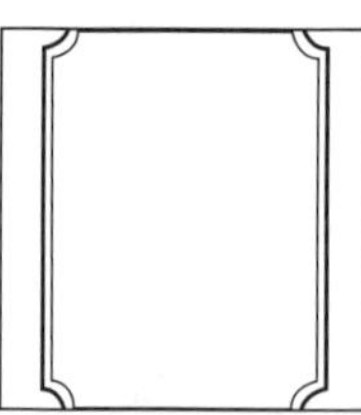
m0002014.eps

m0002015.eps

m0002016.eps

m0002017.eps

m0002018.eps

m0002019.eps

m0002020.eps

m0002021.eps

m0002022.eps

m0002023.eps

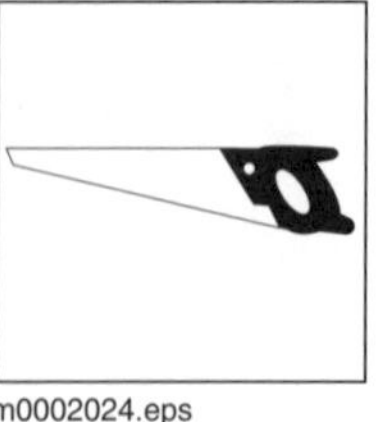
m0002024.eps

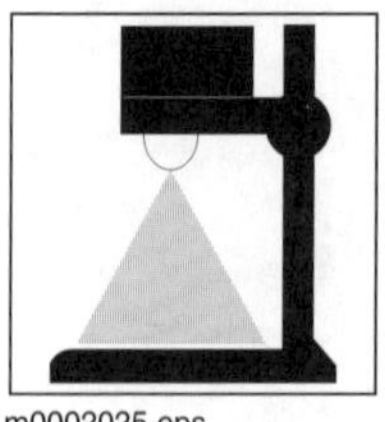
m0002025.eps

m0002026.eps

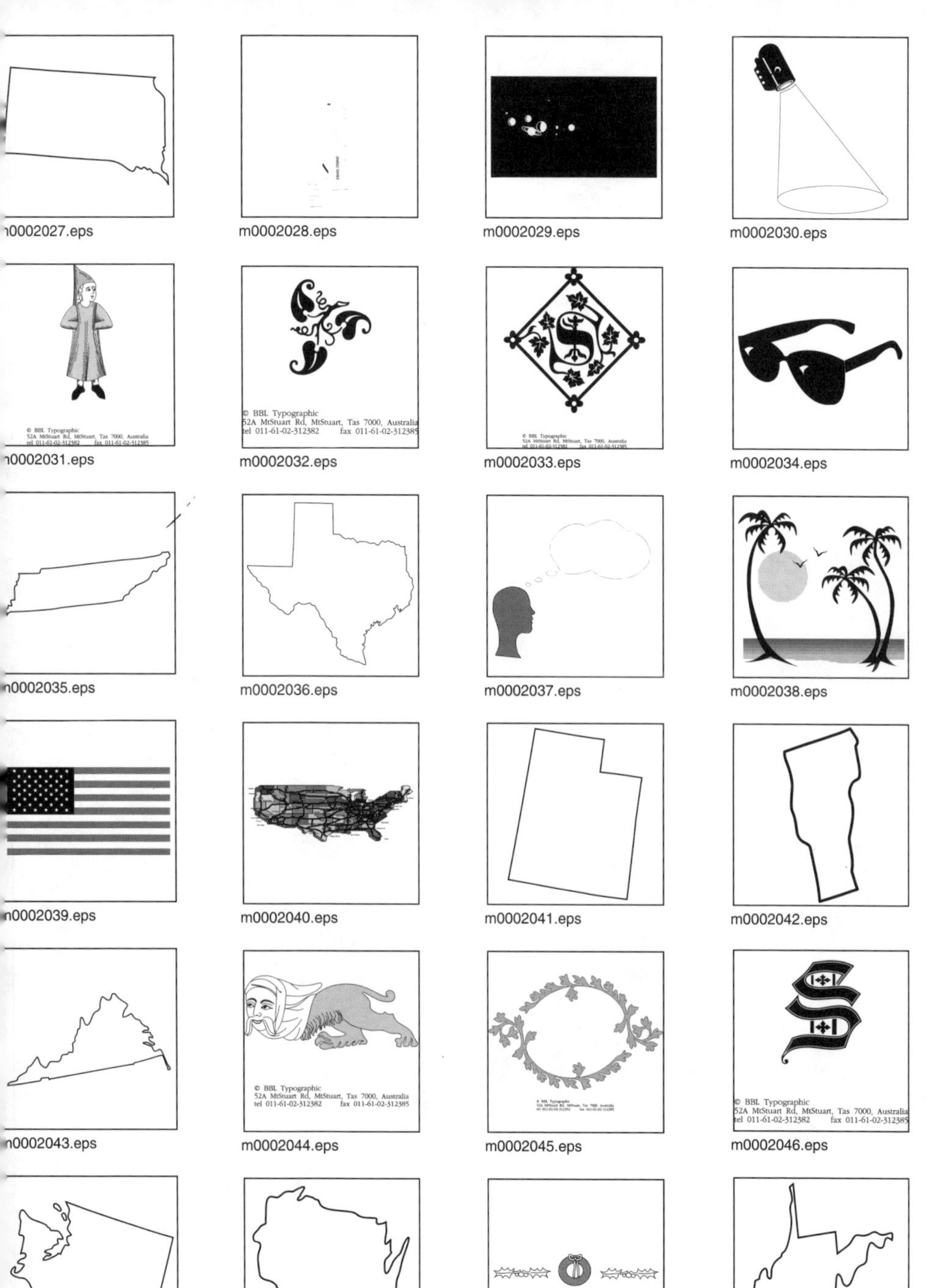

0002027.eps m0002028.eps m0002029.eps m0002030.eps

0002031.eps m0002032.eps m0002033.eps m0002034.eps

0002035.eps m0002036.eps m0002037.eps m0002038.eps

0002039.eps m0002040.eps m0002041.eps m0002042.eps

0002043.eps m0002044.eps m0002045.eps m0002046.eps

0002047.eps m0002048.eps m0002049.eps m0002050.eps

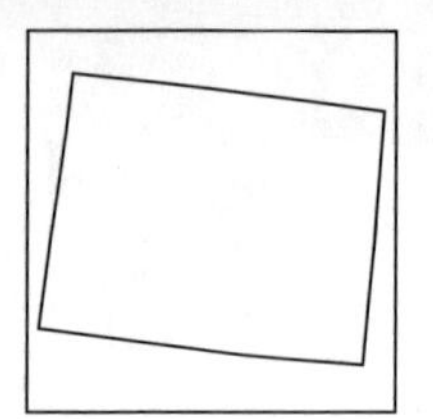

m0002051.eps

m0002052.eps

m0002053.eps

m0002054.tif

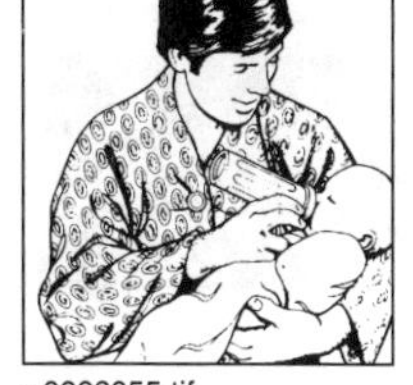
m0002055.tif

m0002056.tif

m0002057.tif

m0002058.tif

m0002059.tif

m0002060.tif

m0002061.tif

m0002062.tif

m0002063.tif

m0002064.tif

m0002065.tif

m0002066.tif

m0002067.tif

m0002068.tif

m0002069.tif

m0002070.tif

m0002071.tif

m0002072.tif

m0002073.tif

m0002074.tif

m0002075.tif

m0002076.tif

d:\images\family

c0002120.tif

c0002122.tif

c0002123.tif

c0002128.tif

c0002154.tif

m0002078.tif

m0002079.tif

m0002080.tif

m0002081.tif

m0002082.tif

m0002083.tif

m0002084.tif

m0002085.tif

m0002086.tif

m0002087.tif

m0002088.tif

m0002089.tif

m0002090.tif

m0002091.tif

m0002092.tif

m0002093.tif

m0002094.tif

m0002095.tif

m0002096.tif

0002097.tif

m0002098.tif

m0002099.tif

m0002100.tif

0002101.tif

m0002102.tif

m0002103.tif

m0002104.tif

0002105.tif

m0002109.tif

m0002112.tif

m0002113.tif

0002114.tif

m0002115.tif

m0002116.tif

m0002117.tif

0002118.tif

m0002119.tif

m0002121.tif

m0002124.tif

0002125.tif

m0002126.tif

m0002129.tif

m0002130.tif

:\images\famous

m0002131.tif

m0002132.tif

m0002134.tif

m0002135.tif

m0002136.tif

m0002137.tif

m0002138.tif

m0002139.tif

m0002140.tif

m0002141.tif

m0002143.tif

m0002144.tif

m0002145.tif

m0002147.tif

m0002148.tif

m0002149.tif

m0002151.tif

m0002152.tif

m0002153.tif

m0002155.tif

m0002156.tif

m0002157.tif

m0002158.tif

m0002159.tif

m0002161.tif

m0002162.tif

m0002163.tif

m0002164.tif

m0002167.tif

m0002168.tif

m0002169.tif

m0002170.tif

m0002171.tif

m0002172.tif

m0002173.tif

m0002174.tif

m0002175.tif

m0002176.tif

m0002177.tif

m0002178.tif

m0002179.tif

m0002180.tif

m0002181.tif

m0002182.tif

m0002183.tif

m0002184.tif

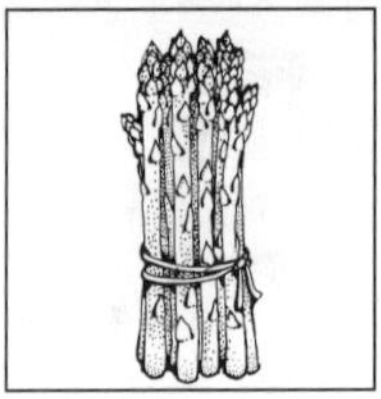

m0002185.tif

m0002186.tif

m0002187.tif

m0002188.tif

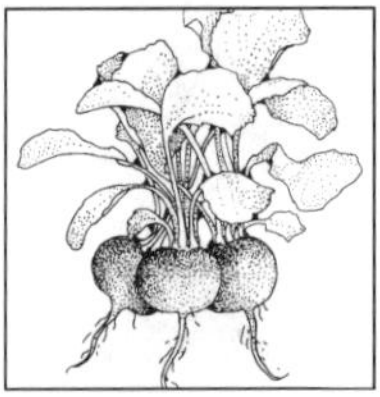

m0002189.tif

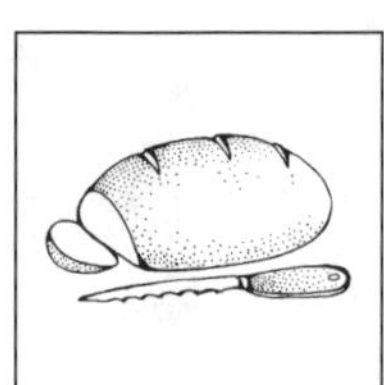
m0002190.tif

m0002191.tif

m0002192.tif

m0002193.tif

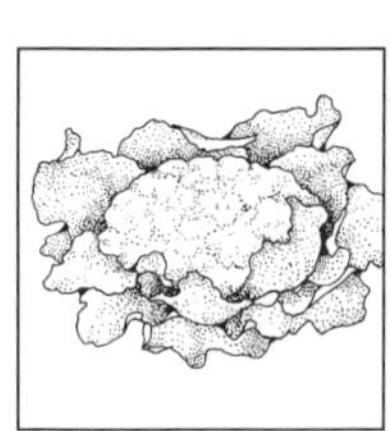
m0002194.tif

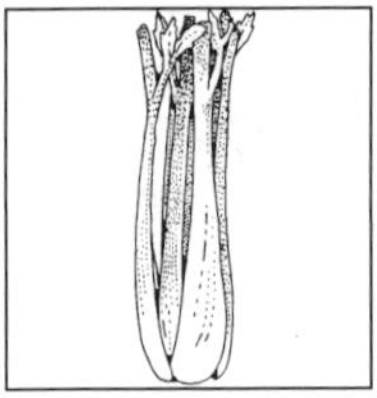

m0002195.tif

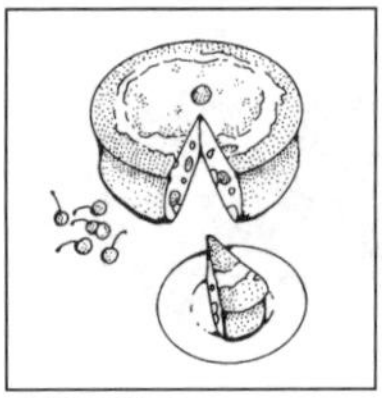

m0002196.tif

m0002197.tif

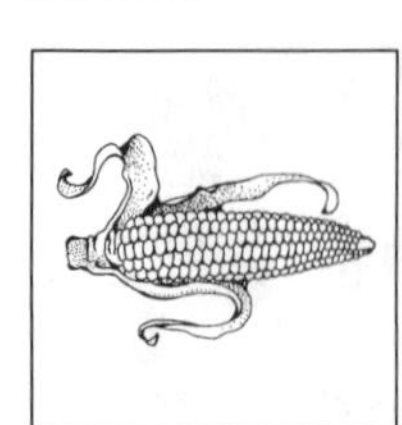
m0002198.tif

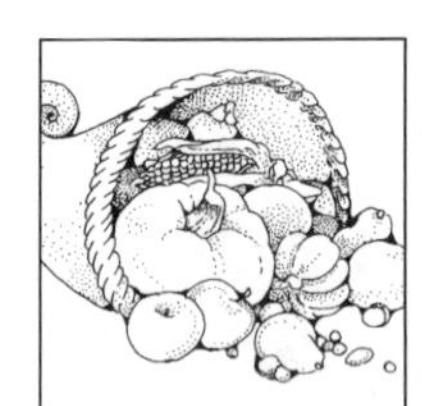
m0002199.tif

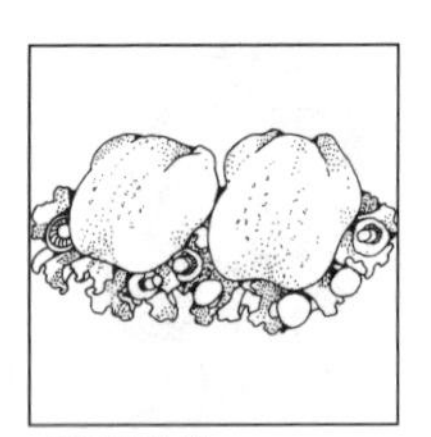
m0002200.tif

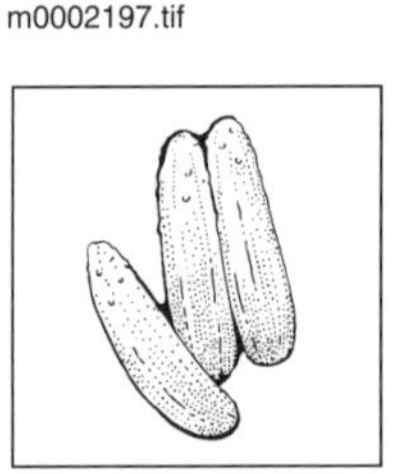
m0002201.tif

m0002202.tif

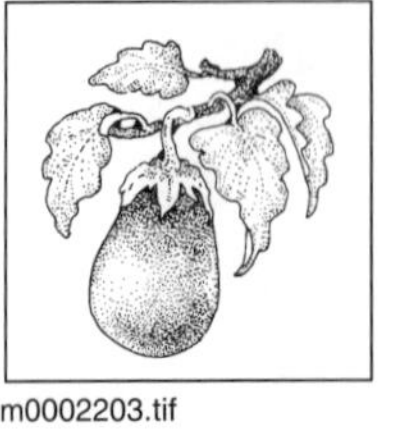
m0002203.tif

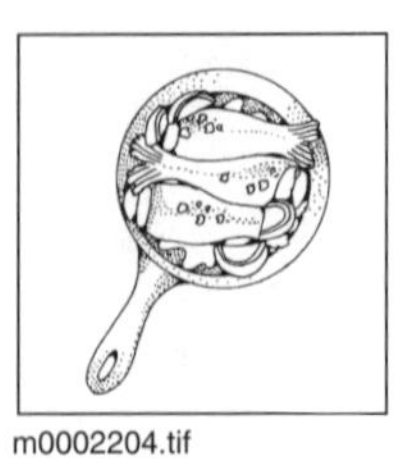
m0002204.tif

m0002205.tif

m0002206.tif

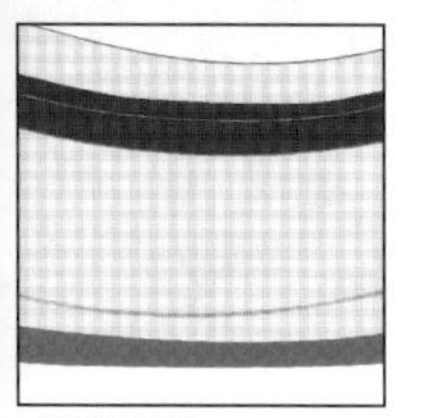
m0002207.tif

m0002208.tif

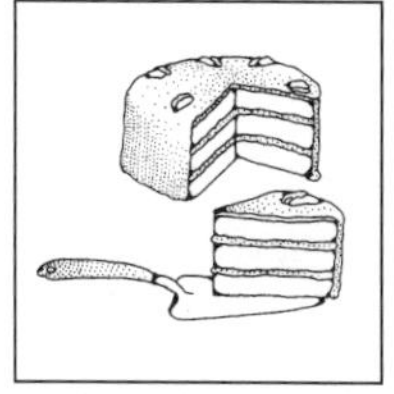
m0002209.tif

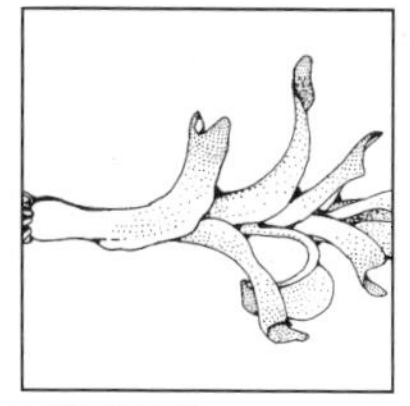
m0002210.tif

m0002211.tif

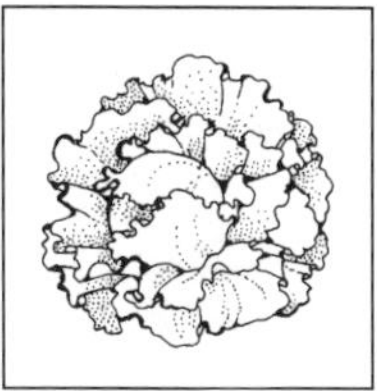
m0002212.tif

m0002213.tif

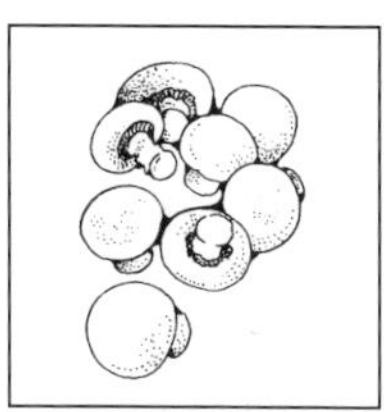
m0002214.tif

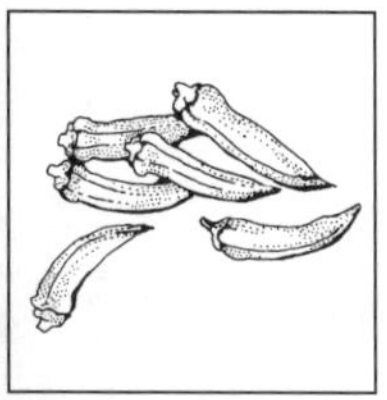
m0002215.tif

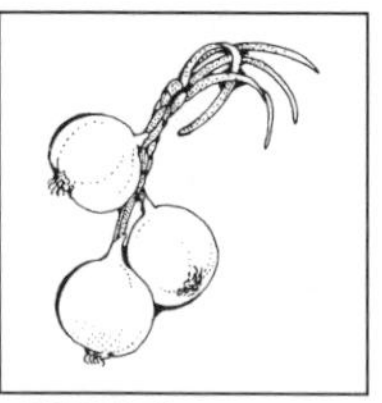
m0002216.tif

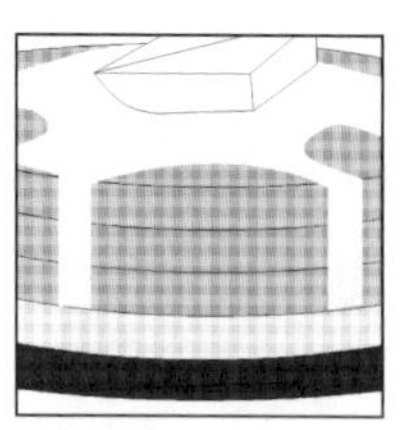
m0002217.tif

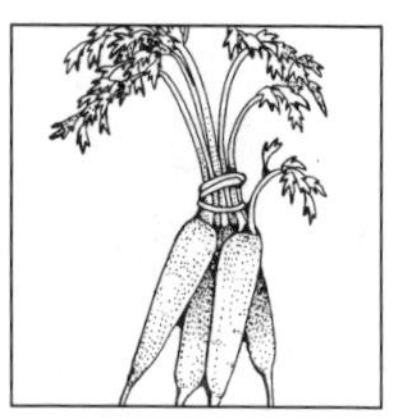
m0002218.tif

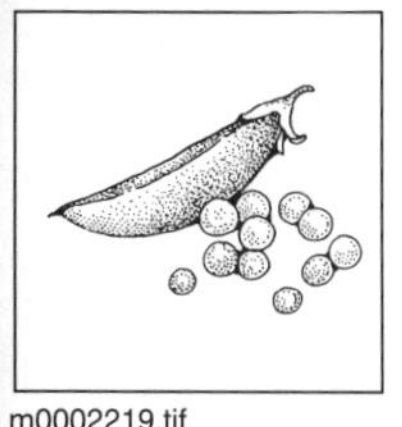
m0002219.tif

m0002220.tif

m0002221.tif

m0002222.tif

m0002223.tif

m0002224.tif

m0002225.tif

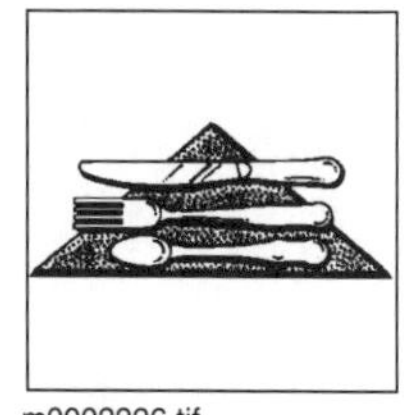
m0002226.tif

m0002227.tif

m0002228.tif

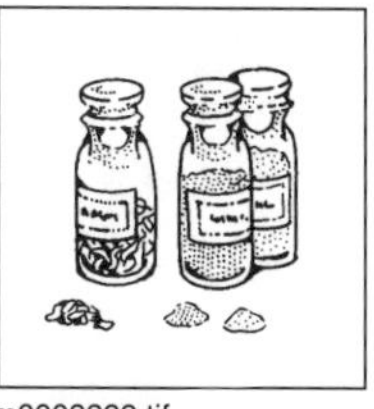
m0002229.tif

m0002230.tif

m0002231.tif

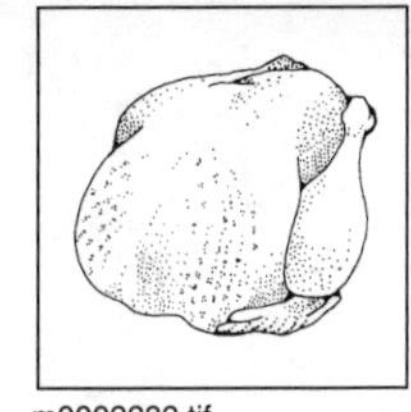
m0002232.tif

m0002233.tif

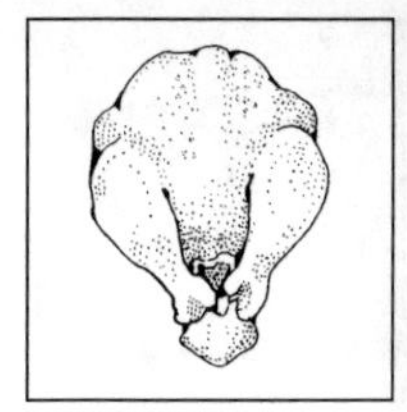
m0002234.tif

m0002235.tif

m0002236.tif

m0002237.tif

m0002238.tif

m0002239.tif

m0002240.tif

m0002241.tif

m0002242.tif

m0002243.tif

m0002244.tif

m0002245.tif

m0002246.tif

m0002247.tif

m0002248.tif

m0002249.tif

m0002250.tif

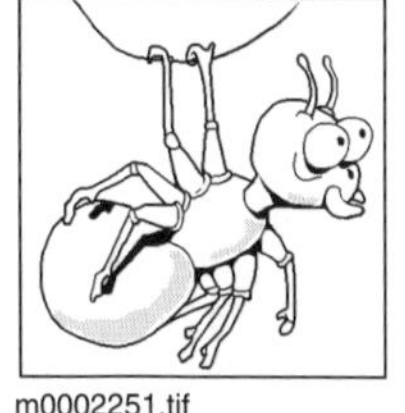
m0002251.tif

m0002252.tif

m0002253.tif

m0002254.tif

m0002255.tif

m0002256.tif

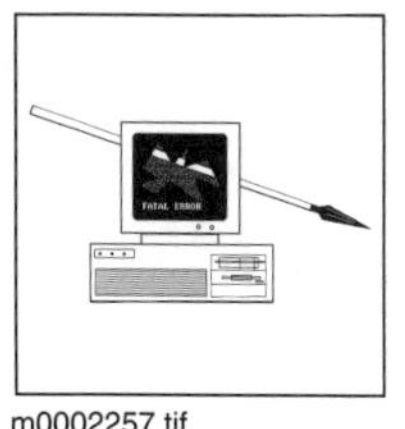

m0002257.tif

m0002258.tif

m0002259.tif

m0002260.tif

m0002261.tif

d:\images\grin1

m0002262.tif

m0002263.tif

m0002264.tif

m0002265.tif

m0002266.tif

m0002267.tif

m0002268.tif

m0002269.tif

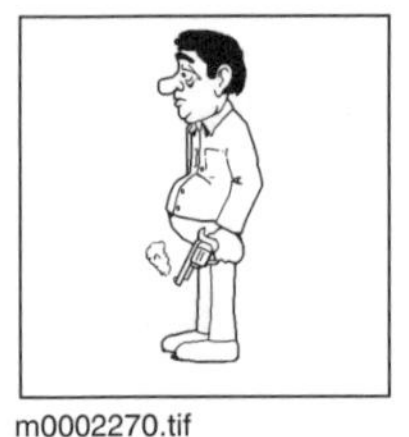
m0002270.tif

m0002271.tif

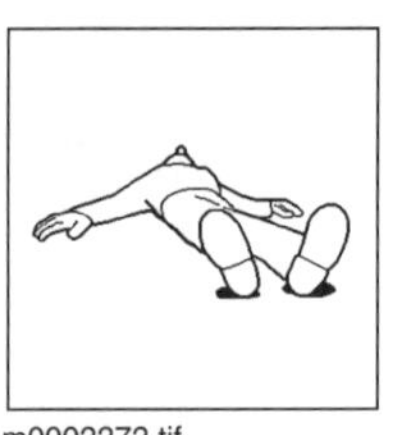
m0002272.tif

m0002273.tif

m0002274.tif

m0002275.tif

m0002276.tif

m0002277.tif

m0002278.tif

m0002279.tif

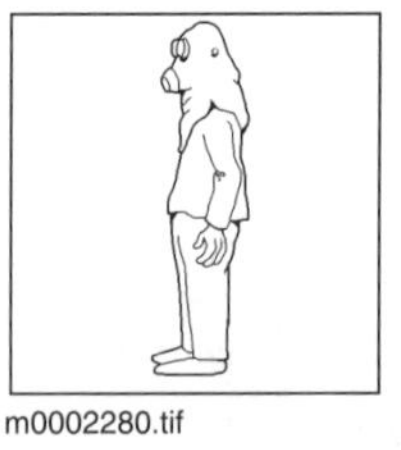
m0002280.tif

m0002281.tif

m0002282.tif

m0002283.tif

m0002284.tif

m0002285.tif

d:\images\grin1

m0002286.tif

m0002287.tif

m0002288.tif

m0002289.tif

m0002290.tif

m0002291.tif

m0002292.tif

m0002293.tif

m0002294.tif

m0002295.tif

m0002296.tif

m0002297.tif

m0002298.tif

m0002299.tif

m0002300.tif

m0002301.tif

m0002302.tif

m0002303.tif

m0002304.tif

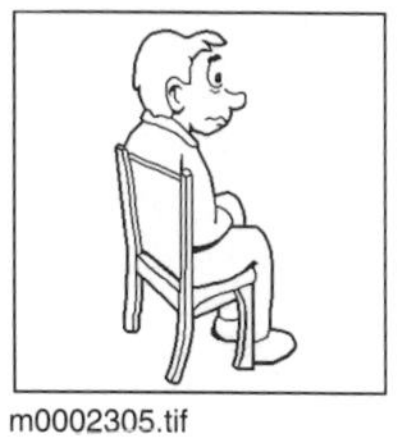
m0002305.tif

m0002306.tif

m0002307.tif

m0002308.tif

m0002309.tif

d:\images\grin1

m0002310.tif

m0002311.tif

m0002312.tif

m0002313.tif

m0002314.tif

m0002315.tif

m0002316.tif

m0002317.tif

m0002318.tif

m0002319.tif

m0002320.tif

m0002321.tif

m0002322.tif

m0002323.tif

m0002324.tif

m0002325.tif

m0002326.tif

m0002327.tif

m0002328.tif

m0002329.tif

m0002330.tif

m0002331.tif

m0002332.tif

m0002333.tif

m0002334.tif

m0002335.tif

m0002336.tif

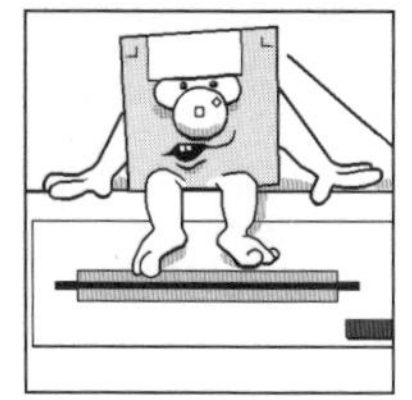
m0002337.tif

m0002338.tif

m0002339.tif

m0002340.tif

m0002341.tif

m0002342.tif

m0002343.tif

m0002344.tif

m0002345.tif

m0002346.tif

m0002347.tif

m0002348.tif

m0002349.tif

m0002350.tif

m0002351.tif

m0002352.tif

m0002353.tif

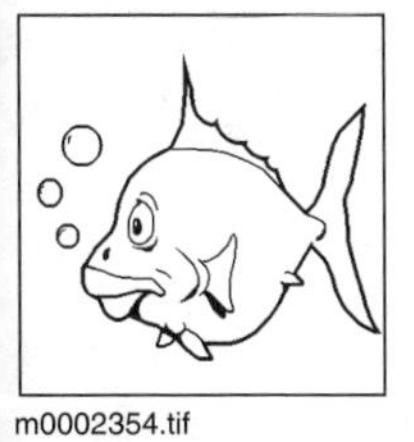
m0002354.tif

m0002355.tif

m0002356.tif

m0002357.tif

d:\images\grin1

m0002358.tif m0002359.tif m0002360.tif m0002361.tif

m0002362.tif m0002363.tif m0002364.tif m0002365.tif

m0002366.tif m0002367.tif m0002368.tif m0002369.tif

m0002370.tif m0002371.tif m0002372.tif m0002373.tif

m0002374.tif m0002375.tif m0002376.tif m0002377.tif

m0002378.tif m0002379.tif m0002380.tif m0002381.tif

m0002382.tif m0002383.tif m0002384.tif m0002385.tif

m0002386.tif m0002387.tif m0002388.tif m0002389.tif

m0002390.tif m0002391.tif m0002392.tif m0002393.tif

m0002238.tif

m0002394.tif

m0002395.tif

m0002396.tif

m0002397.tif

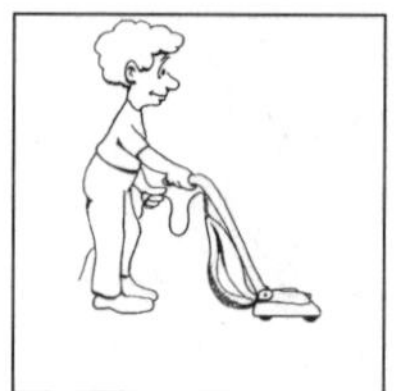
m0002398.tif

m0002399.tif

m0002400.tif

m0002401.tif

m0002402.tif

m0002403.tif

m0002404.tif

m0002405.tif

m0002406.tif

m0002407.tif

m0002408.tif

m0002409.tif

m0002410.tif

m0002411.tif

m0002412.tif

m0002413.tif

m0002414.tif

m0002415.tif

m0002416.tif

m0002417.tif

m0002418.tif

m0002419.tif

m0002420.tif

m0002421.tif

m0002422.tif

m0002423.tif

m0002424.tif

m0002425.tif

m0002426.tif

m0002427.tif

m0002428.tif

m0002429.tif

m0002430.tif

m0002431.tif

m0002432.tif

m0002433.tif

m0002434.tif

m0002435.tif

m0002436.tif

m0002437.tif

m0002438.tif

m0002439.tif

m0002440.tif

d:\images\grin2

m0002441.tif 
m0002442.tif 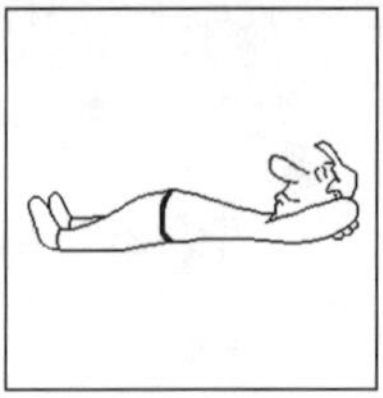
m0002443.tif 
m0002444.tif

m0002445.tif 
m0002446.tif 
m0002447.tif 
m0002448.tif

m0002449.tif 
m0002450.tif 
m0002451.tif 
m0002452.tif

m0002453.tif 
m0002454.tif 
m0002455.tif 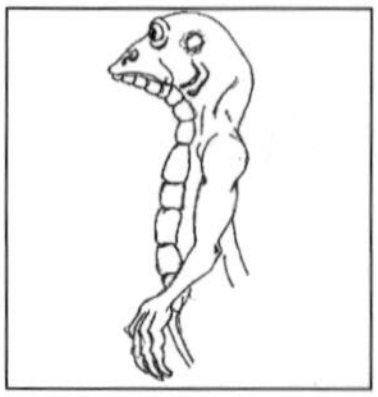
m0002456.tif

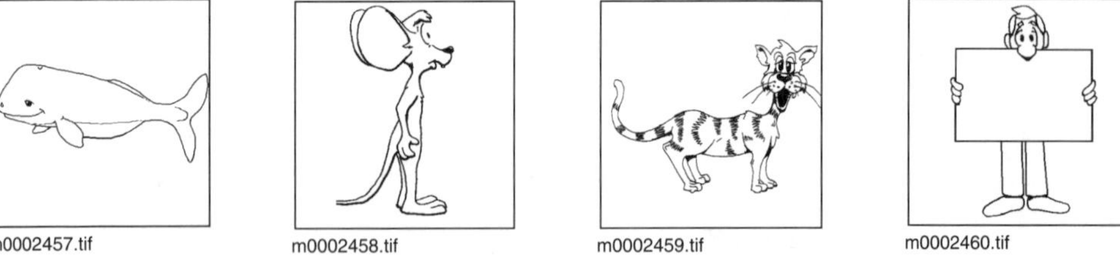

m0002457.tif
m0002458.tif
m0002459.tif
m0002460.tif

m0002461.tif
m0002462.tif 
m0002463.tif 
m0002464.tif

m0002465.tif

m0002466.tif

m0002467.tif

m0002468.tif

m0002469.tif

m0002470.tif

m0002471.tif

m0002472.tif

m0002473.tif

m0002474.tif

m0002475.tif

m0002476.tif

m0002477.tif

m0002478.tif

m0002479.tif

m0002480.tif

m0002481.tif

m0002482.tif

m0002483.tif

m0002484.tif

m0002485.tif

m0002486.tif

m0002487.tif

m0002488.tif

d:\images\grin2

m0002489.tif

m0002490.tif

m0002491.tif

m0002492.tif

m0002493.tif

m0002494.tif

m0002495.tif

m0002496.tif

m0002497.tif

m0002498.tif

m0002499.tif

m0002500.tif

m0002501.tif

m0002502.tif

m0002503.tif

m0002504.tif

m0002505.tif

m0002506.tif

m0002507.tif

m0002508.tif

m0002509.tif

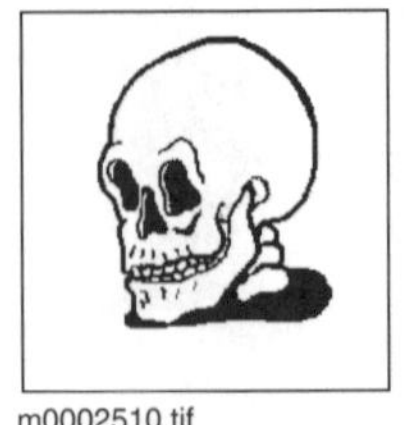
m0002510.tif

m0002511.tif

m0002512.tif

m0002513.tif

m0002514.tif

m0002515.tif

m0002516.tif

m0002517.tif

m0002518.tif

m0002519.tif

m0002520.tif

m0002521.tif

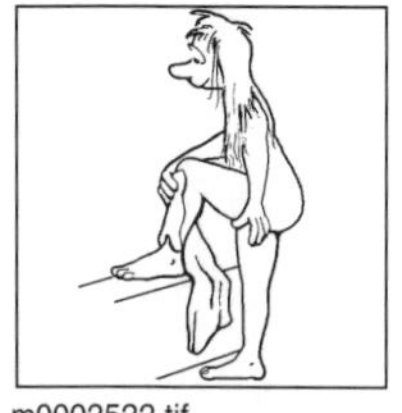
m0002522.tif

m0002523.tif

m0002524.tif

m0002525.tif

m0002526.tif

m0002527.tif

m0002528.tif

m0002529.tif

m0002530.tif

m0002531.tif

m0002532.tif

m0002533.tif

m0002534.tif

m0002535.tif

m0002536.tif

d:\images\grin2

m0002537.tif

m0002538.tif

m0002539.tif

m0002540.tif

m0002541.tif

m0002542.tif

m0002543.tif

m0002544.tif

m0002545.tif

ı0002550.tif

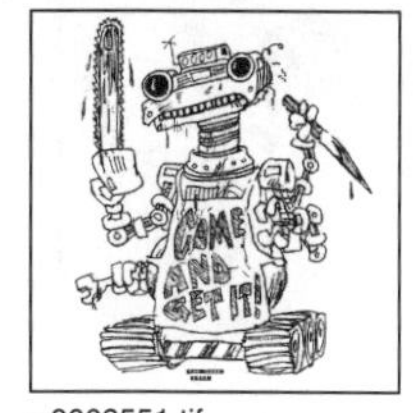

m0002551.tif

m0002552.tif

m0002553.tif

m0002557.tif

m0002558.tif

m0002559.tif

m0002560.tif

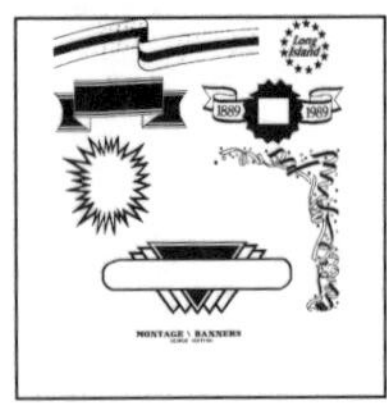
m0002561.tif

m0002562.tif

m0002563.tif

m0002564.tif

m0002565.tif

m0002566.tif

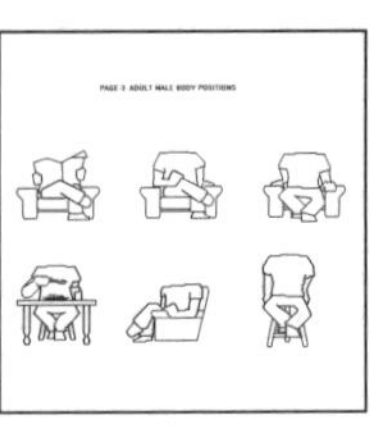
m0002567.tif

m0002568.tif

m0002569.tif

m0002570.tif

m0002571.tif

m0002572.tif

m0002573.tif

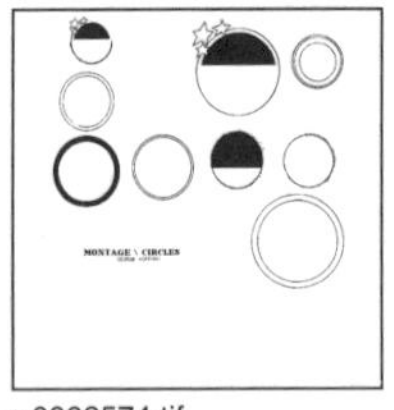
m0002574.tif

m0002575.tif

m0002576.tif

m0002577.tif

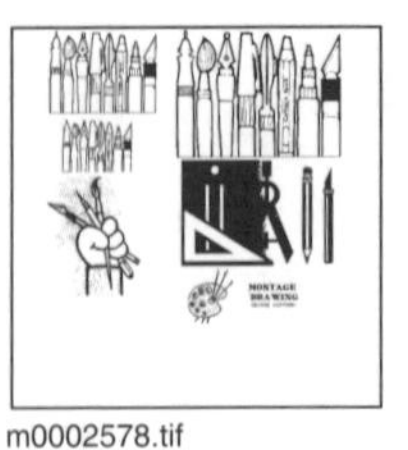
m0002578.tif

m0002579.tif

m0002580.tif

0002581.tif

m0002582.tif

m0002583.tif

m0002584.tif

0002590.tif

m0002591.tif

m0002592.tif

m0002593.tif

0002594.tif

m0002595.tif

m0002596.tif

m0002597.tif

0002598.tif

m0002602.tif

m0002606.tif

m0002609.tif

m0002610.tif

m0002611.tif

m0002612.tif

m0002613.tif

m0002614.tif

m0002615.tif

m0002616.tif

m0002617.tif

m0002618.tif

m0002619.tif

m0002620.tif

m0002621.tif

m0002622.tif

m0002623.tif

m0002624.tif

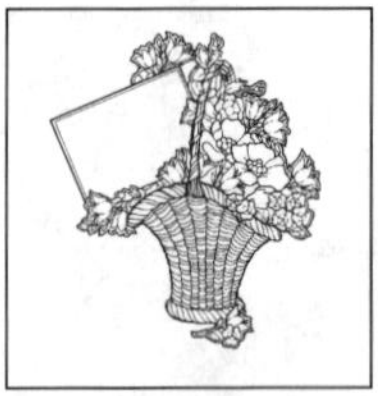

m0002625.tif

m0002626.tif

m0002627.tif

m0002628.tif

m0002629.tif

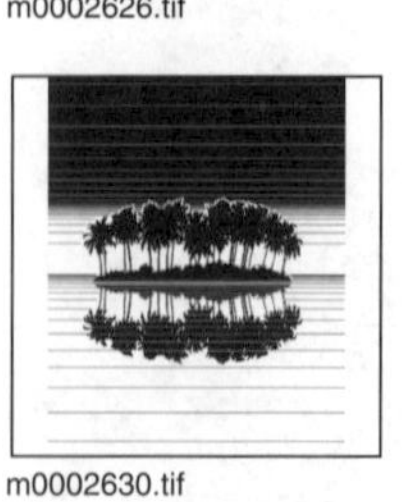

m0002630.tif

m0002631.tif

m0002632.tif

0002633.tif

m0002634.tif

m0002635.tif

m0002636.tif

0002637.tif

m0002638.tif

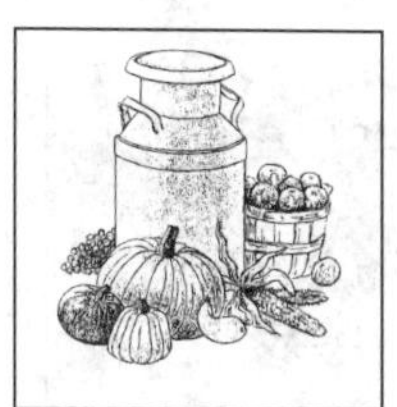
m0002639.tif

m0002640.tif

0002641.tif

m0002642.tif

m0002643.tif

m0002644.tif

0002645.tif

m0002646.tif

m0002647.tif

m0002648.tif

0002649.tif

m0002650.tif

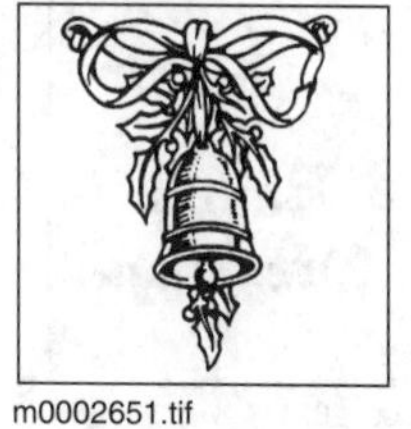
m0002651.tif

m0002652.tif

0002653.tif

m0002654.tif

m0002655.tif

m0002656.tif

:\images\holiday

m0002657.tif

m0002658.tif

m0002659.tif

m0002660.tif

m0002661.tif

m0002662.tif

m0002663.tif

m0002664.tif

m0002665.tif

m0002666.tif

m0002667.tif

m0002668.tif

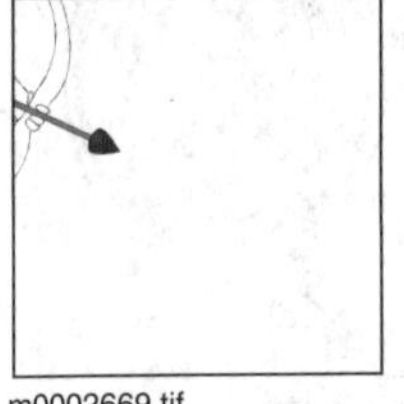
m0002669.tif

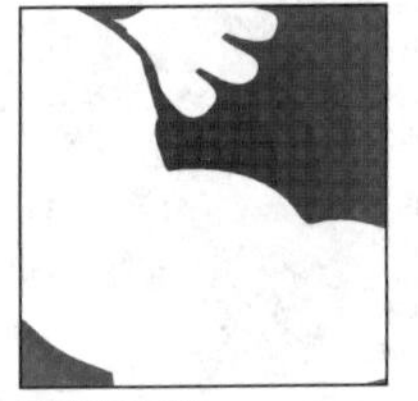
m0002670.tif

m0002671.tif

m0002672.tif

m0002673.tif

m0002674.tif

m0002675.tif

m0002676.tif

m0002677.tif

m0002678.tif

m0002679.tif

m0002680.tif

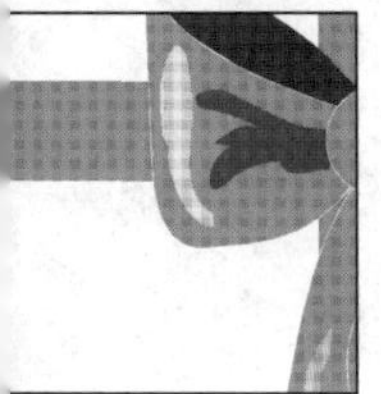
0002681.tif

m0002682.tif

m0002683.tif

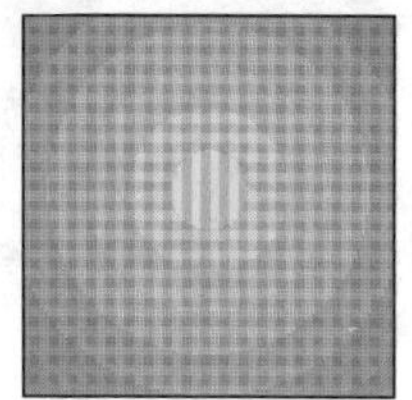
m0002684.tif

0002685.tif

m0002686.tif

m0002689.tif

m0002690.tif

0002691.tif

m0002692.tif

m0002693.tif

m0002694.tif

0002695.tif

m0002698.tif

m0002699.tif

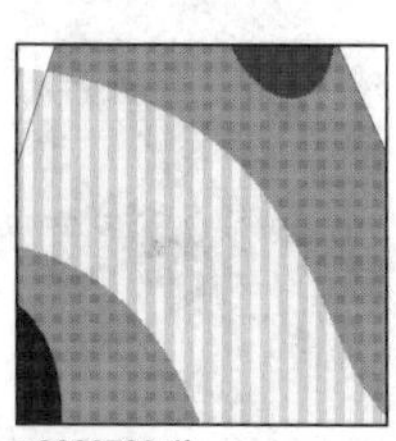
m0002700.tif

0002701.tif

m0002702.tif

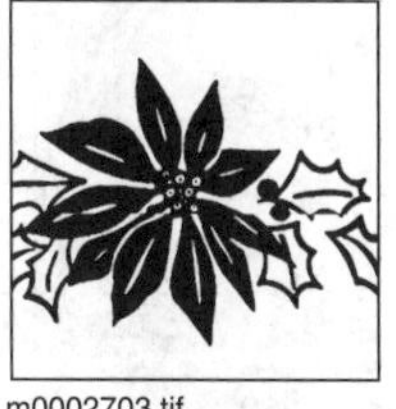
m0002703.tif

m0002704.tif

0002705.tif

m0002706.tif

m0002707.tif

m0002708.tif

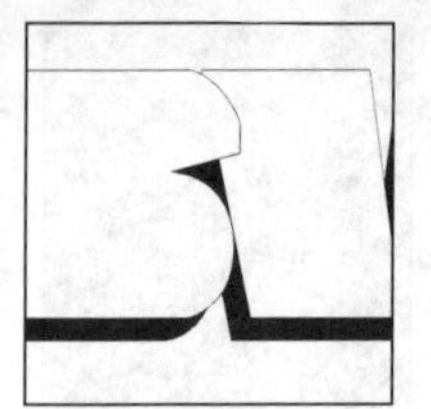
m0002709.tif

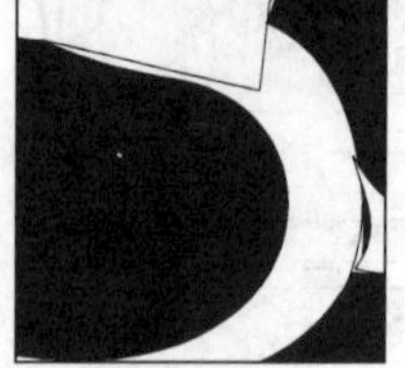
m0002710.tif

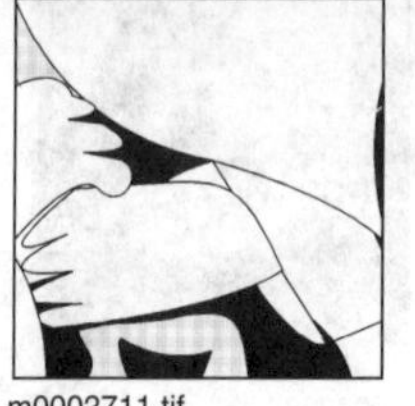
m0002711.tif

m0002712.tif

m0002713.tif

m0002714.tif

m0002715.tif

m0002716.tif

m0002717.tif

m0002718.tif

m0002719.tif

m0002720.tif

m0002721.tif

m0002722.tif

m0002723.tif

m0002724.tif

m0002725.tif

m0002726.tif

m0002727.tif

m0002728.tif

m0002729.tif

m0002730.tif

m0002731.tif

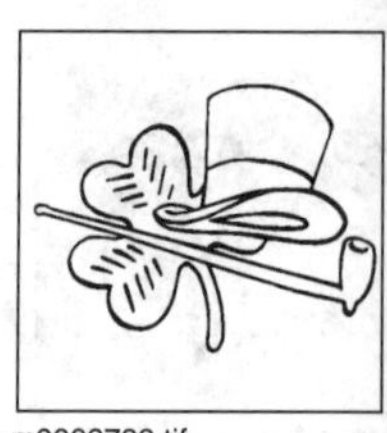
m0002732.tif

0002733.tif

m0002734.tif

m0002735.tif

m0002736.tif

0002737.tif

m0002738.tif

m0002739.tif

m0002740.tif

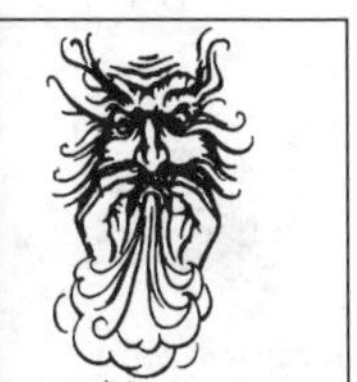
0002741.tif

m0002742.tif

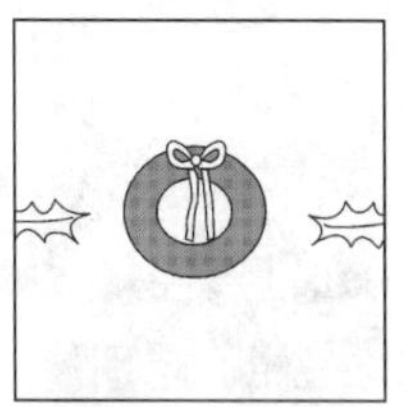
m0002743.tif

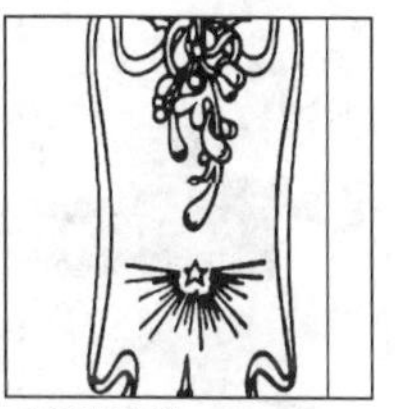
m0002744.tif

0002745.tif

m0002746.tif

m0002747.tif

m0002748.tif

0002749.tif

m0002750.tif

m0002751.tif

m0002752.tif

m0002753.tif

m0002754.tif

m0002755.tif

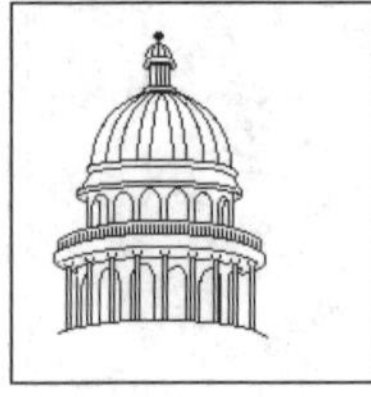
m0002756.tif

m0002757.tif

m0002758.tif

m0002759.tif

m0002760.tif

m0002761.tif

m0002762.tif

m0002763.tif

m0002764.tif

m0002765.tif

m0002766.tif

m0002767.tif

m0002768.tif

m0002769.tif

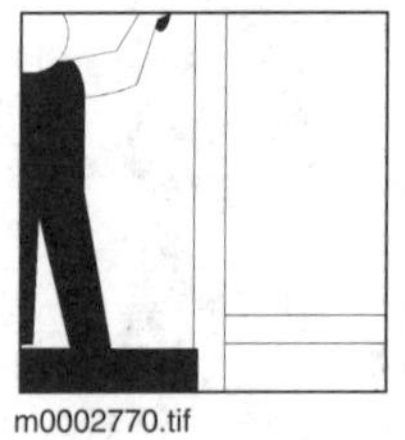
m0002770.tif

m0002771.tif

m0002772.tif

m0002773.tif

m0002774.tif

m0002775.tif

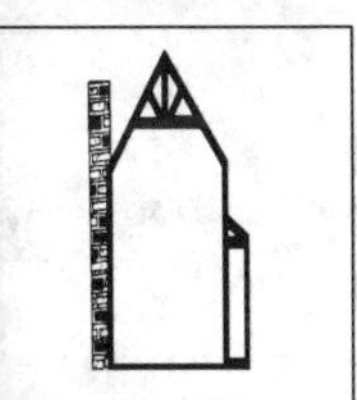
0002776.tif

m0002777.tif

m0002778.tif

m0002779.tif

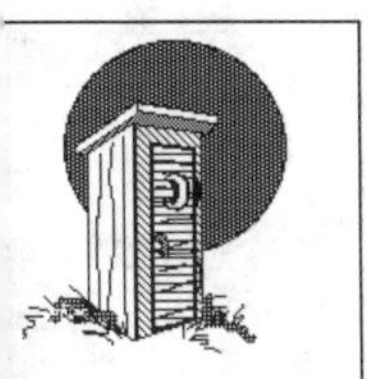
0002780.tif

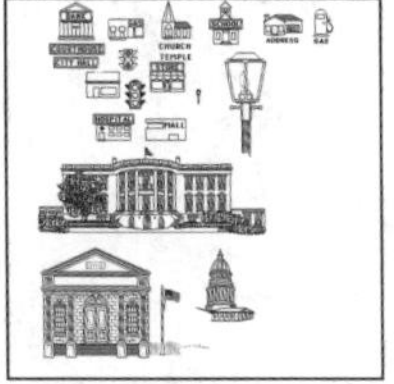
m0002781.tif

m0002782.tif

m0002783.tif

0002784.tif

m0002785.tif

m0002786.tif

m0002787.tif

m0002788.tif	 m0002789.tif	 m0002790.tif	 m0002791.tif
 m0002792.tif	 m0002793.tif	 m0002794.tif	m0002795.tif
 m0002796.tif	 m0002797.tif	 m0002798.tif	m0002799.tif
m0002800.tif	 m0002801.tif	m0002802.tif	 m0002803.tif
 m0002804.tif	 m0002805.tif	 m0002806.tif	 m0002807.tif
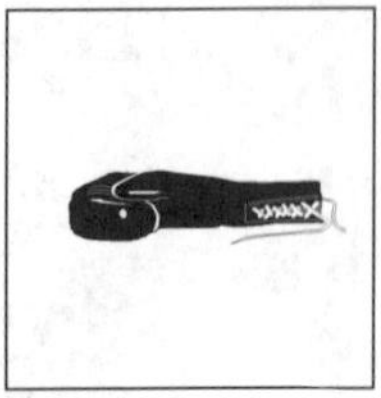 m0002808.tif	 m0002809.tif	 m0002810.tif	m0002811.tif

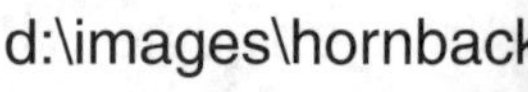

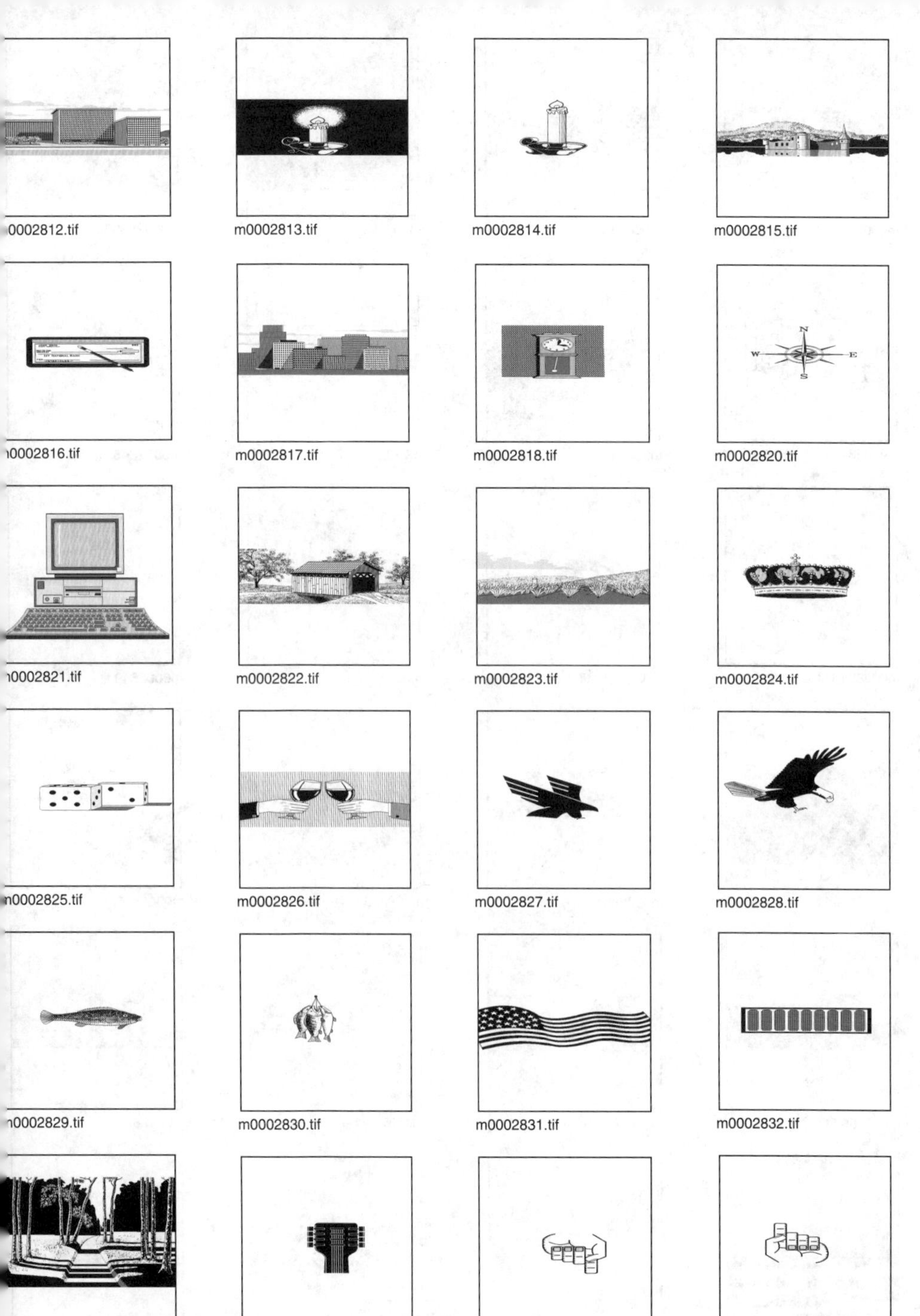

0002812.tif | m0002813.tif | m0002814.tif | m0002815.tif

0002816.tif | m0002817.tif | m0002818.tif | m0002820.tif

0002821.tif | m0002822.tif | m0002823.tif | m0002824.tif

0002825.tif | m0002826.tif | m0002827.tif | m0002828.tif

0002829.tif | m0002830.tif | m0002831.tif | m0002832.tif

0002833.tif | m0002834.tif | m0002835.tif | m0002836.tif

d:\images\hornback

m0002837.tif

m0002838.tif

m0002839.tif

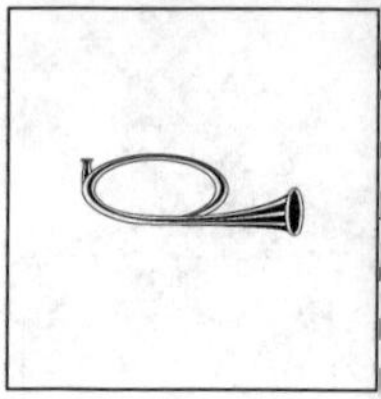

m0002840.tif

m0002841.tif

m0002842.tif

m0002844.tif

m0002845.tif

m0002846.tif

m0002847.tif

m0002848.tif

m0002849.tif

m0002850.tif

m0002851.tif

m0002852.tif

m0002853.tif

m0002854.tif

m0002855.tif

m0002856.tif

m0002857.tif

m0002858.tif

m0002859.tif

m0002860.tif

m0002861.tif

m0002862.tif

m0002863.tif

m0002864.tif

m0002865.tif

m0002866.tif

m0002867.tif

m0002868.tif

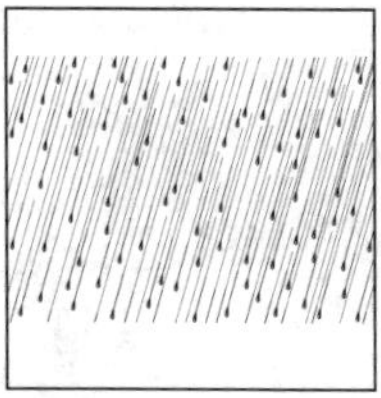

m0002869.tif

m0002870.tif

m0002871.tif

m0002872.tif

m0002873.tif

m0002874.tif

m0002875.tif

m0002876.tif

m0002877.tif

I'm such a loser!
The world stinks!
I'll never get out
of this place!

m0002878.tif

m0002879.tif

m0002880.tif

m0002881.tif

m0002882.tif

m0002883.tif

m0002884.tif

m0002885.tif

d:\images\hornback

m0002886.tif

m0002887.tif

m0002888.tif

9.tif

m0002890.tif

m0002891.tif

m0002892.tif

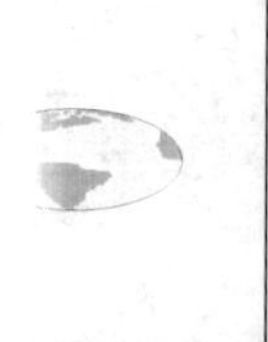
3.tif

m0002897.tif

m0002900.tif

m0002917.tif

m0002918.tif

m0002919.tif

m0002920.tif

m0002921.tif

m0002922.tif

m0002923.tif

m0002924.tif

m0002925.tif

m0002926.tif

m0002927.tif

m0002928.tif

m0002929.tif

m0002930.tif

m0002931.tif

m0002932.tif

m0002933.tif

m0002934.tif

m0002937.tif

m0002938.tif

m0002939.tif

m0002940.tif

m0002941.tif

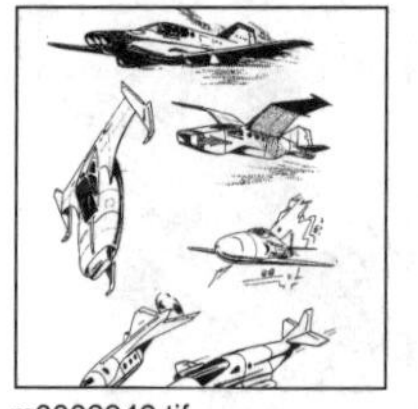
m0002942.tif

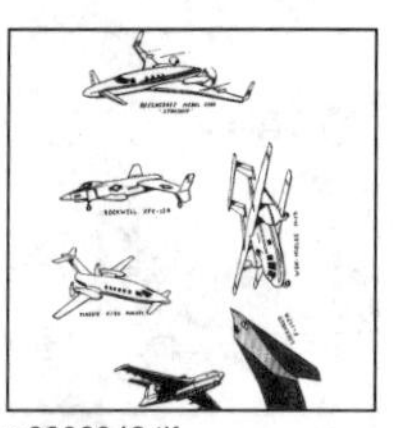
m0002943.tif

m0002944.tif

m0002945.tif

m0002946.tif

m0002947.tif

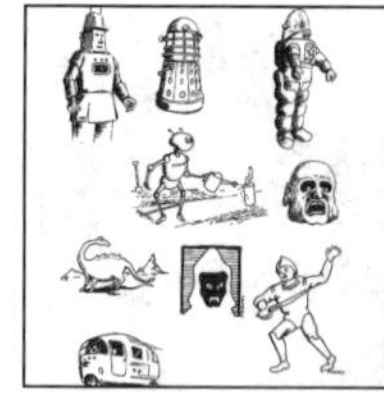
m0002948.tif

d:\images\jeeves

m0002950.tif

m0002951.tif

m0002952.tif

m0002953.tif

m0002954.tif

m0002955.tif

m0002956.tif

m0002957.tif

m0002958.tif

m0002959.tif

m0002960.tif

m0002961.tif

m0002962.tif

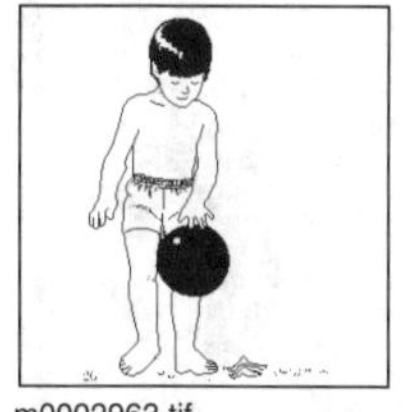
m0002963.tif

m0002964.tif

m0002965.tif

m0002966.tif

m0002967.tif

m0002968.tif

m0002969.tif

m0002970.tif

m0002971.tif

m0002972.tif

m0002973.tif

m0002974.tif

m0002975.tif

m0002976.tif

m0002977.tif

m0002978.tif

m0002979.tif

m0002980.tif

m0002981.tif

m0002982.tif

m0002983.tif

m0002984.tif

m0002985.tif

m0002986.tif

m0002987.tif

m0002988.tif

m0002989.tif

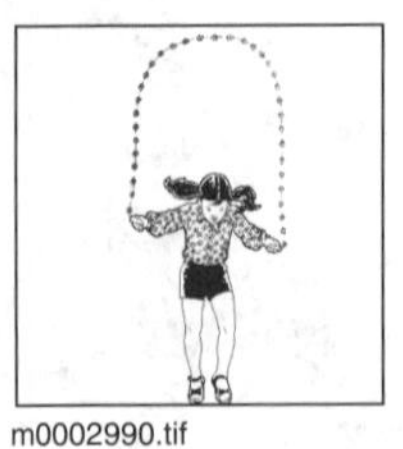
m0002990.tif

m0002991.tif

m0002992.tif

m0002993.tif

m0002994.tif

m0002995.tif

m0002996.tif

m0002997.tif

m0002998.tif

m0002999.tif

m0003000.tif

m0003001.tif

m0003002.tif

m0003003.tif

m0003004.tif

m0003005.tif

m0003006.tif

m0003007.tif

m0003008.tif

m0003009.tif

m0003010.tif

m0003011.tif

m0003012.tif

m0003013.tif

m0003014.tif

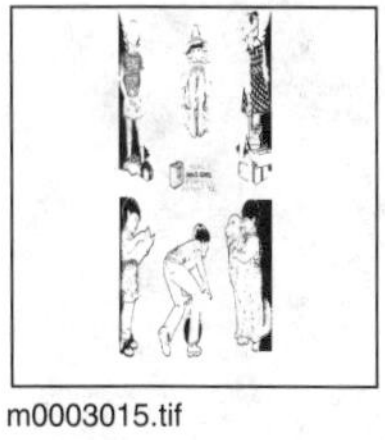
m0003015.tif

m0003016.tif

m0003017.tif

m0003018.tif

m0003019.tif

m0003020.tif

m0003021.tif

m0003022.tif

m0003023.tif

m0003024.tif

m0003025.tif

m0003026.tif

m0003027.tif

m0003028.tif

m0003029.tif

m0003030.tif

m0003031.tif

m0003032.tif

m0003033.tif

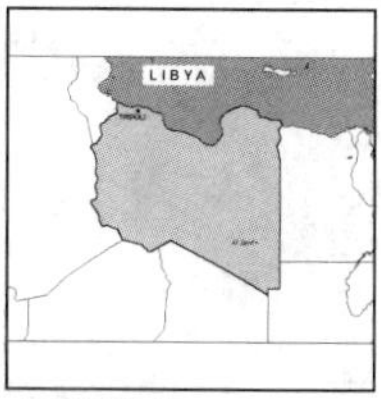

m0003034.tif

m0003035.tif

m0003036.tif

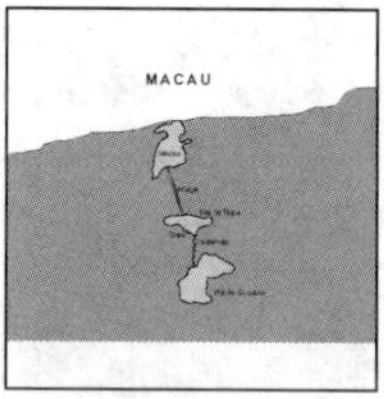

m0003037.tif

m0003038.tif

m0003039.tif

m0003040.tif

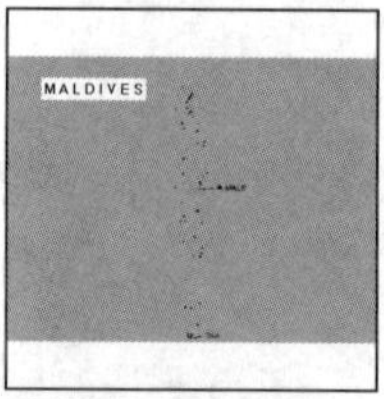

m0003041.tif

m0003042.tif

m0003043.tif

m0003044.tif

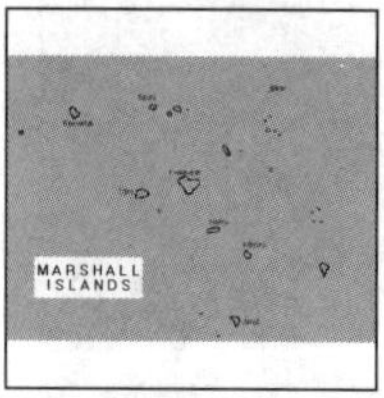

m0003045.tif

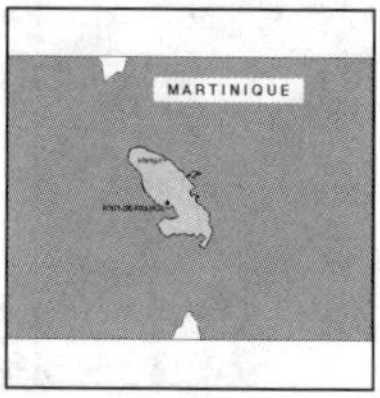

m0003046.tif

m0003047.tif

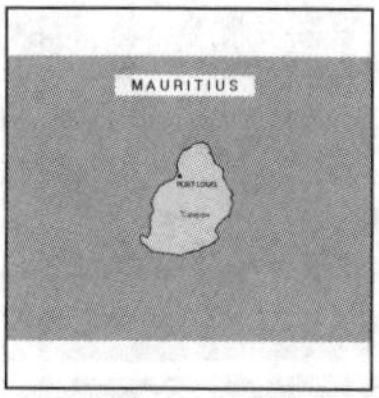

m0003048.tif

m0003049.tif

m0003050.tif

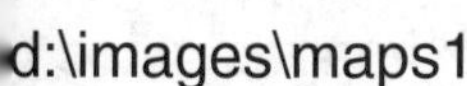

d:\images\maps1

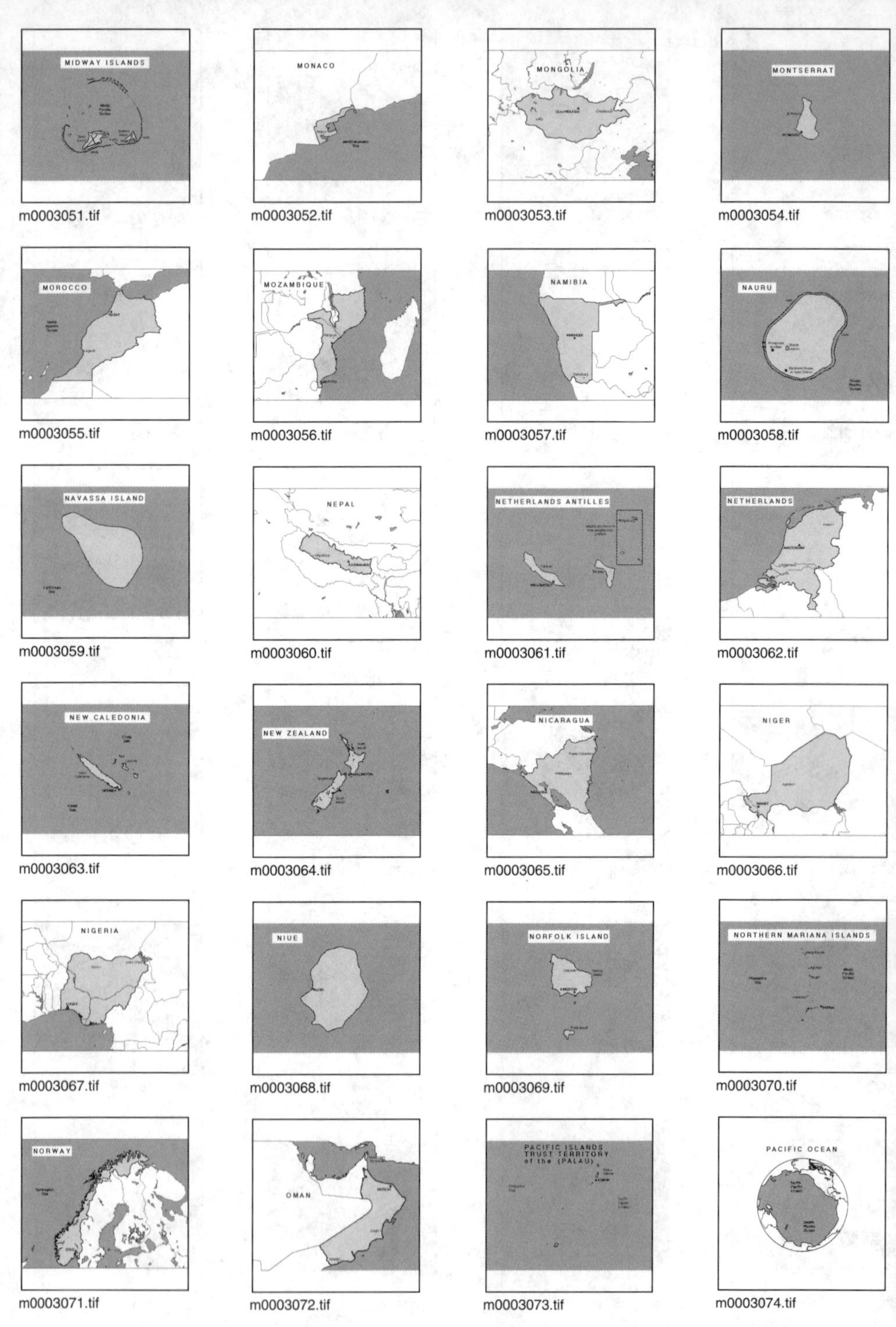

m0003051.tif m0003052.tif m0003053.tif m0003054.tif

m0003055.tif m0003056.tif m0003057.tif m0003058.tif

m0003059.tif m0003060.tif m0003061.tif m0003062.tif

m0003063.tif m0003064.tif m0003065.tif m0003066.tif

m0003067.tif m0003068.tif m0003069.tif m0003070.tif

m0003071.tif m0003072.tif m0003073.tif m0003074.tif

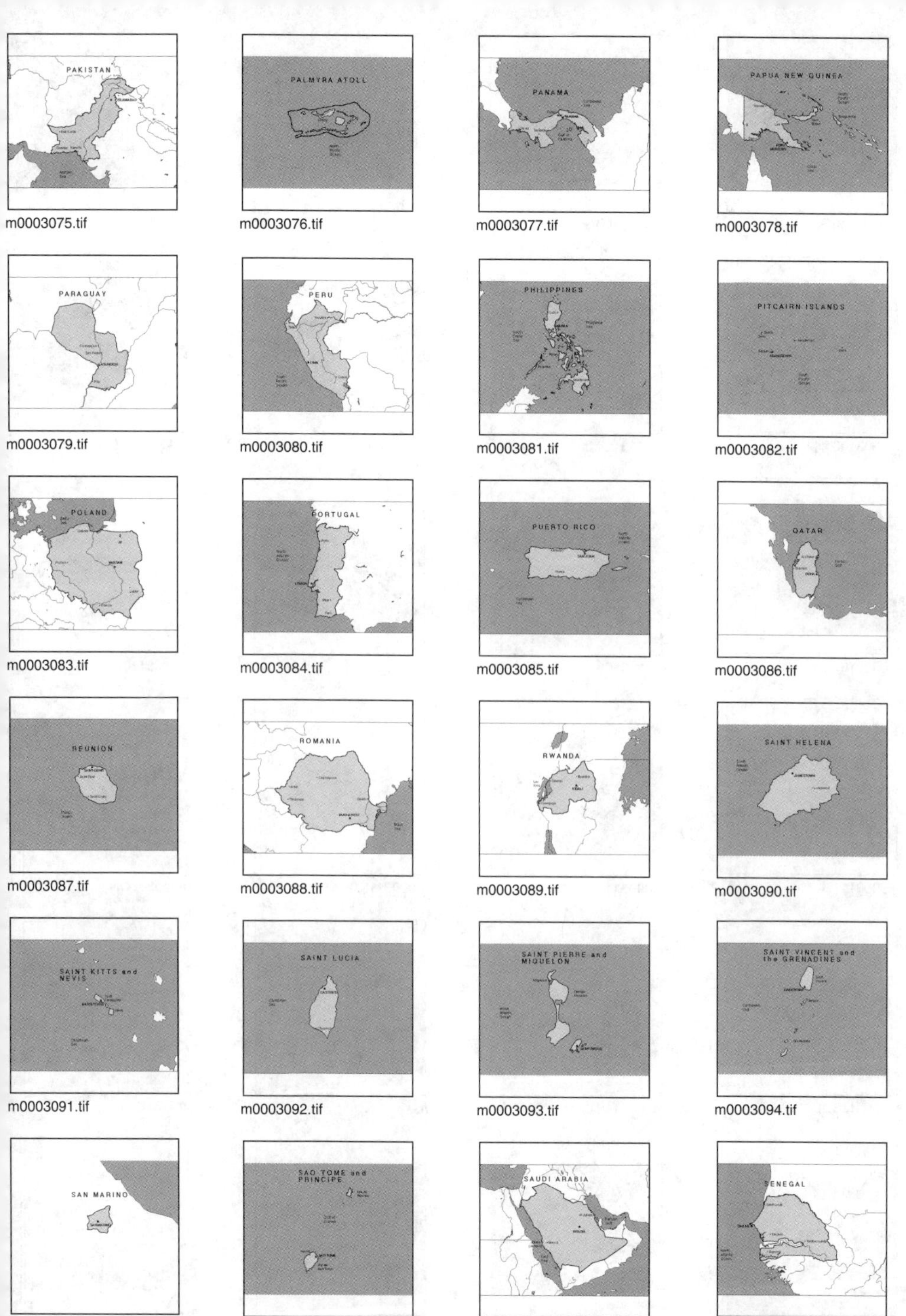

m0003075.tif m0003076.tif m0003077.tif m0003078.tif

m0003079.tif m0003080.tif m0003081.tif m0003082.tif

m0003083.tif m0003084.tif m0003085.tif m0003086.tif

m0003087.tif m0003088.tif m0003089.tif m0003090.tif

m0003091.tif m0003092.tif m0003093.tif m0003094.tif

m0003095.tif m0003096.tif m0003097.tif m0003098.tif

d:\images\maps1

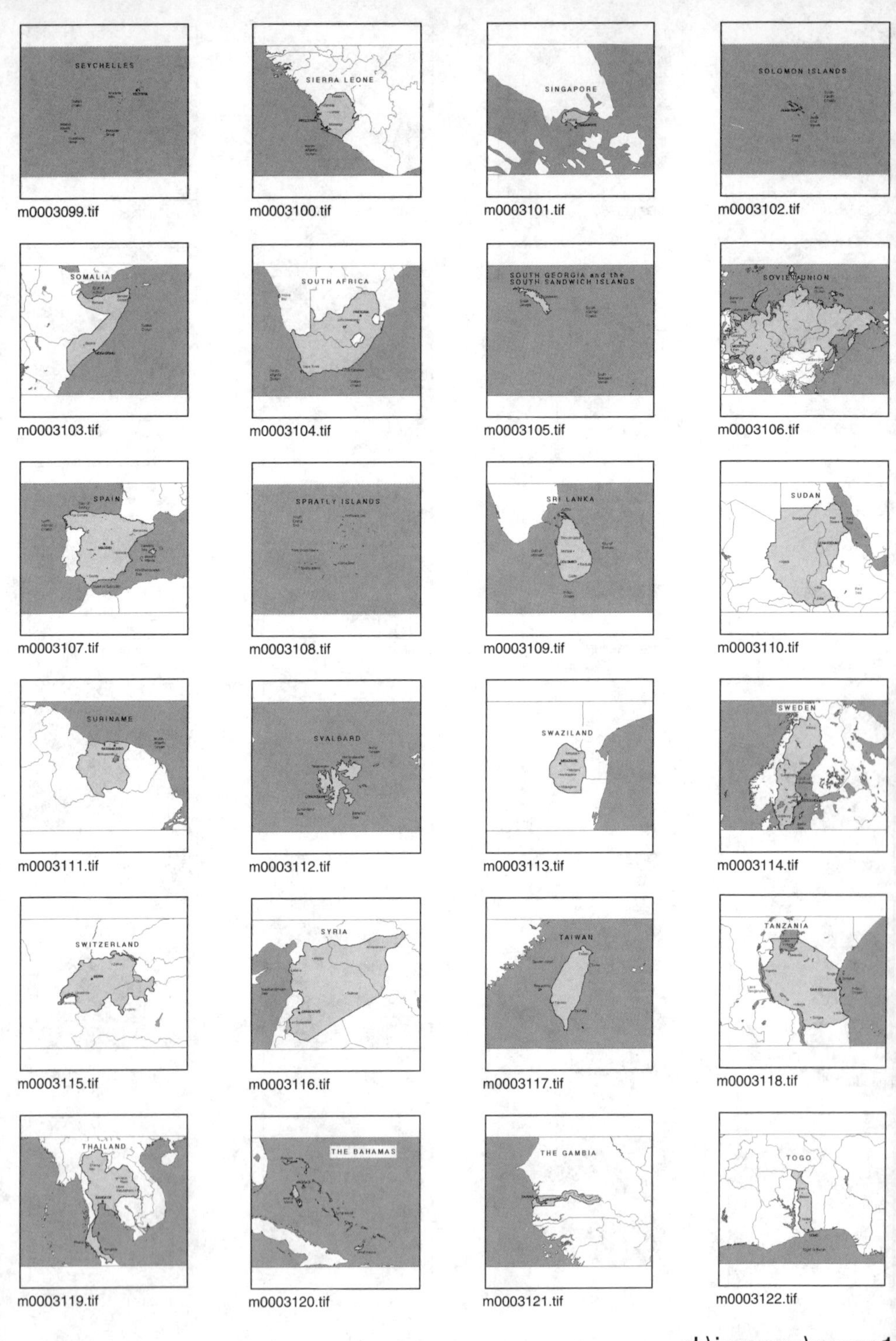

m0003099.tif m0003100.tif m0003101.tif m0003102.tif

m0003103.tif m0003104.tif m0003105.tif m0003106.tif

m0003107.tif m0003108.tif m0003109.tif m0003110.tif

m0003111.tif m0003112.tif m0003113.tif m0003114.tif

m0003115.tif m0003116.tif m0003117.tif m0003118.tif

m0003119.tif m0003120.tif m0003121.tif m0003122.tif

d:\images\maps1

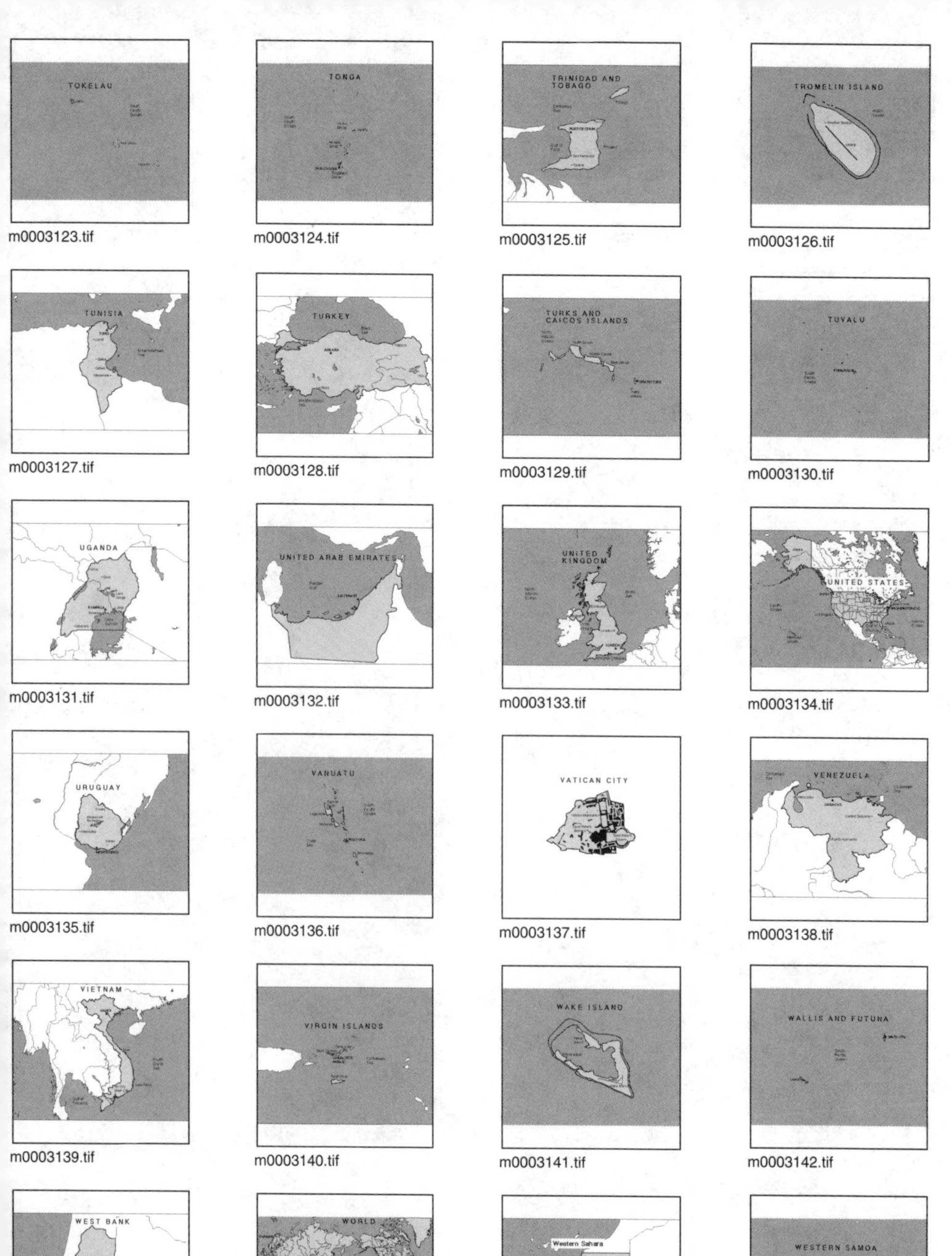

m0003123.tif m0003124.tif m0003125.tif m0003126.tif

m0003127.tif m0003128.tif m0003129.tif m0003130.tif

m0003131.tif m0003132.tif m0003133.tif m0003134.tif

m0003135.tif m0003136.tif m0003137.tif m0003138.tif

m0003139.tif m0003140.tif m0003141.tif m0003142.tif

m0003143.tif m0003144.tif m0003145.tif m0003146.tif

d:\images\maps1

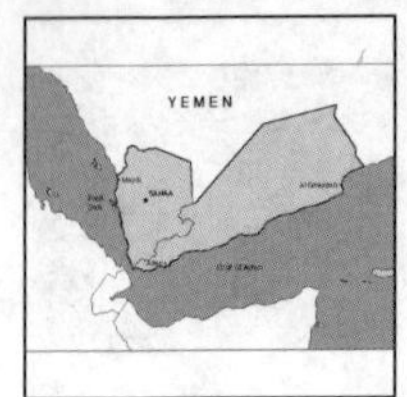

m0003147.tif

m0003148.tif

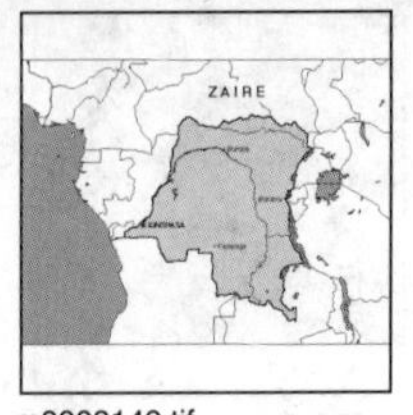

m0003149.tif

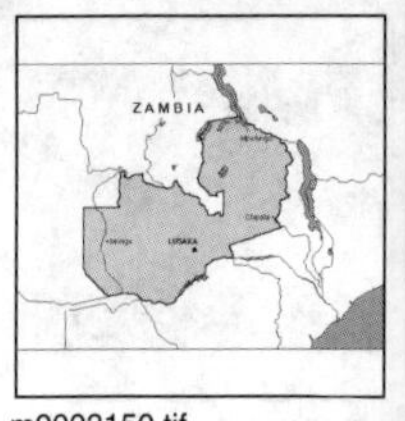

m0003150.tif

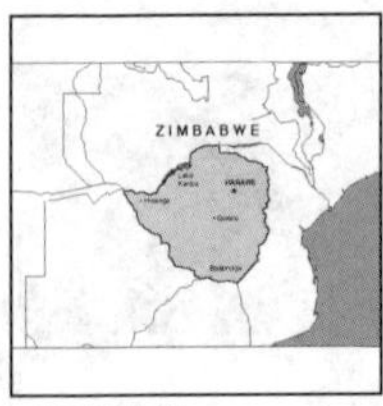

m0003151.tif

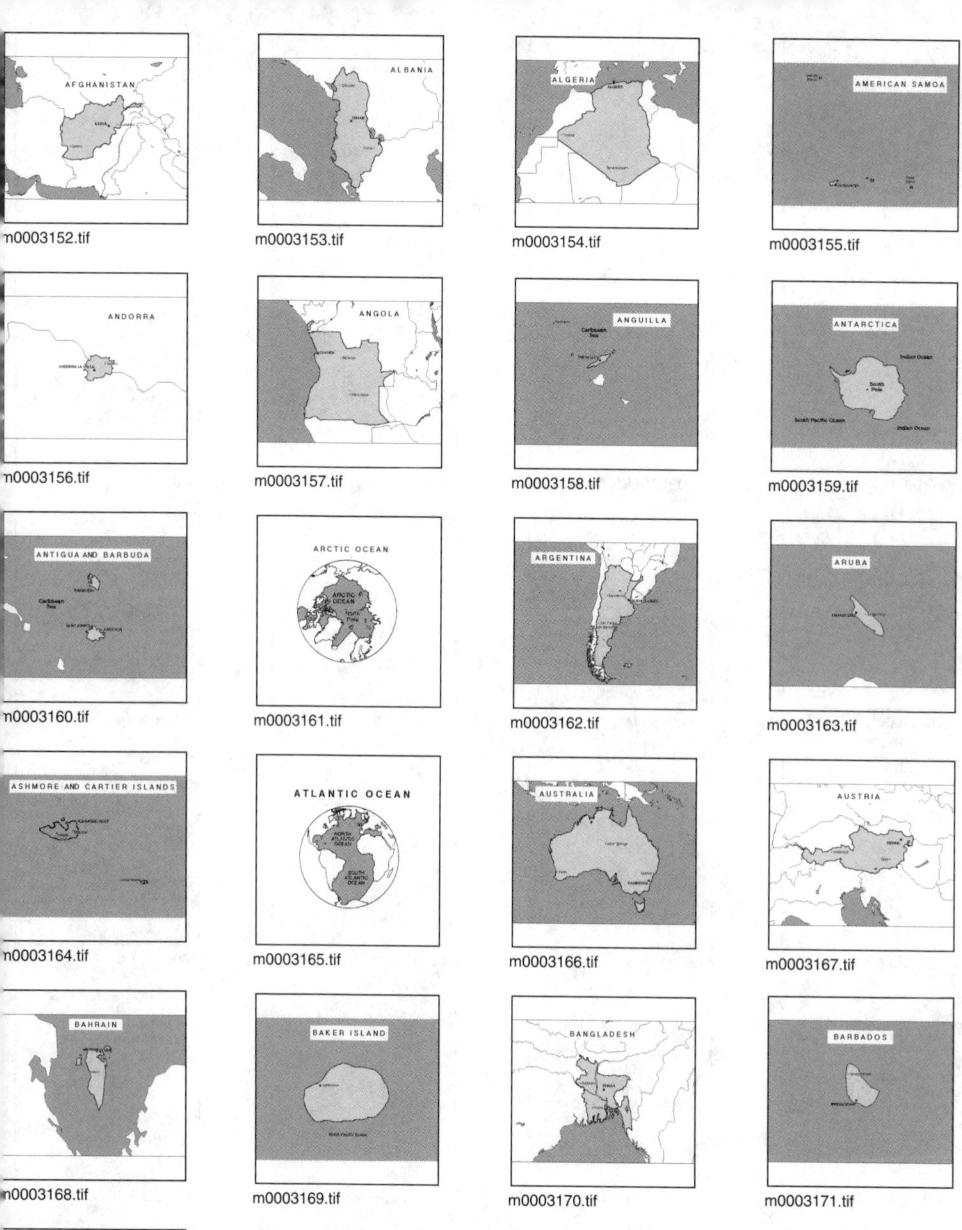

m0003152.tif m0003153.tif m0003154.tif m0003155.tif

m0003156.tif m0003157.tif m0003158.tif m0003159.tif

m0003160.tif m0003161.tif m0003162.tif m0003163.tif

m0003164.tif m0003165.tif m0003166.tif m0003167.tif

m0003168.tif m0003169.tif m0003170.tif m0003171.tif

m0003172.tif m0003173.tif m0003174.tif m0003175.tif

d:\images\maps2

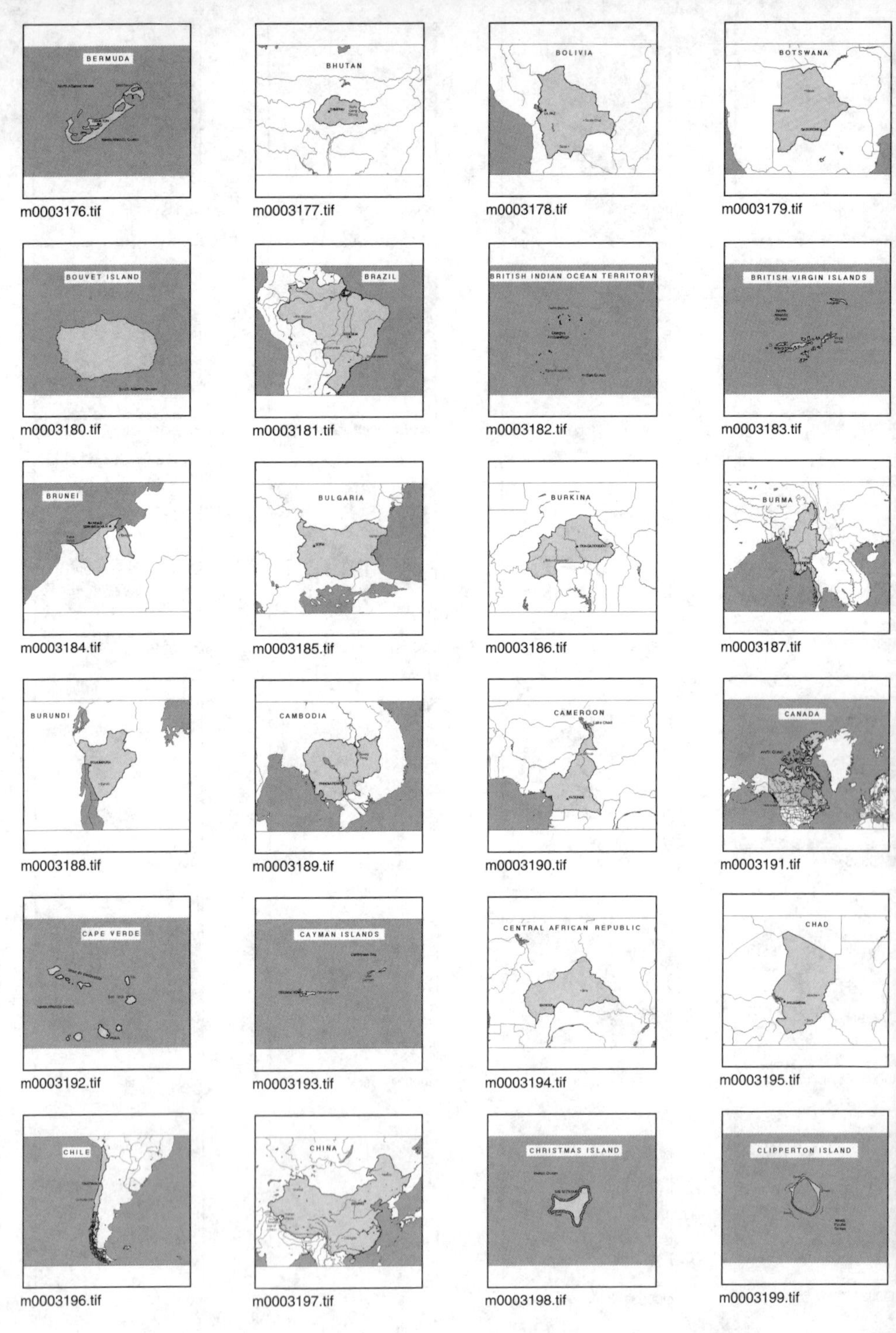

m0003176.tif m0003177.tif m0003178.tif m0003179.tif
m0003180.tif m0003181.tif m0003182.tif m0003183.tif
m0003184.tif m0003185.tif m0003186.tif m0003187.tif
m0003188.tif m0003189.tif m0003190.tif m0003191.tif
m0003192.tif m0003193.tif m0003194.tif m0003195.tif
m0003196.tif m0003197.tif m0003198.tif m0003199.tif

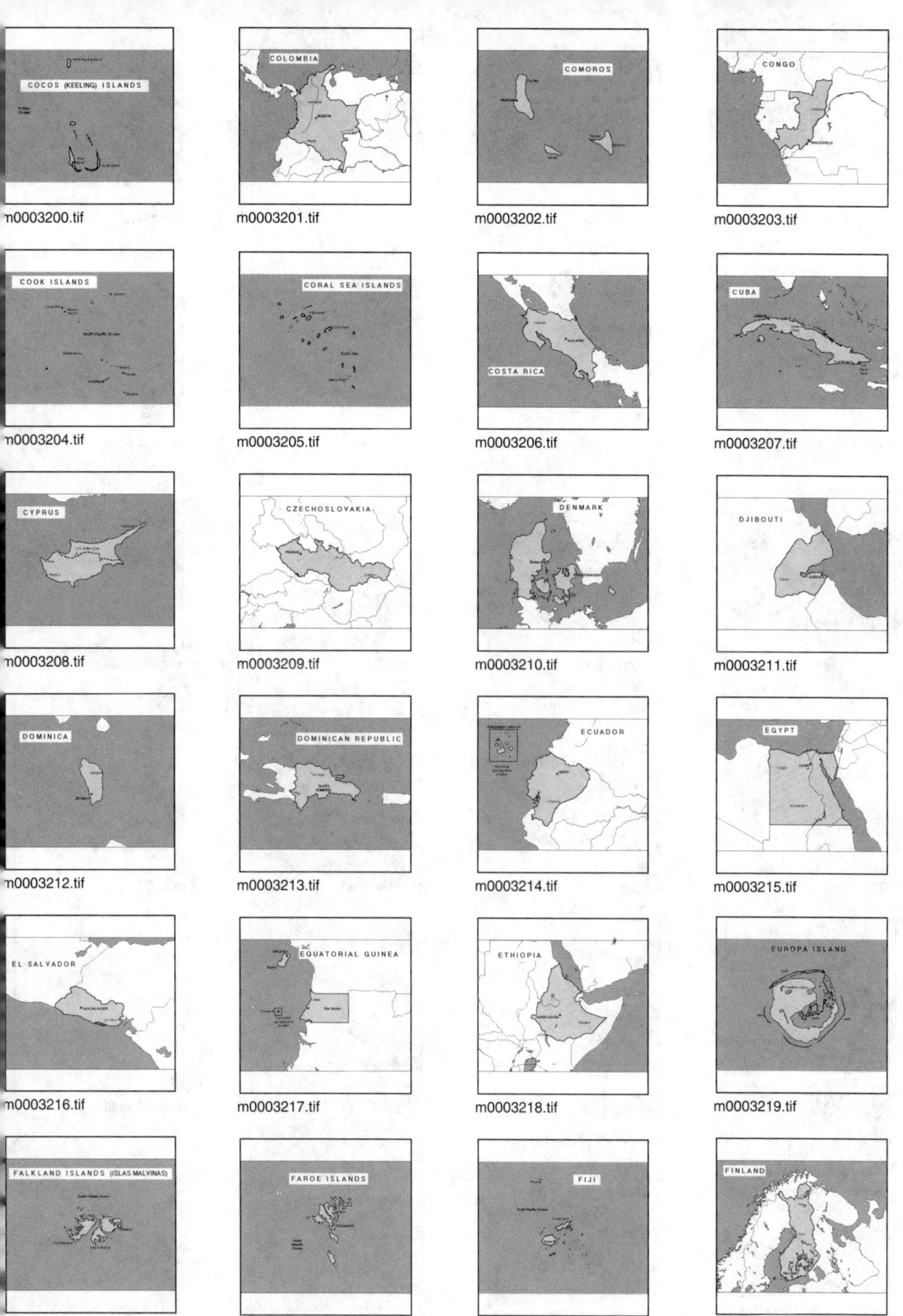

m0003200.tif m0003201.tif m0003202.tif m0003203.tif

m0003204.tif m0003205.tif m0003206.tif m0003207.tif

m0003208.tif m0003209.tif m0003210.tif m0003211.tif

m0003212.tif m0003213.tif m0003214.tif m0003215.tif

m0003216.tif m0003217.tif m0003218.tif m0003219.tif

m0003220.tif m0003221.tif m0003222.tif m0003223.tif

d:\images\maps2

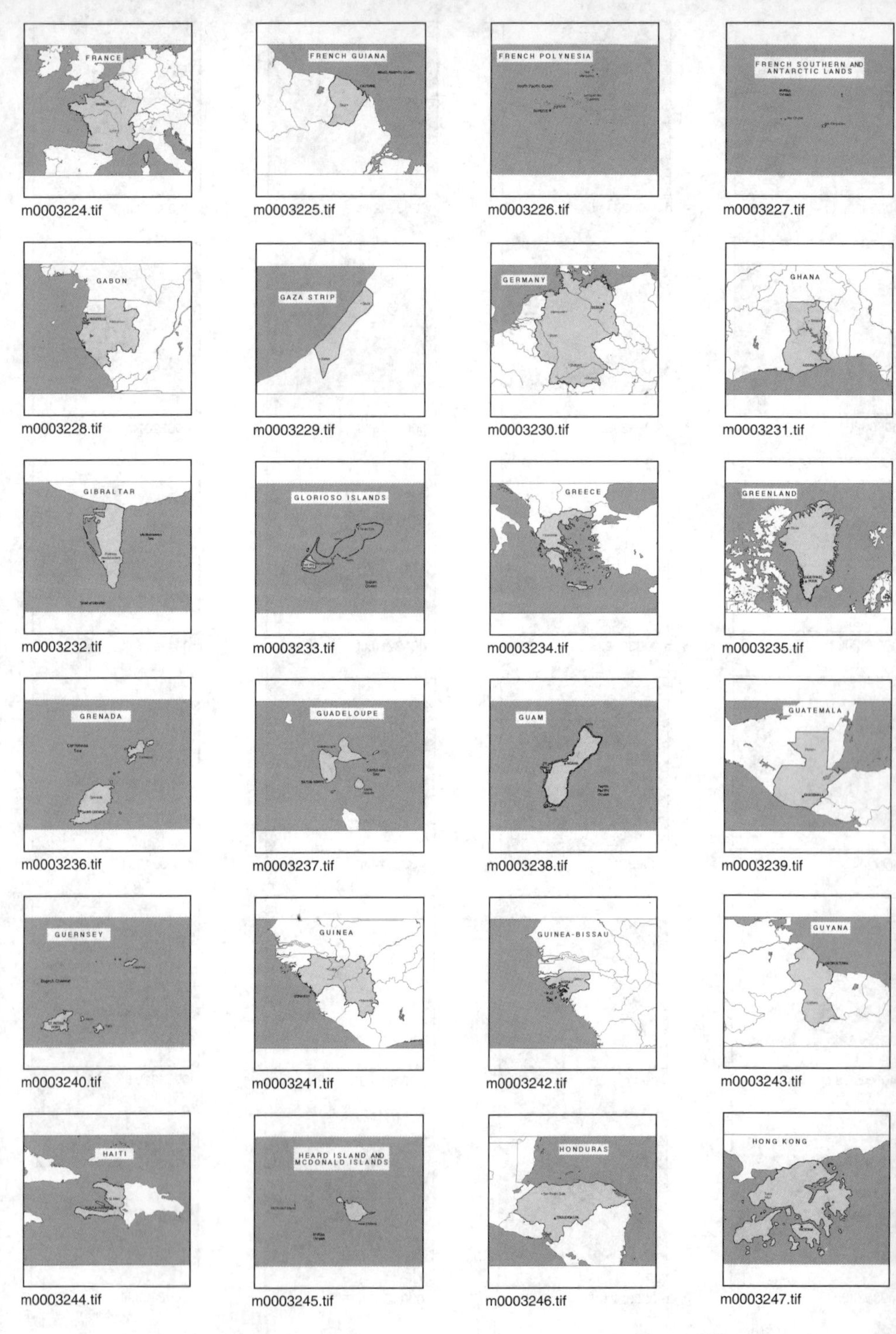

m0003224.tif m0003225.tif m0003226.tif m0003227.tif
m0003228.tif m0003229.tif m0003230.tif m0003231.tif
m0003232.tif m0003233.tif m0003234.tif m0003235.tif
m0003236.tif m0003237.tif m0003238.tif m0003239.tif
m0003240.tif m0003241.tif m0003242.tif m0003243.tif
m0003244.tif m0003245.tif m0003246.tif m0003247.tif

d:\images\maps2

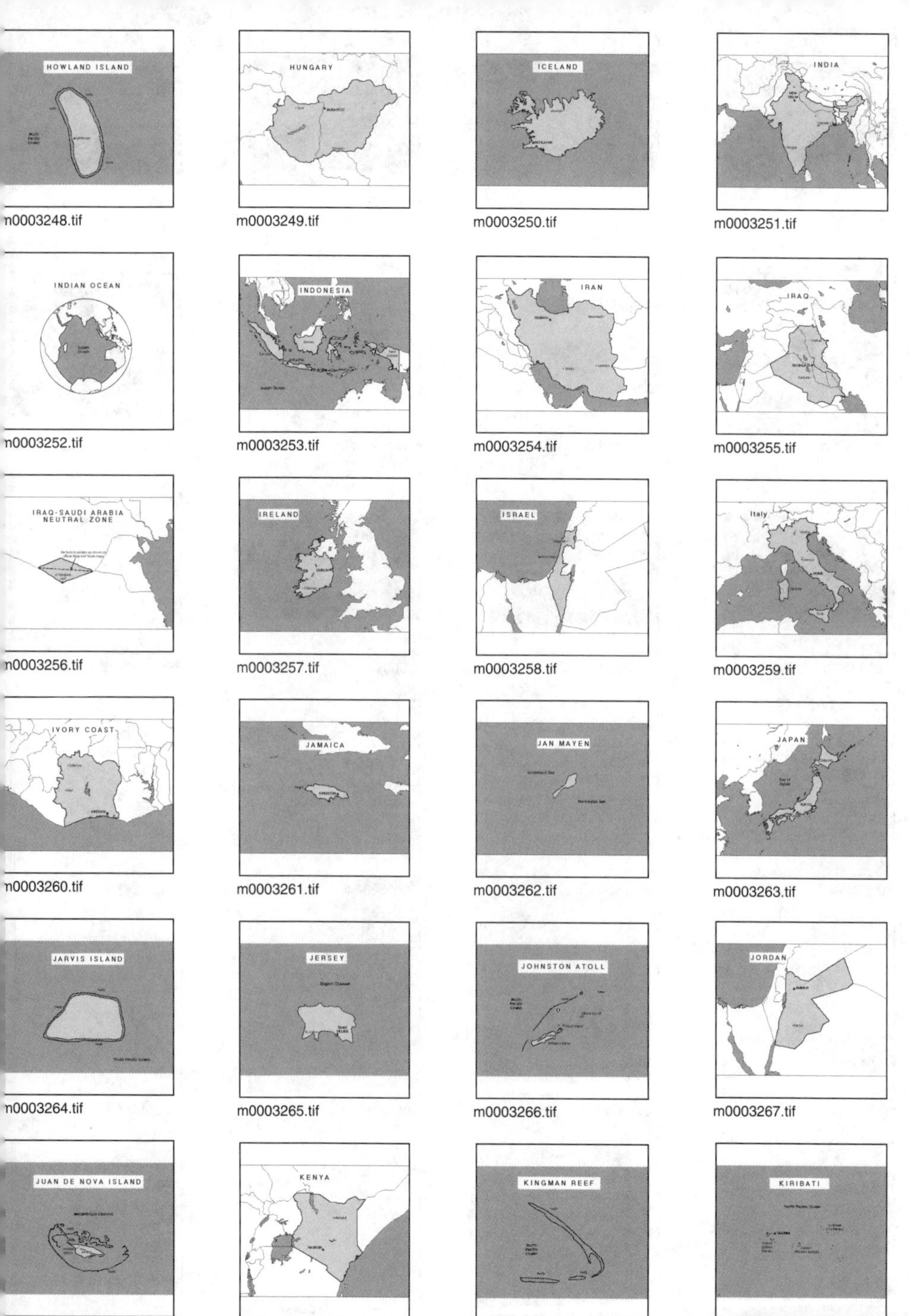

d:\images\maps2

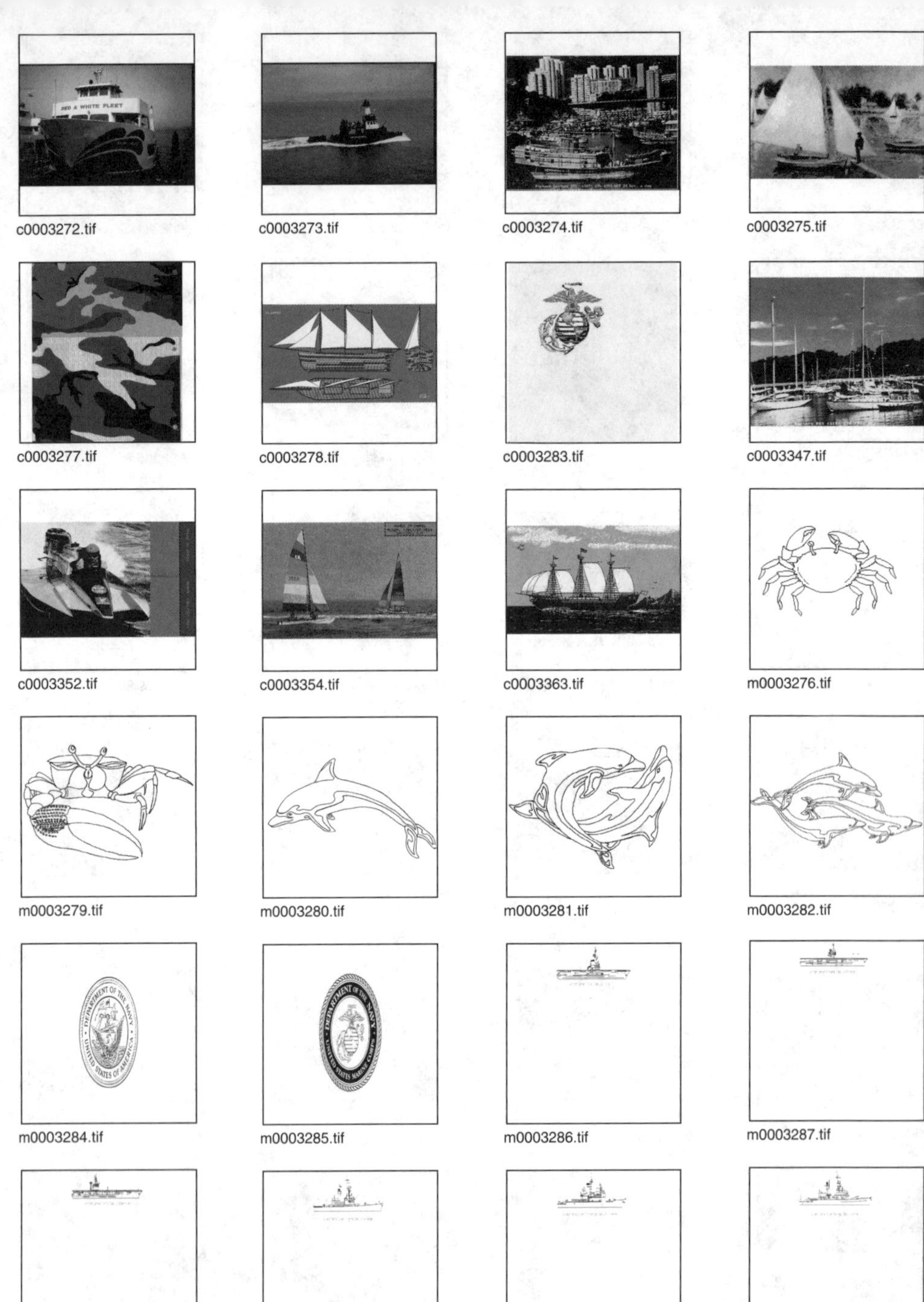

c0003272.tif c0003273.tif c0003274.tif c0003275.tif

c0003277.tif c0003278.tif c0003283.tif c0003347.tif

c0003352.tif c0003354.tif c0003363.tif m0003276.tif

m0003279.tif m0003280.tif m0003281.tif m0003282.tif

m0003284.tif m0003285.tif m0003286.tif m0003287.tif

m0003288.tif m0003289.tif m0003290.tif m0003291.tif

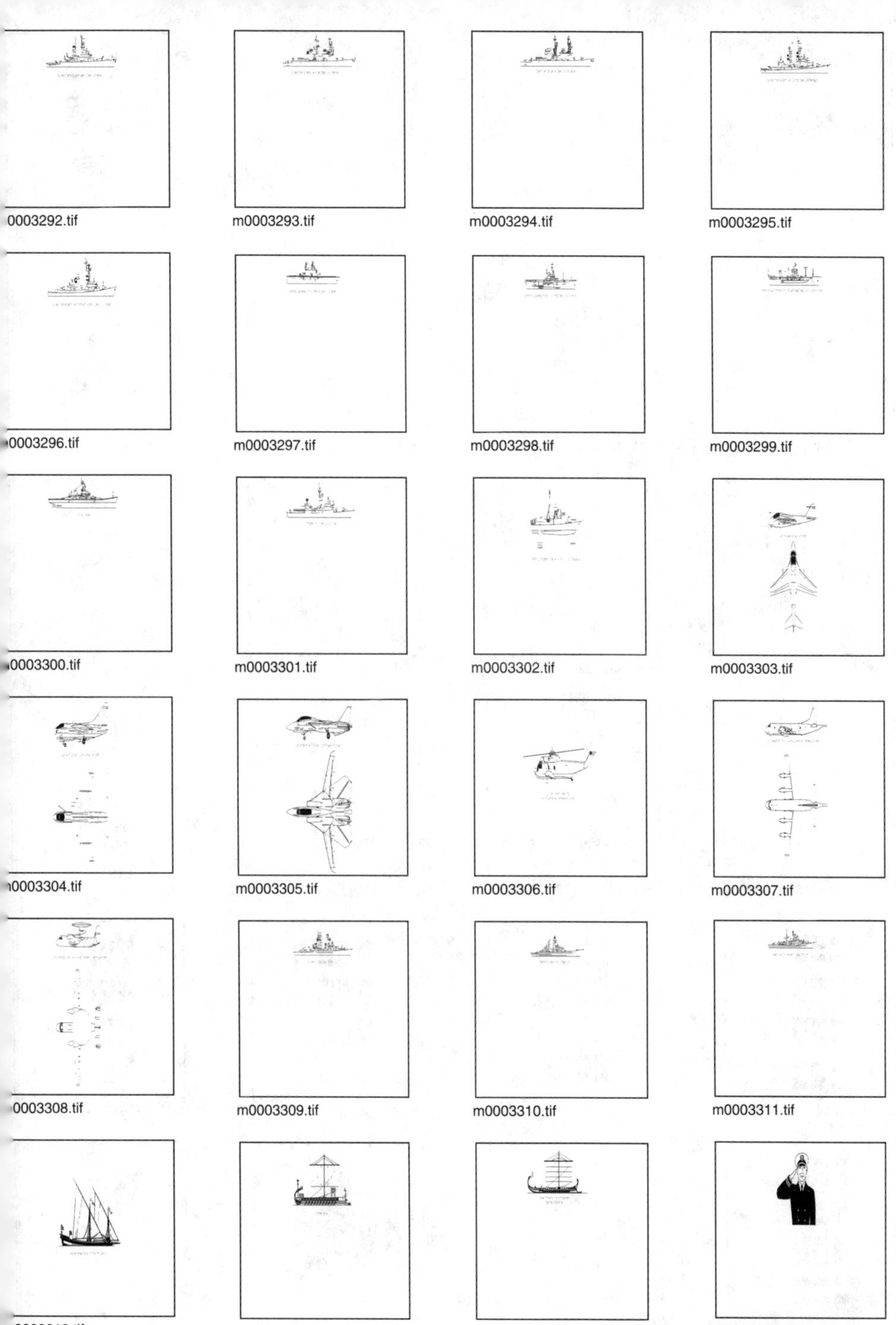

0003292.tif m0003293.tif m0003294.tif m0003295.tif

0003296.tif m0003297.tif m0003298.tif m0003299.tif

0003300.tif m0003301.tif m0003302.tif m0003303.tif

0003304.tif m0003305.tif m0003306.tif m0003307.tif

0003308.tif m0003309.tif m0003310.tif m0003311.tif

0003312.tif m0003313.tif m0003314.tif m0003315.tif

:\images\animal1

m0003316.tif

m0003317.tif

m0003318.tif

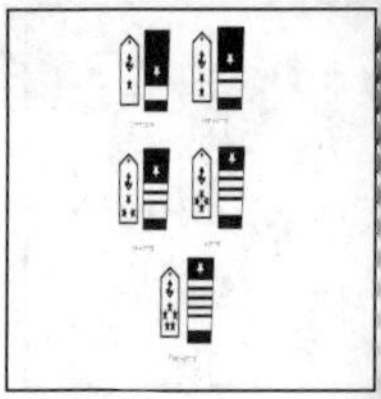

m0003319.tif

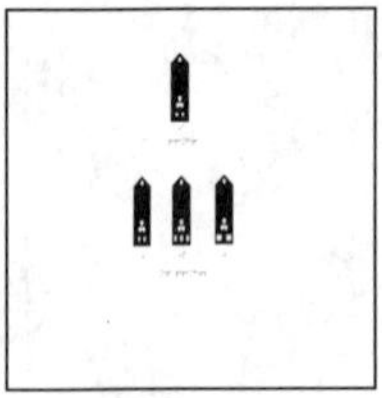

m0003320.tif

m0003321.tif

m0003322.tif

m0003323.tif

m0003324.tif

m0003325.tif

m0003326.tif

m0003327.tif

m0003328.tif

m0003329.tif

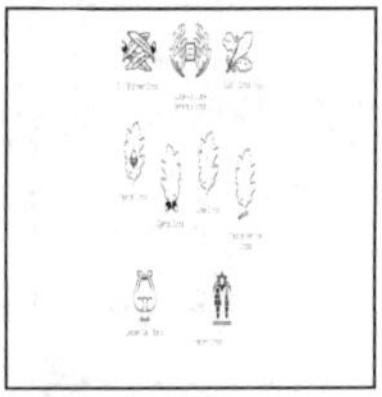

m0003330.tif

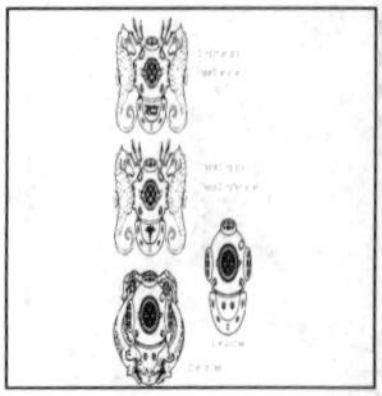

m0003331.tif

m0003332.tif

m0003333.tif

m0003334.tif

m0003335.tif

m0003336.tif

m0003337.tif

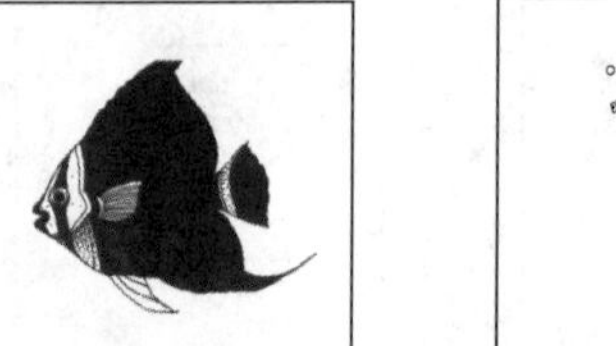

m0003338.tif

m0003339.tif

0003340.tif m0003341.tif m0003342.tif m0003343.tif

0003344.tif m0003345.tif m0003346.tif m0003348.tif

0003349.tif m0003350.tif m0003351.tif m0003353.tif

0003355.tif m0003356.tif m0003357.tif m0003358.tif

0003359.tif m0003360.tif m0003361.tif m0003362.tif

0003364.tif m0003365.tif m0003366.tif m0003367.tif

:\images\marine

m0003368.tif

m0003369.tif

m0003370.tif

m0003371.tif

m0003372.tif

m0003373.tif

m0003374.tif

m0003375.tif

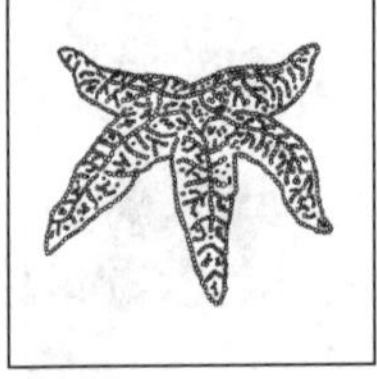
m0003376.tif

m0003377.tif

0003378.tif

m0003379.tif

m0003380.tif

m0003381.tif

0003382.tif

m0003383.tif

m0003384.tif

m0003385.tif

0003386.tif

m0003387.tif

m0003388.tif

m0003389.tif

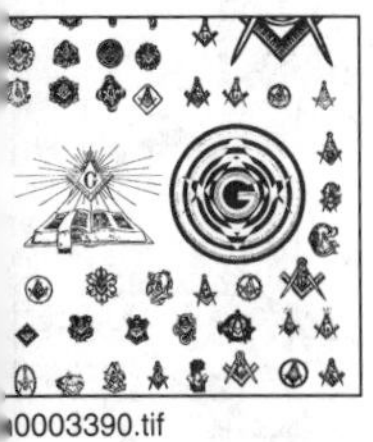
0003390.tif

m0003391.tif

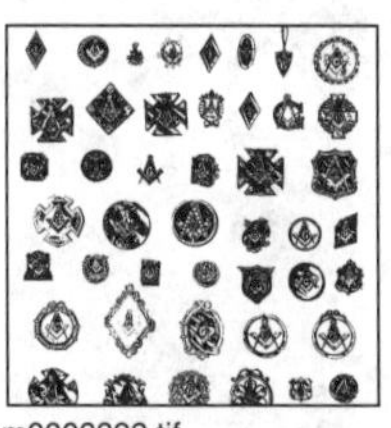
m0003392.tif

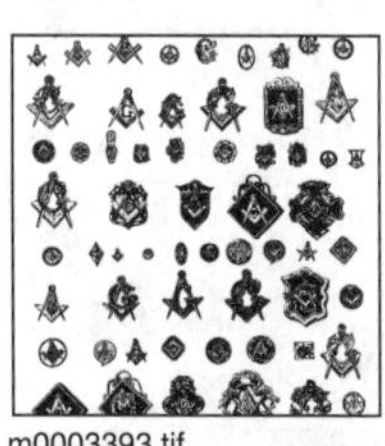
m0003393.tif

0003394.tif

m0003395.tif

m0003396.tif

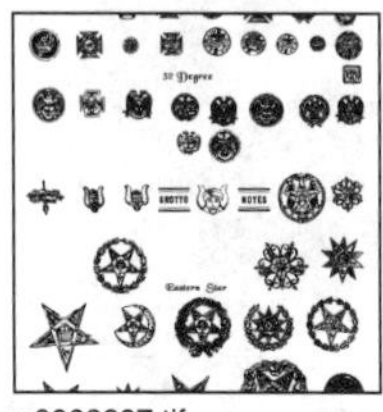
m0003397.tif

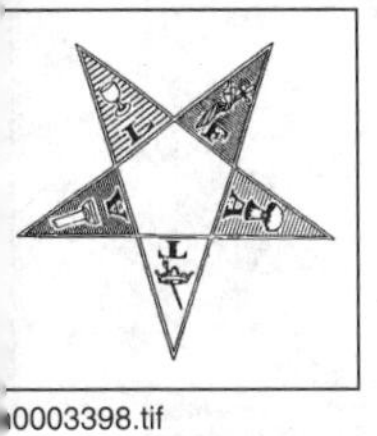
0003398.tif

m0003399.tif

:\images\mason

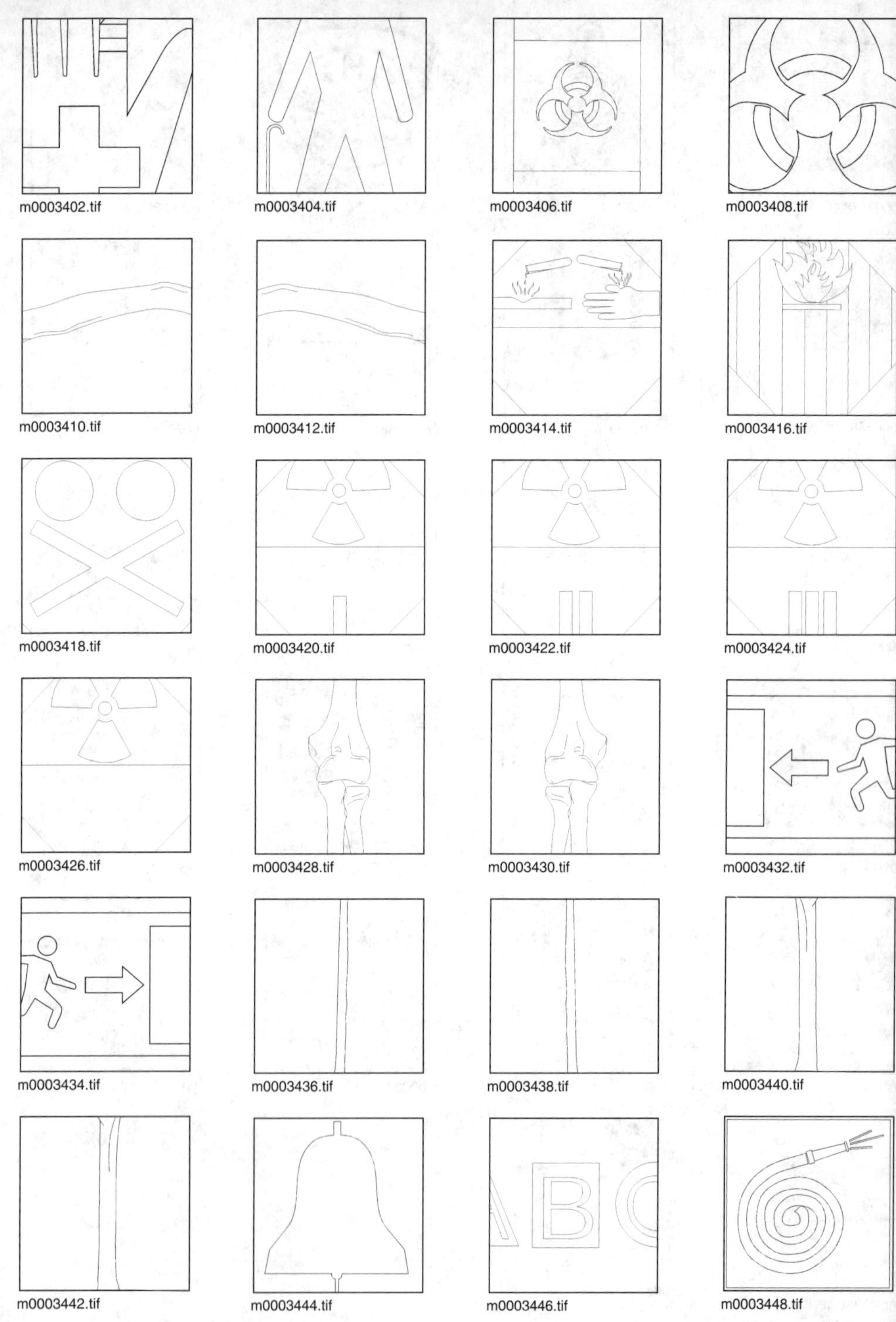

m0003402.tif m0003404.tif m0003406.tif m0003408.tif
m0003410.tif m0003412.tif m0003414.tif m0003416.tif
m0003418.tif m0003420.tif m0003422.tif m0003424.tif
m0003426.tif m0003428.tif m0003430.tif m0003432.tif
m0003434.tif m0003436.tif m0003438.tif m0003440.tif
m0003442.tif m0003444.tif m0003446.tif m0003448.tif

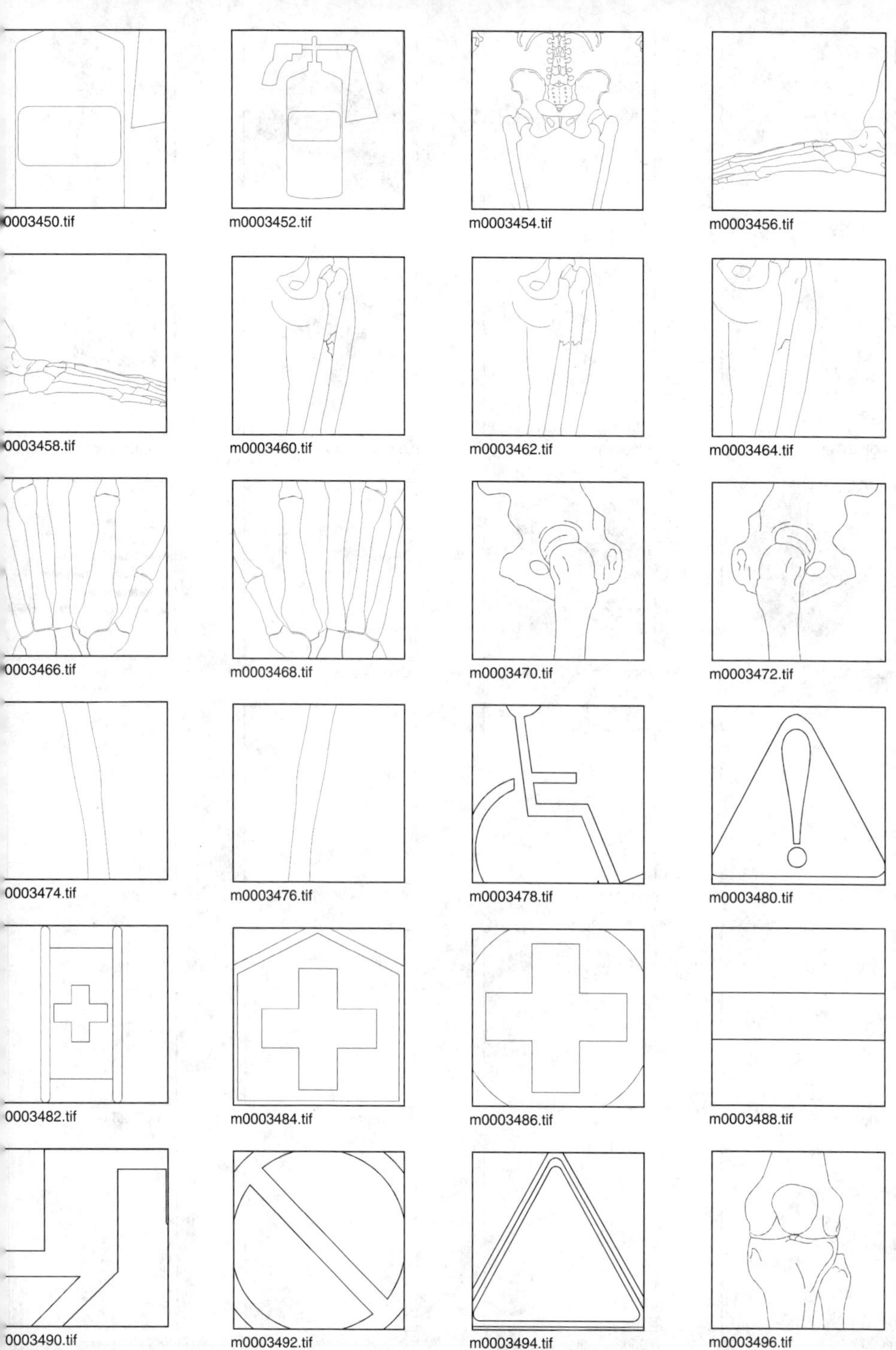
0003450.tif
m0003452.tif
m0003454.tif
m0003456.tif
0003458.tif
m0003460.tif
m0003462.tif
m0003464.tif
0003466.tif
m0003468.tif
m0003470.tif
m0003472.tif
0003474.tif
m0003476.tif
m0003478.tif
m0003480.tif
0003482.tif
m0003484.tif
m0003486.tif
m0003488.tif
0003490.tif
m0003492.tif
m0003494.tif
m0003496.tif

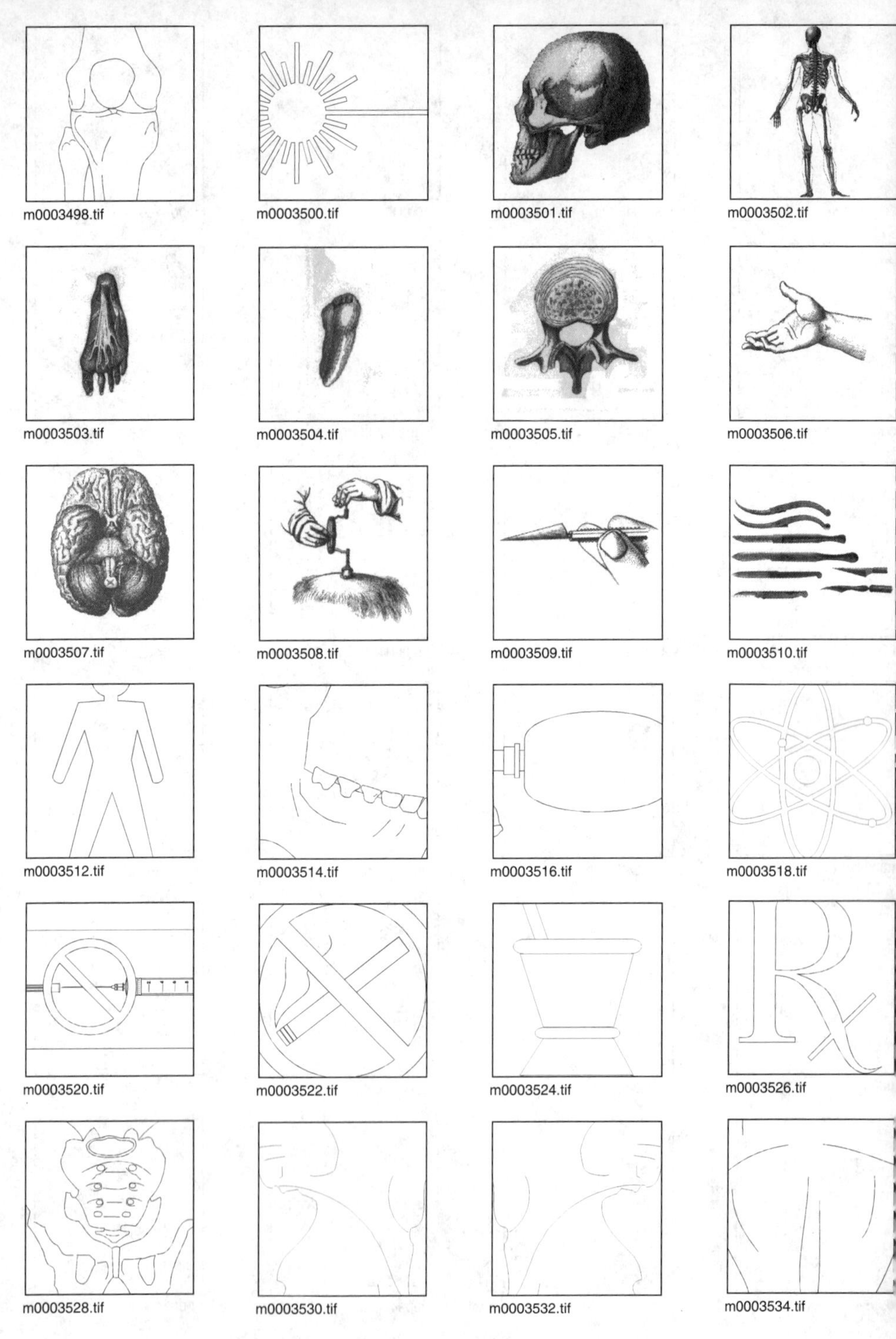

m0003498.tif
m0003500.tif
m0003501.tif
m0003502.tif
m0003503.tif
m0003504.tif
m0003505.tif
m0003506.tif
m0003507.tif
m0003508.tif
m0003509.tif
m0003510.tif
m0003512.tif
m0003514.tif
m0003516.tif
m0003518.tif
m0003520.tif
m0003522.tif
m0003524.tif
m0003526.tif
m0003528.tif
m0003530.tif
m0003532.tif
m0003534.tif

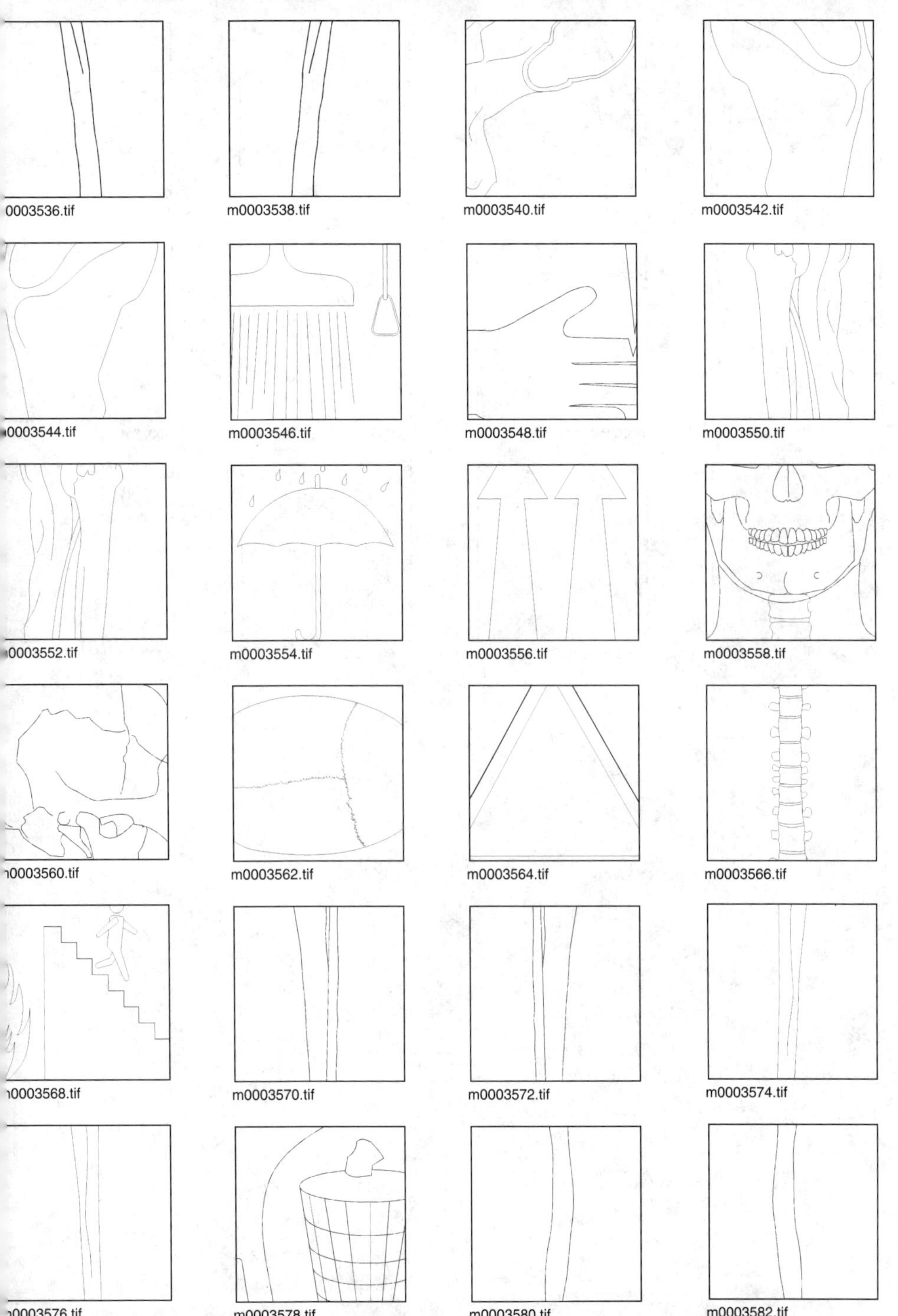

0003536.tif m0003538.tif m0003540.tif m0003542.tif

0003544.tif m0003546.tif m0003548.tif m0003550.tif

0003552.tif m0003554.tif m0003556.tif m0003558.tif

0003560.tif m0003562.tif m0003564.tif m0003566.tif

0003568.tif m0003570.tif m0003572.tif m0003574.tif

0003576.tif m0003578.tif m0003580.tif m0003582.tif

m0003584.tif m0003586.tif m0003588.tif m0003590.tif

m0003591.tif m0003593.tif m0003596.tif m0003598.tif

m0003600.tif m0003602.tif m0003604.tif m0003606.tif

003701.tif

c0003702.tif

c0003703.tif

c0003704.tif

003705.tif

c0003706.tif

c0003707.tif

c0003709.tif

003710.tif

c0003711.tif

c0003712.tif

c0003715.tif

003716.tif

c0003719.tif

c0003720.tif

c0003721.tif

003722.tif

c0003723.tif

c0003725.tif

c0003726.tif

003727.tif

c0003729.tif

c0003730.tif

c0003731.tif

:\images\militar

c0003732.tif

c0003733.tif

c0003734.tif

c0003736.tif

c0003737.tif

c0003739.tif

c0003740.tif

c0003741.tif

c0003742.tif

c0003750.tif

c0003751.tif

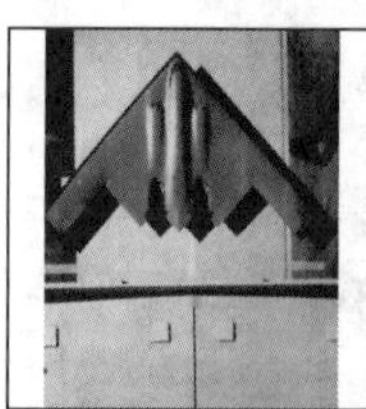
c0003753.tif

c0003754.tif

c0003755.tif

c0003756.tif

c0003757.tif

c0003758.tif

c0003759.tif

c0003760.tif

m0003708.tif

m0003713.tif

m0003718.tif

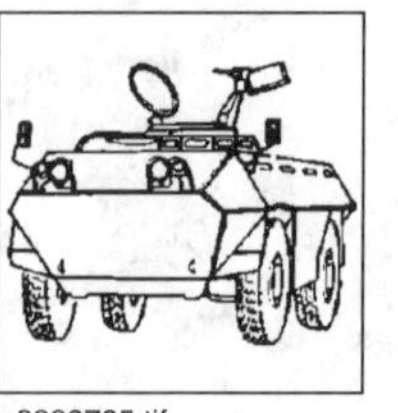
m0003735.tif

m0003738.tif

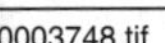
0003748.tif

m0003752.tif

m0003762.tif

c0003793.tif

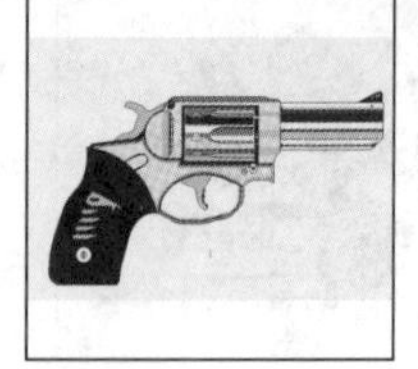
c0003795.tif

c0003801.tif

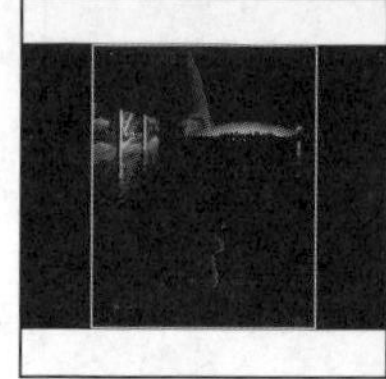
c0003805.tif

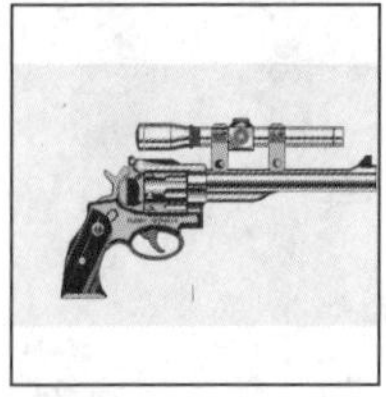
c0003811.tif

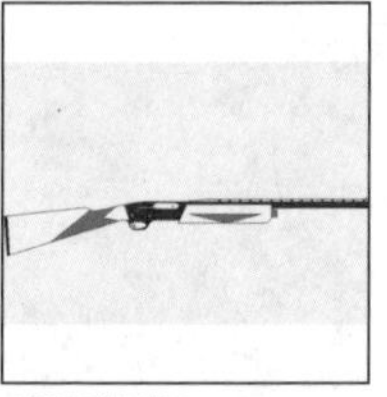
c0003812.tif

c0003823.tif

c0003824.tif

c0003825.tif

c0003826.tif

c0003827.tif

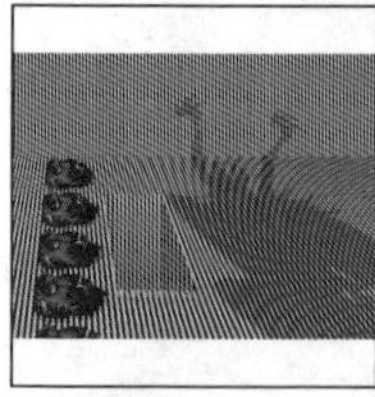
c0003833.tif

m0003763.tif

m0003764.tif

m0003766.tif

m0003767.tif

m0003768.tif

m0003769.tif

m0003770.tif

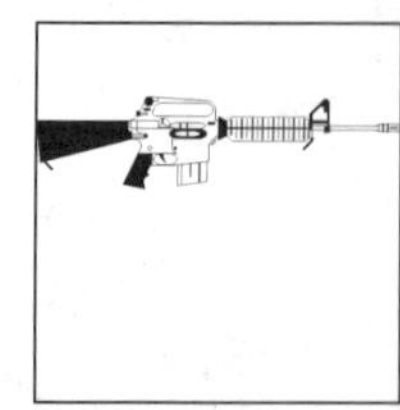
m0003771.tif

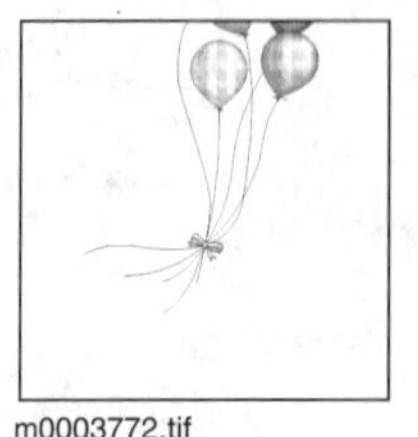
m0003772.tif

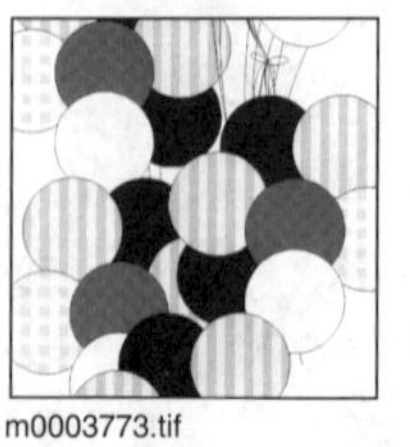
m0003773.tif

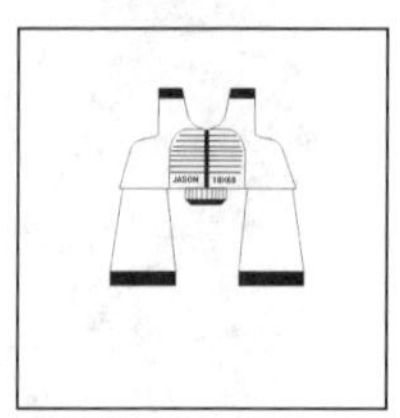
m0003774.tif

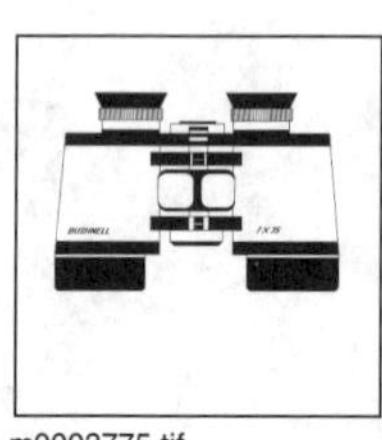
m0003775.tif

n0003776.tif

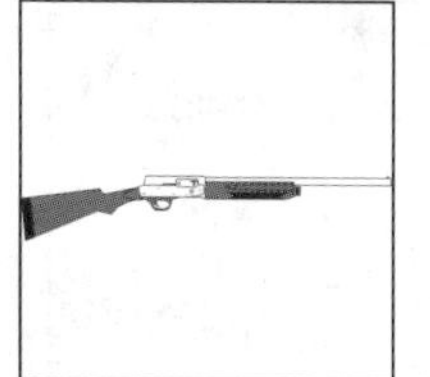
m0003777.tif

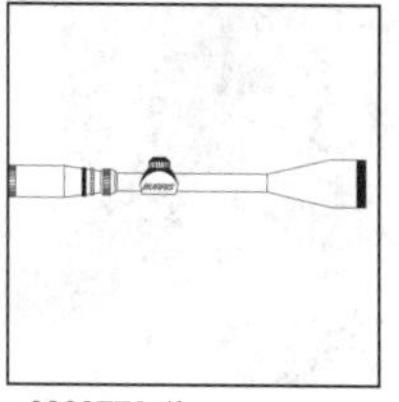
m0003778.tif

m0003779.tif

n0003780.tif

m0003781.tif

m0003782.tif

m0003783.tif

n0003784.tif

m0003785.tif

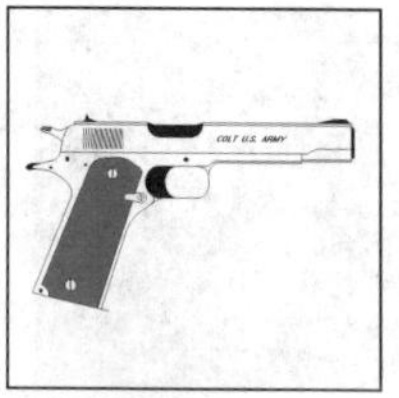

m0003786.tif

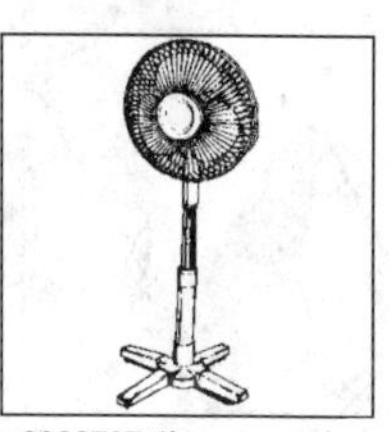
m0003787.tif

n0003788.tif

m0003790.tif

m0003791.tif

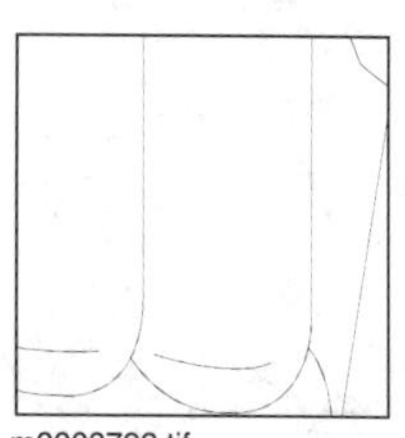
m0003792.tif

n0003794.tif

m0003796.tif

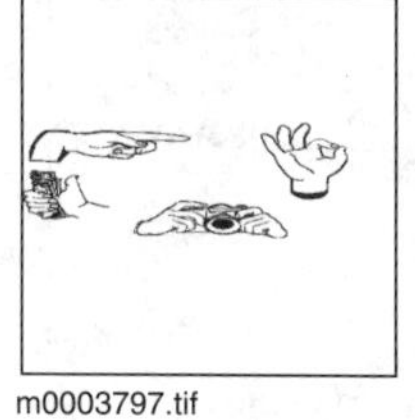
m0003797.tif

m0003798.tif

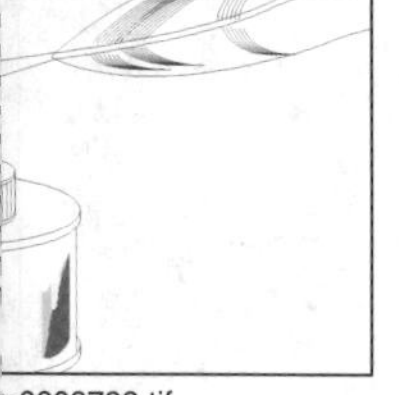
n0003799.tif

m0003800.tif

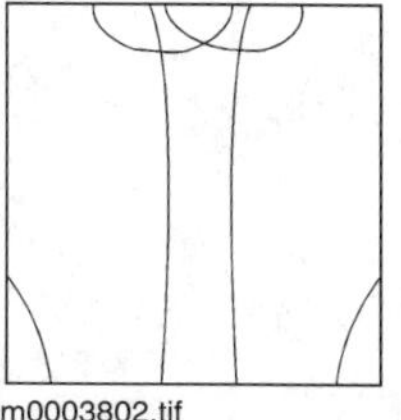
m0003802.tif

m0003803.tif

:\images\misc

m0003804.tif 
m0003807.tif 
m0003808.tif 
m0003810.tif

m0003813.tif 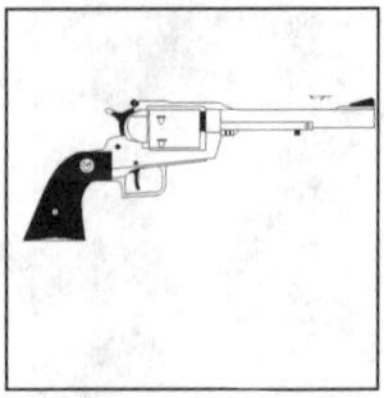
m0003814.tif 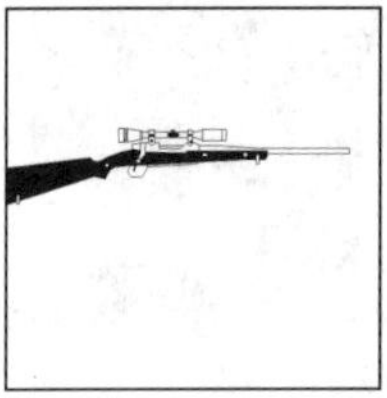
m0003815.tif 
m0003816.tif

m0003817.tif 
m0003818.tif 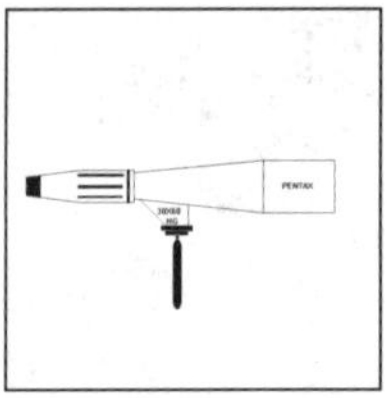
m0003819.tif 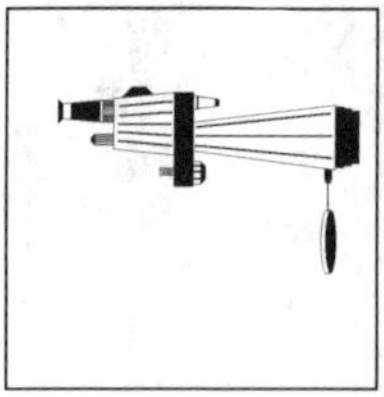
m0003820.tif

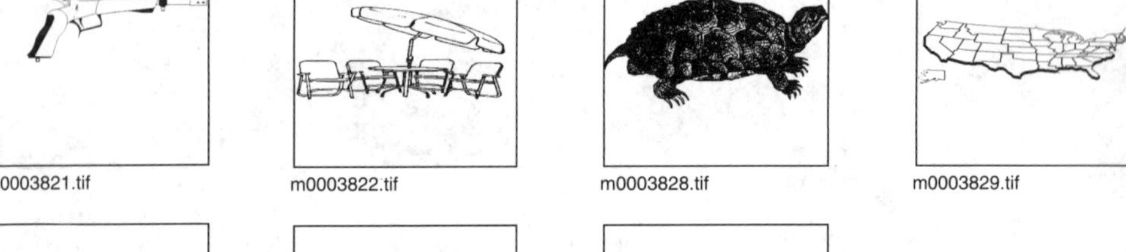

m0003821.tif
m0003822.tif
m0003828.tif
m0003829.tif

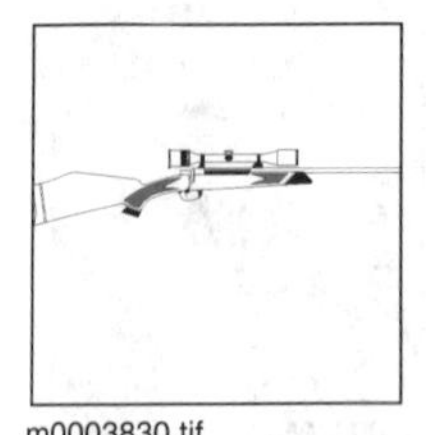

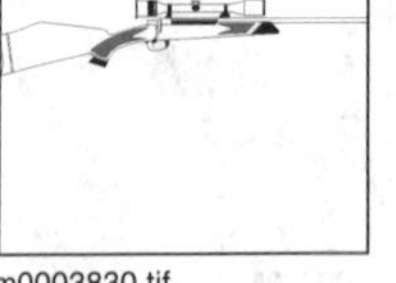

m0003830.tif

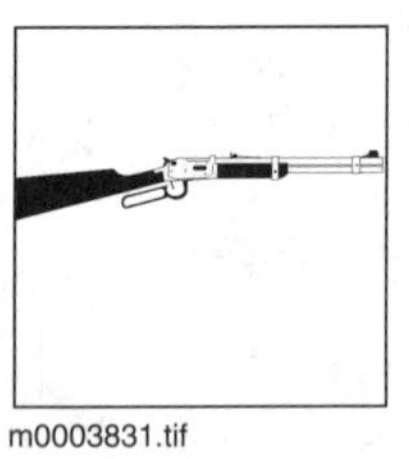

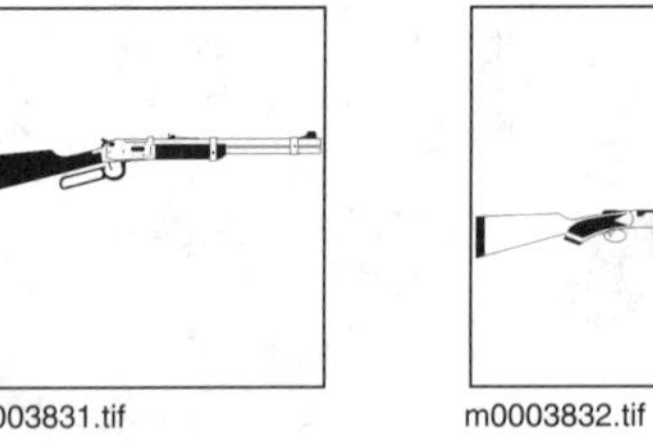

m0003831.tif

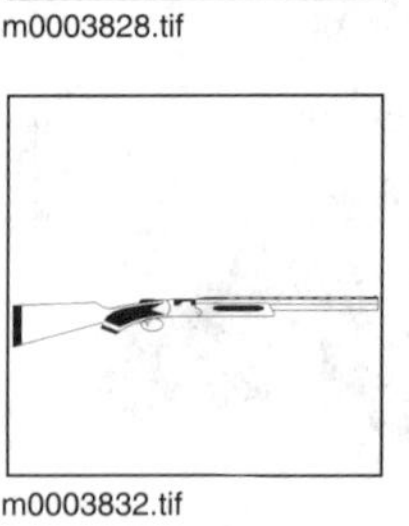

m0003832.tif

m0003834.tif

m0003835.tif

m0003836.tif

m0003837.tif

m0003838.tif

m0003839.tif

m0003840.tif

m0003841.tif

m0003842.tif

m0003843.tif

m0003844.tif

m0003845.tif

m0003846.tif

m0003847.tif

m0003848.tif

m0003849.tif

m0003850.tif

m0003851.tif

m0003852.tif

m0003853.tif

m0003854.tif

m0003855.tif

m0003856.tif

m0003857.tif

d:\images\mossburn

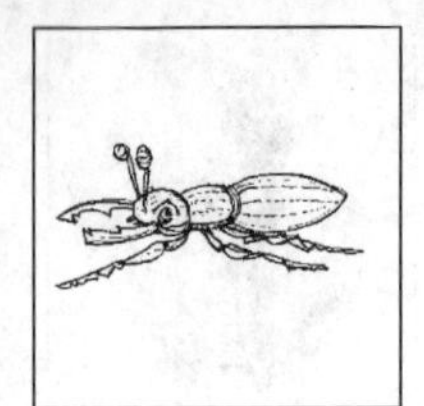
m0003858.tif

m0003859.tif

m0003860.tif

m0003861.tif

m0003862.tif

m0003863.tif

m0003864.tif

m0003865.tif

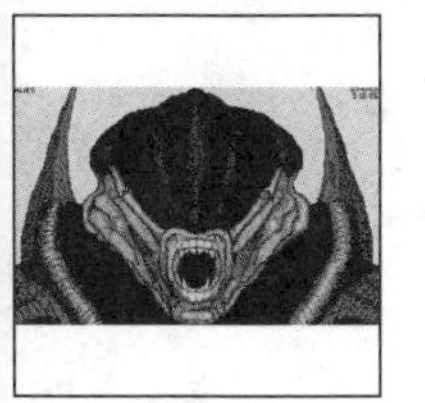
c0003868.tif

c0003869.tif

c0003870.tif

c0003872.tif

c0003875.tif

c0003876.tif

c0003878.tif

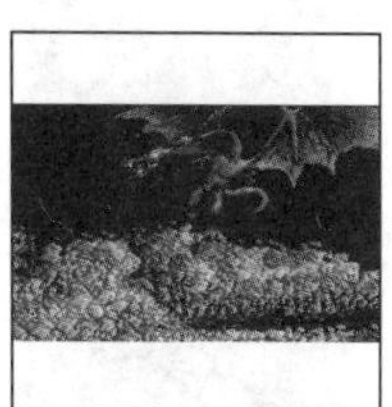
c0003881.tif

c0003884.tif

c0003892.tif

c0003893.tif

c0003894.tif

c0003896.tif

c0003899.tif

c0003902.tif

c0003903.tif

m0003867.tif

m0003877.tif

m0003879.tif

m0003882.tif

m0003886.tif

m0003888.tif

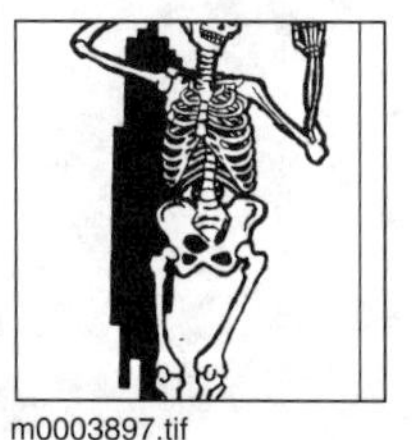
m0003897.tif

m0003900.tif

d:\images\myth

m0003904.tif

d:\images\myth

m0003908.tif

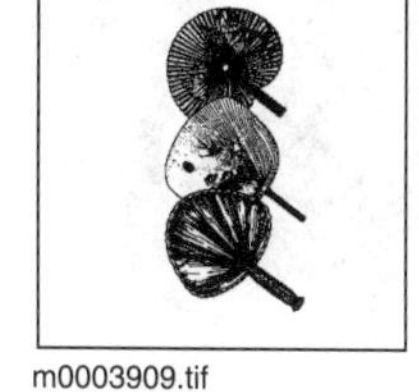
m0003909.tif

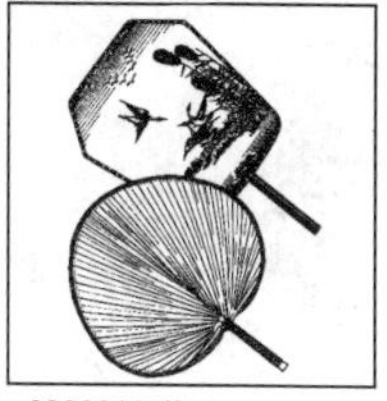
m0003910.tif

m0003911.tif

m0003912.tif

m0003913.tif

m0003914.tif

m0003915.tif

m0003916.tif

m0003917.tif

m0003918.tif

m0003919.tif

m0003920.tif

m0003921.tif

m0003922.tif

m0003923.tif

m0003924.tif

m0003925.tif

m0003926.tif

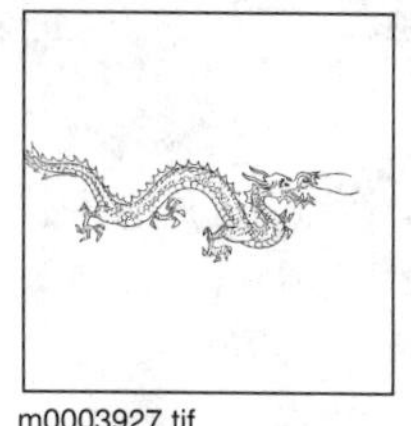
m0003927.tif

m0003928.tif

m0003929.tif

m0003930.tif

m0003931.tif

d:\images\orient

m0003932.tif

m0003933.tif

m0003934.tif

m0003935.tif

m0003936.tif

m0003937.tif

m0003938.tif

m0003939.tif

m0003940.tif

m0003941.tif

m0003942.tif

m0003943.tif

m0003944.tif

m0003945.tif

m0003946.tif

m0003947.tif

m0003948.tif

m0003949.tif

m0003950.tif

m0003951.tif

m0003952.tif

m0003953.tif

m0003954.tif

m0003955.tif

m0003956.tif

m0003957.tif

m0003958.tif

m0003959.tif

m0003960.tif

m0003961.tif

m0003962.tif

m0003963.tif

m0003964.tif

m0003965.tif

m0003966.tif

m0003967.tif

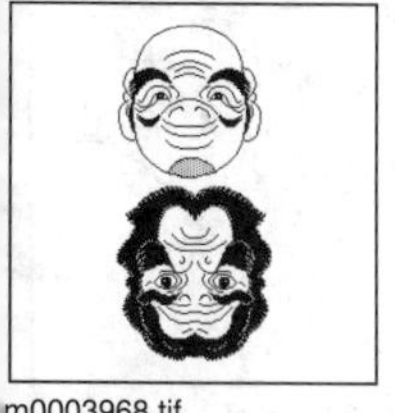
m0003968.tif

m0003969.tif

m0003970.tif

m0003971.tif

m0003972.tif

m0003973.tif

m0003974.tif

m0003975.tif

m0003976.tif

m0003977.tif

m0003978.tif

m0003979.tif

m0003980.tif

m0003981.tif

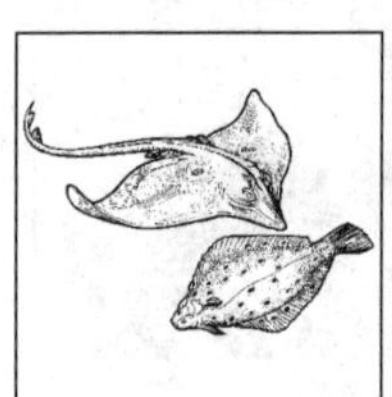
m0003982.tif

m0003983.tif

m0003984.tif

m0003985.tif

m0003986.tif

m0003987.tif

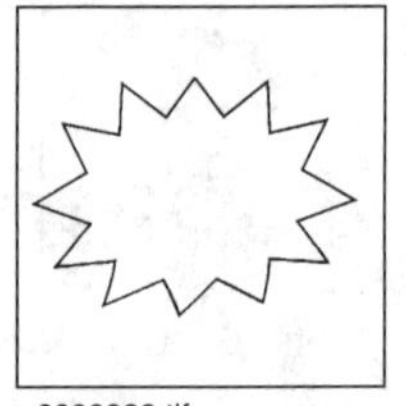
m0003988.tif

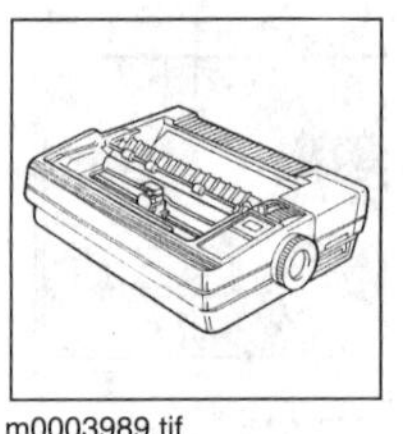
m0003989.tif

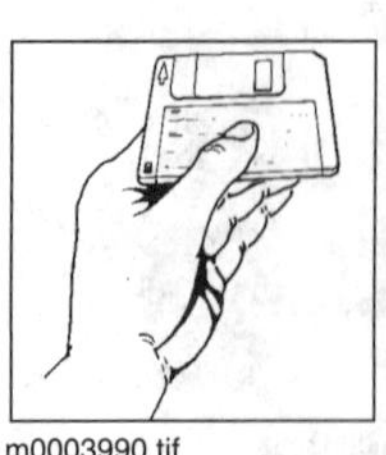
m0003990.tif

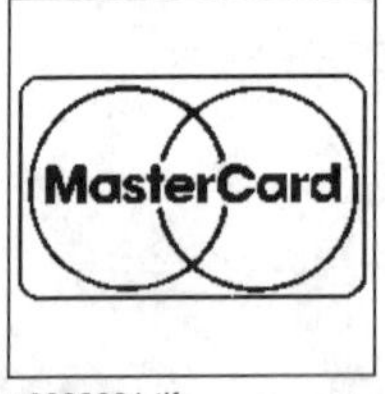

m0003991.tif

m0003992.tif

m0003993.tif

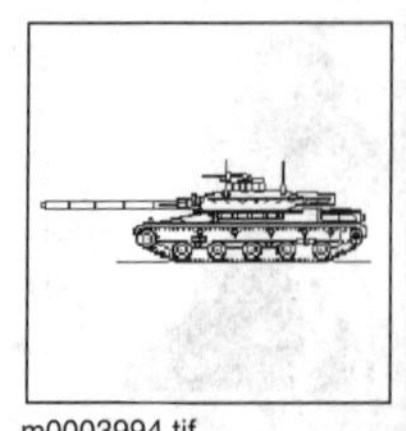
m0003994.tif

m0003995.tif

m0003996.tif

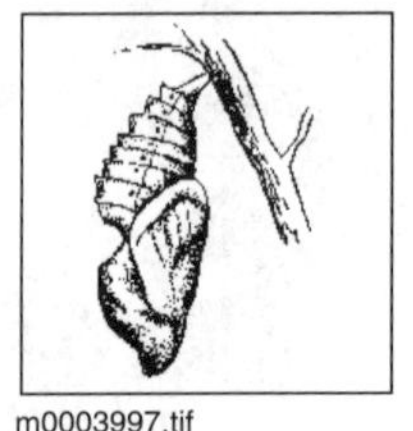
m0003997.tif

m0003998.tif

d:\images\panth1

m0003999.tif

m0004000.tif

m0004001.tif

m0004002.tif

m0004003.tif

m0004004.tif

m0004005.tif

m0004006.tif

m0004007.tif

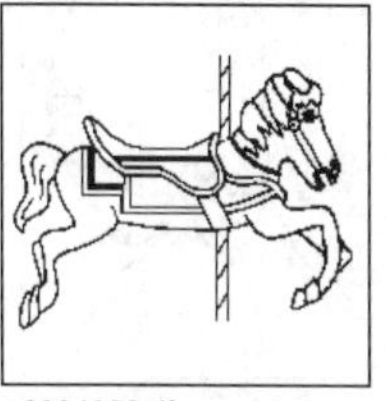
m0004008.tif

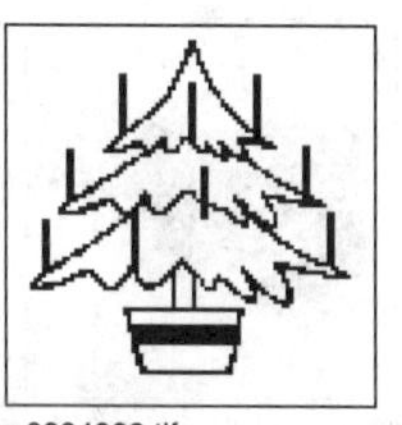
m0004009.tif

m0004010.tif

m0004011.tif

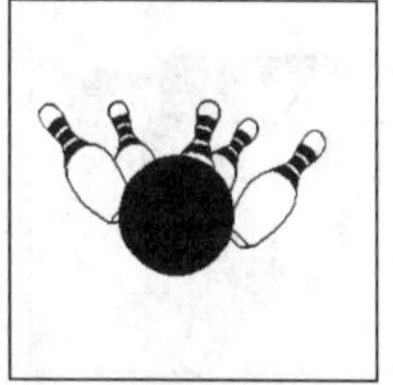
m0004012.tif

m0004013.tif

m0004014.tif

m0004015.tif

m0004016.tif

m0004017.tif

m0004018.tif

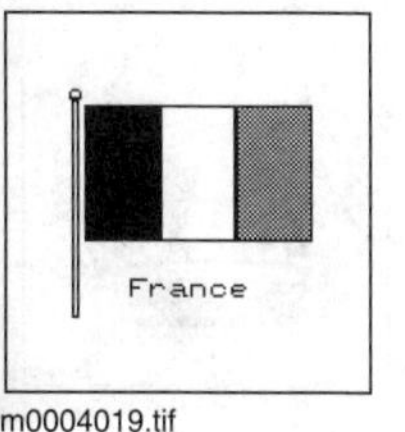

m0004019.tif

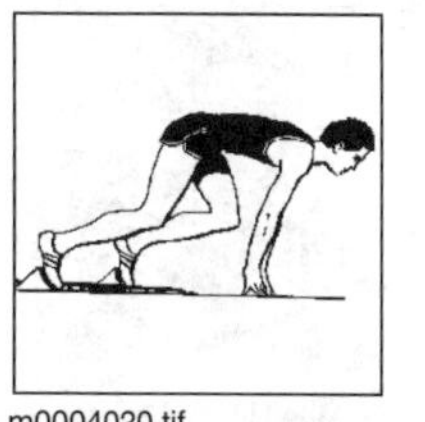
m0004020.tif

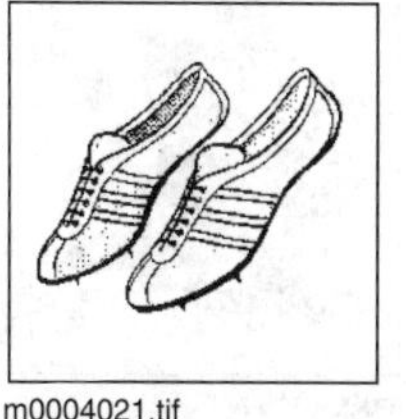
m0004021.tif

m0004022.tif

d:\images\panth1

m0004023.tif

m0004024.tif

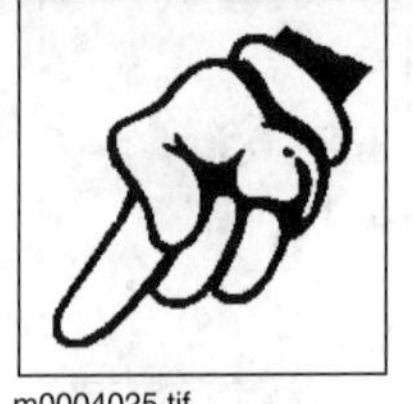
m0004025.tif

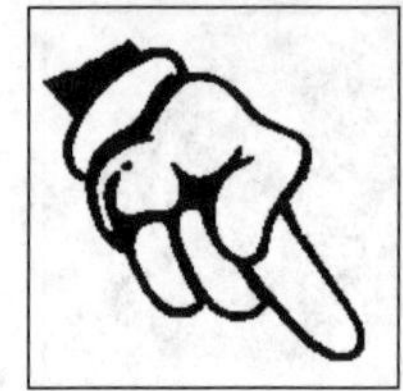
m0004026.tif

m0004027.tif

m0004028.tif

m0004029.tif

m0004030.tif

m0004031.tif

m0004032.tif

m0004033.tif

m0004034.tif

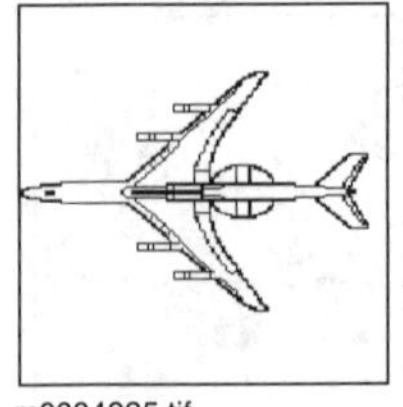
m0004035.tif

m0004036.tif

m0004037.tif

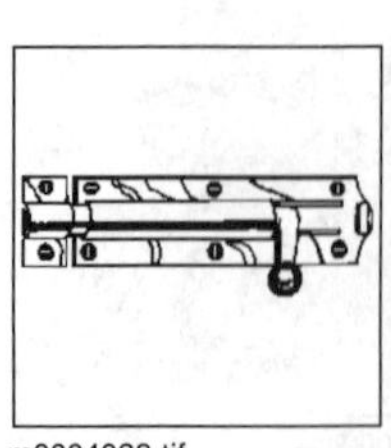
m0004038.tif

m0004039.tif

m0004040.tif

m0004042.tif

m0004043.tif

m0004044.tif

m0004045.tif

m0004046.tif

m0004047.tif

m0004048.tif

m0004049.tif

m0004050.tif

MENU

m0004051.tif

MERRY CHRISTMAS

m0004052.tif

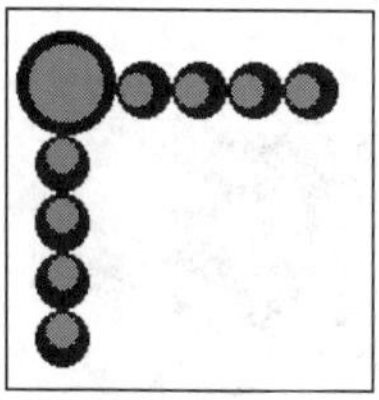

m0004053.tif

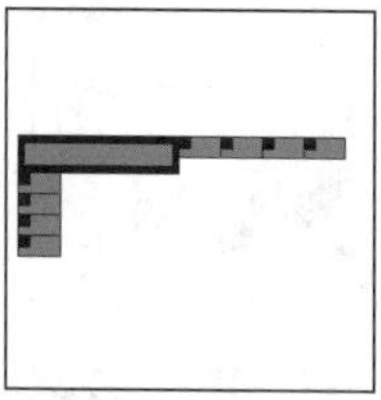

m0004054.tif

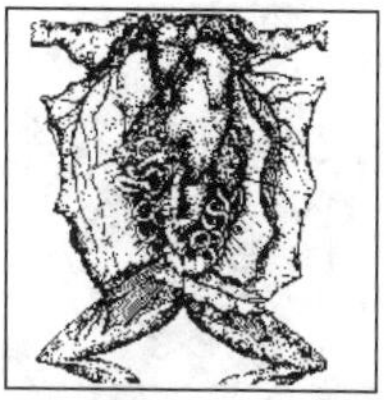

m0004055.tif

m0004056.tif

m0004057.tif

m0004058.tif

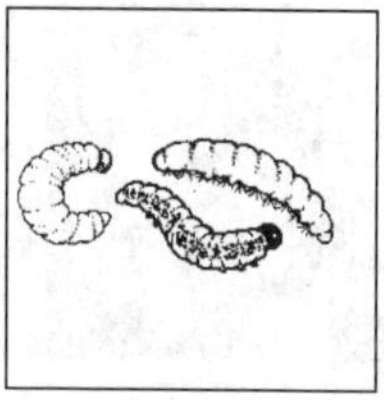

m0004059.tif

m0004060.tif

m0004061.tif

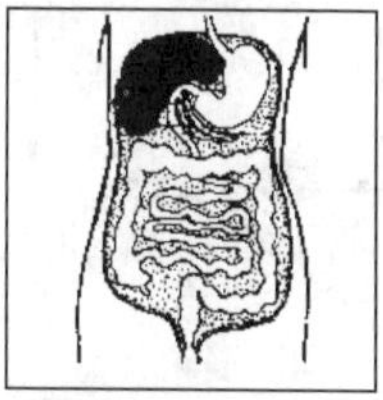

m0004062.tif

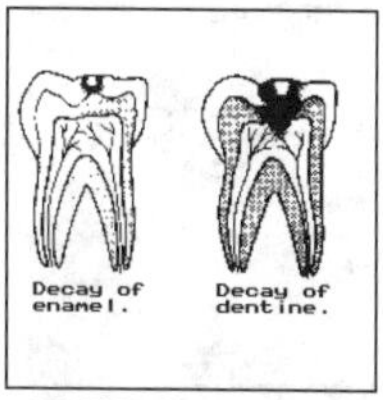

Decay of enamel.

Decay of dentine.

m0004063.tif

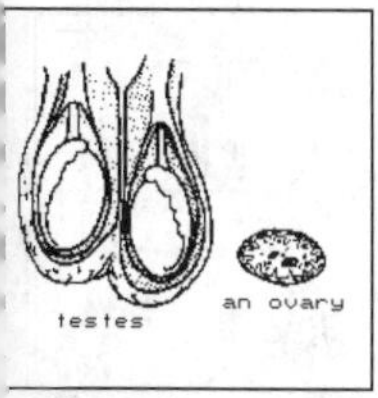

testes

an ovary

m0004064.tif

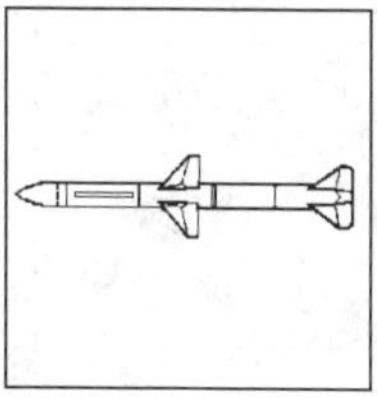

m0004065.tif

m0004066.tif

m0004067.tif

m0004068.tif

m0004069.tif

m0004070.tif

m0004071.tif

d:\images\panth1

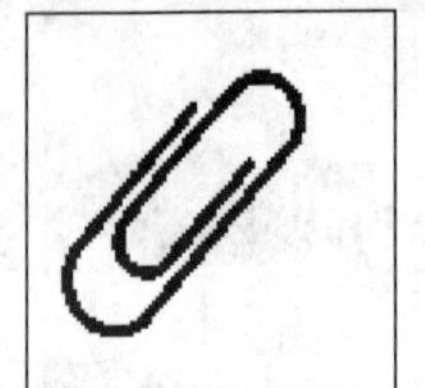
m0004072.tif

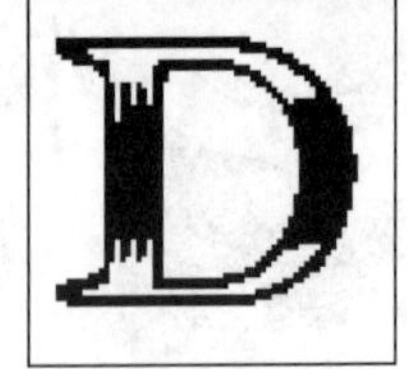
m0004073.tif

m0004074.tif

m0004075.tif

m0004076.tif

m0004077.tif

m0004078.tif

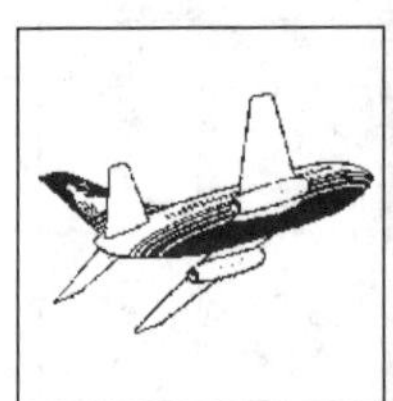
m0004079.tif

m0004081.tif

m0004082.tif

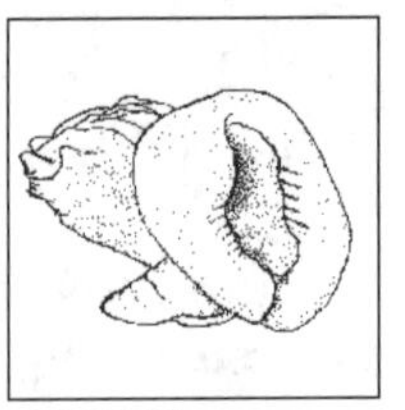
m0004083.tif

m0004084.tif

m0004085.tif

m0004086.tif

m0004087.tif

m0004088.tif

m0004089.tif

m0004090.tif

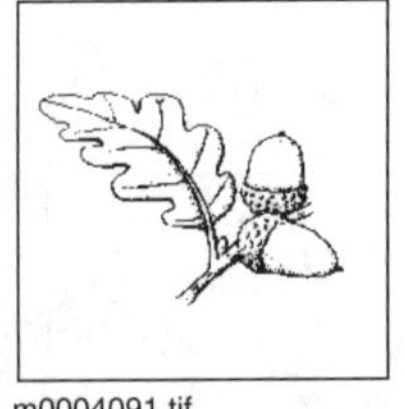
m0004091.tif

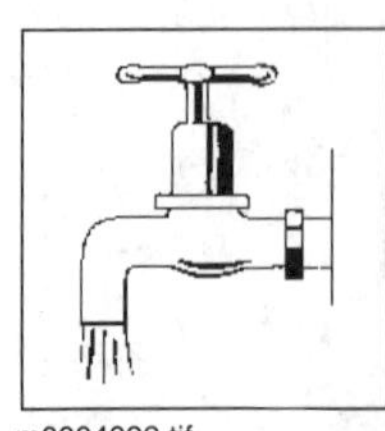
m0004092.tif

m0004093.tif

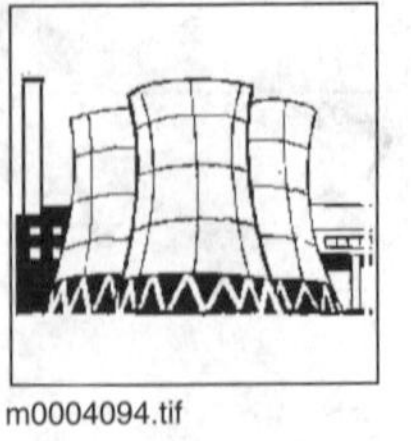
m0004094.tif

m0004095.tif

m0004096.tif

d:\images\panth1

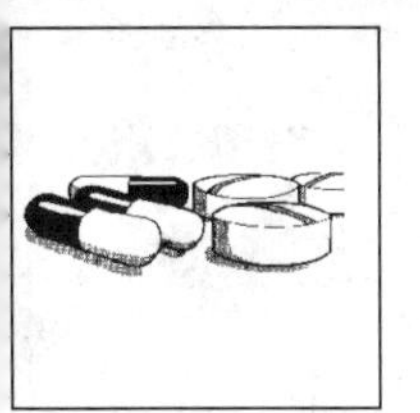
m0004097.tif

m0004098.tif

m0004099.tif

m0004100.tif

m0004101.tif

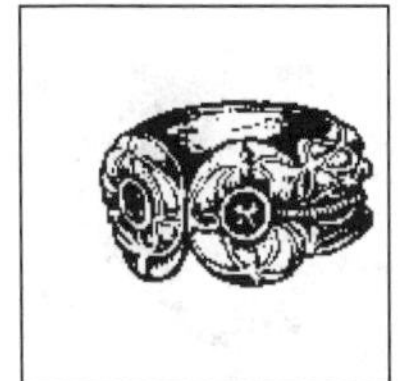
m0004102.tif

m0004103.tif

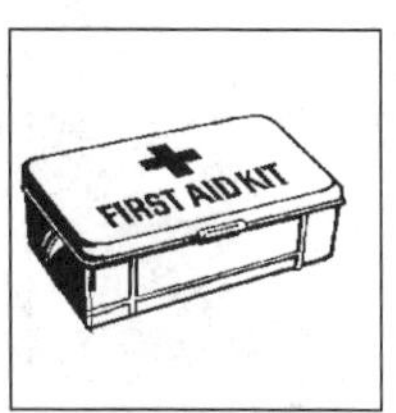

m0004104.tif

m0004105.tif

m0004106.tif

m0004107.tif

m0004108.tif

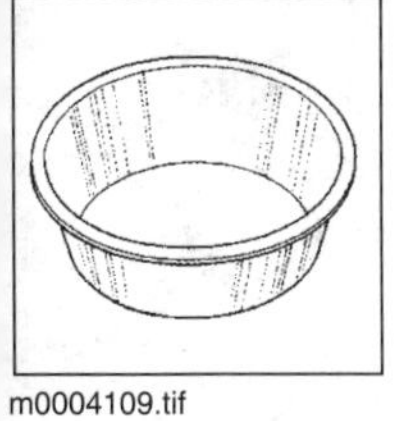
m0004109.tif

m0004110.tif

m0004111.tif

m0004112.tif

m0004113.tif

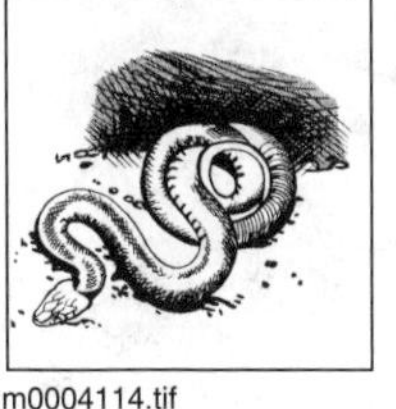
m0004114.tif

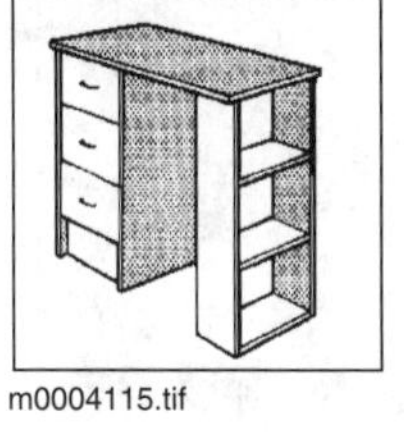
m0004115.tif

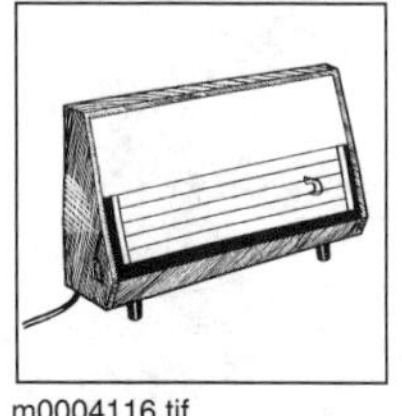
m0004116.tif

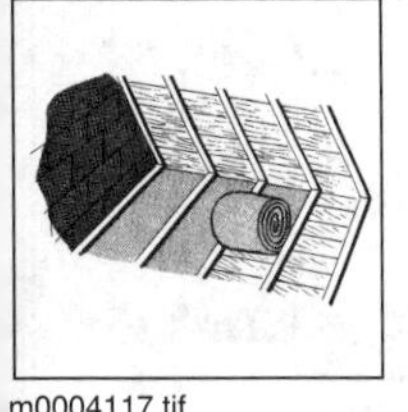
m0004117.tif

m0004118.tif

m0004119.tif

m0004120.tif

d:\images\panth1

m0004121.tif

m0004122.tif

m0004123.tif

m0004124.tif

m0004125.tif

m0004126.tif

m0004127.tif

m0004128.tif

m0004129.tif

m0004130.tif

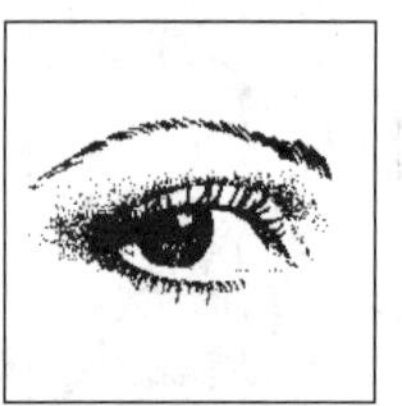
m0004131.tif

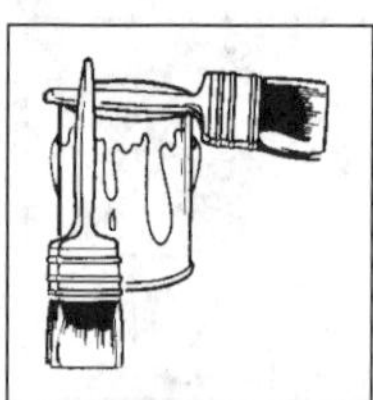
m0004132.tif

m0004133.tif

m0004134.tif

m0004135.tif

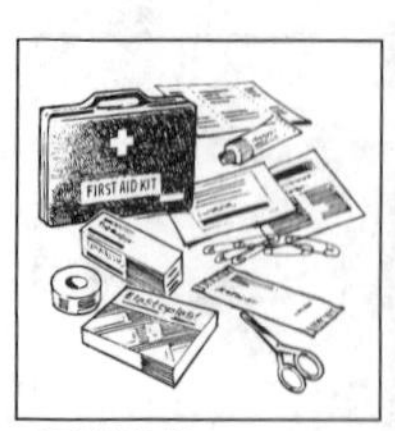

m0004136.tif

m0004137.tif

m0004138.tif

m0004139.tif

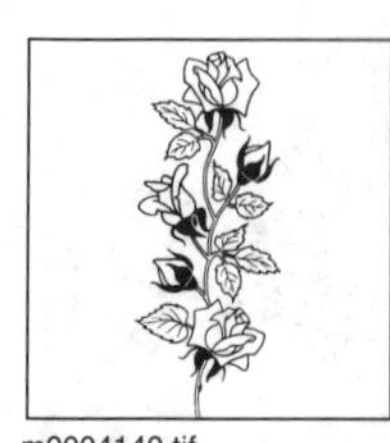
m0004140.tif

m0004141.tif

m0004142.tif

m0004143.tif

m0004144.tif

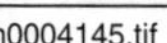
n0004145.tif

m0004146.tif

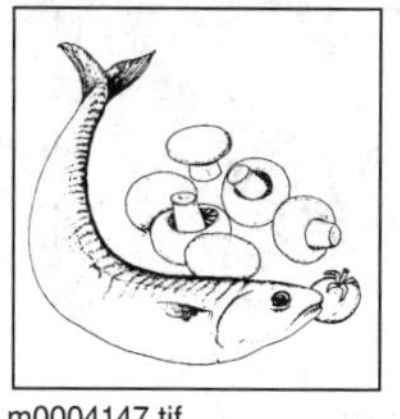
m0004147.tif

m0004148.tif

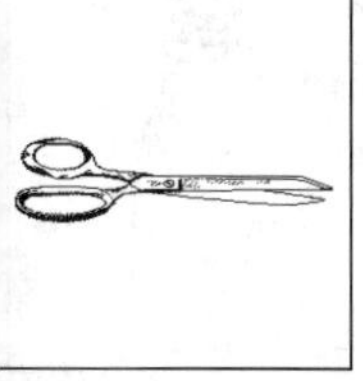
n0004149.tif

m0004150.tif

m0004151.tif

m0004152.tif

m0004153.tif

m0004154.tif

m0004155.tif

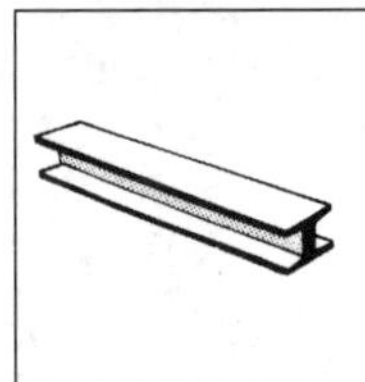
m0004156.tif

m0004157.tif

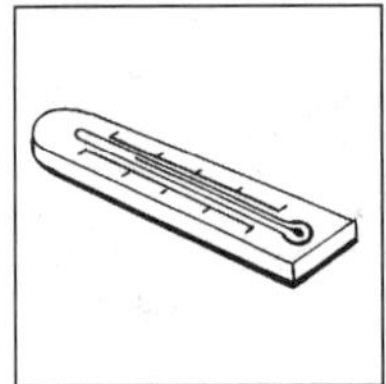
m0004158.tif

m0004159.tif

m0004160.tif

m0004161.tif

m0004162.tif

m0004163.tif

m0004164.tif

m0004165.tif

m0004166.tif

m0004167.tif

m0004168.tif

m0004169.tif

m0004170.tif

m0004171.tif

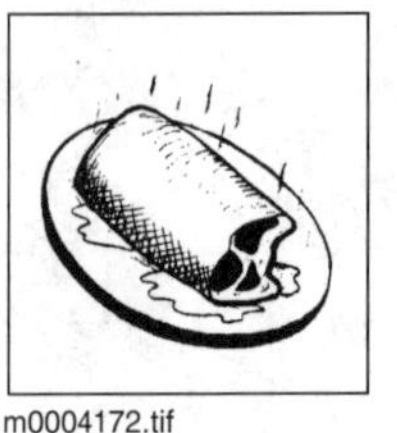
m0004172.tif

m0004173.tif

m0004174.tif

m0004175.tif

m0004176.tif

m0004177.tif

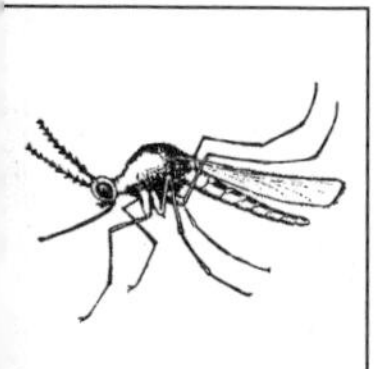
m0004178.tif

m0004179.tif

m0004180.tif

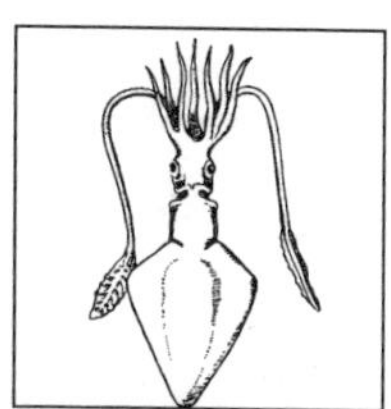
m0004181.tif

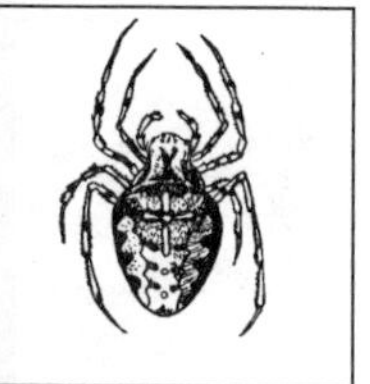
m0004182.tif

m0004183.tif

m0004184.tif

m0004185.tif

m0004186.tif

m0004187.tif

m0004188.tif

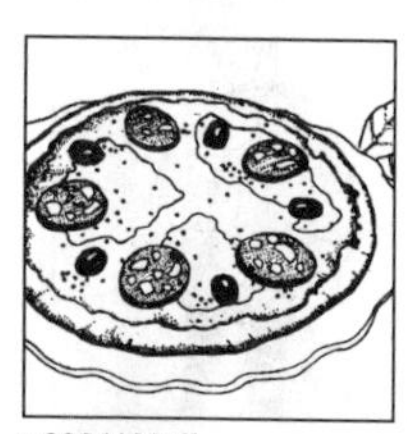
m0004189.tif

m0004190.tif

m0004191.tif

m0004192.tif

m0004193.tif

m0004194.tif

m0004195.tif

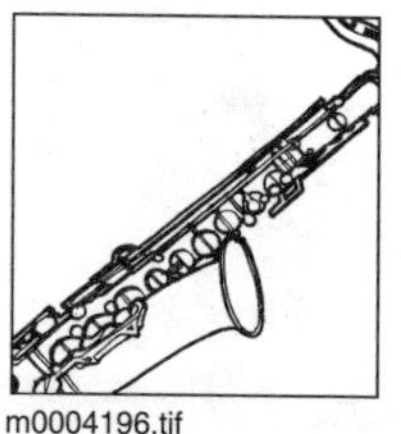
m0004196.tif

m0004197.tif

m0004198.tif

m0004199.tif

m0004200.tif

m0004201.tif

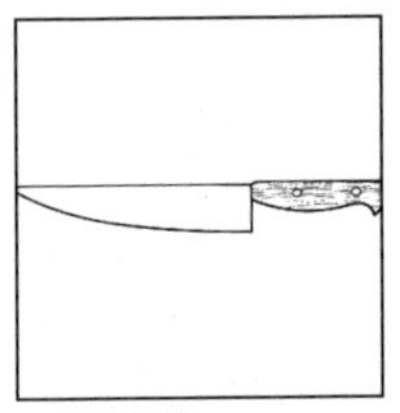
m0004202.tif

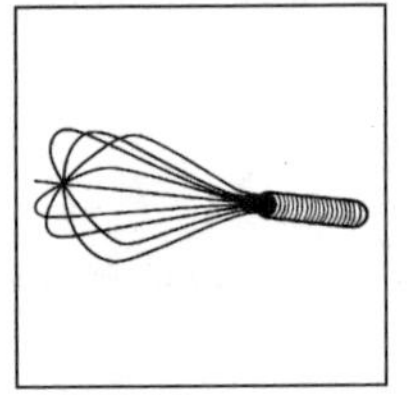
m0004203.tif

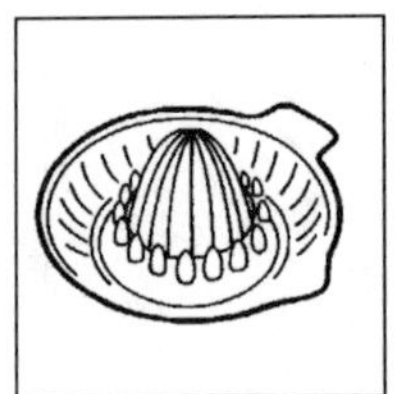
m0004204.tif

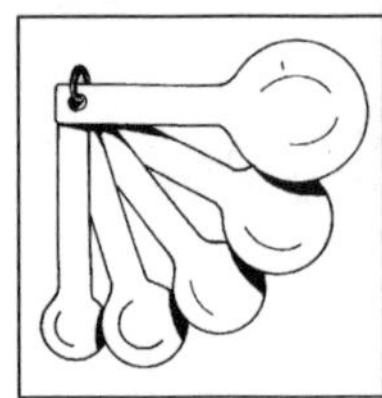
m0004205.tif

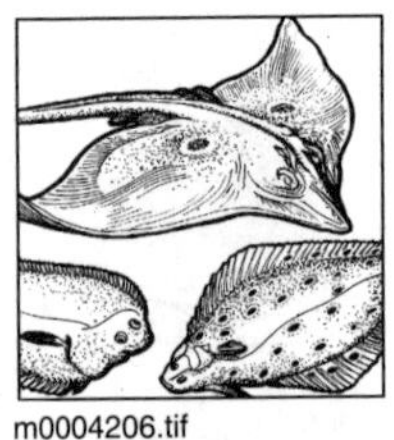
m0004206.tif

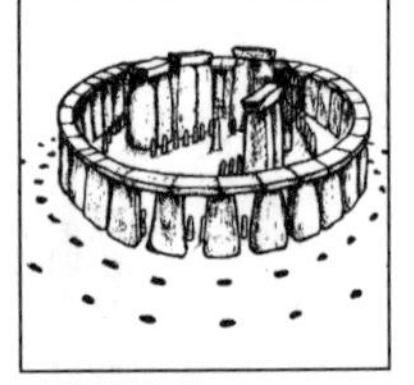
m0004207.tif

m0004208.tif

m0004209.tif

m0004210.tif

m0004211.tif

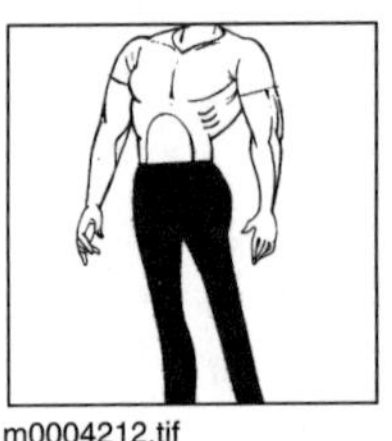
m0004212.tif

m0004213.tif

m0004214.tif

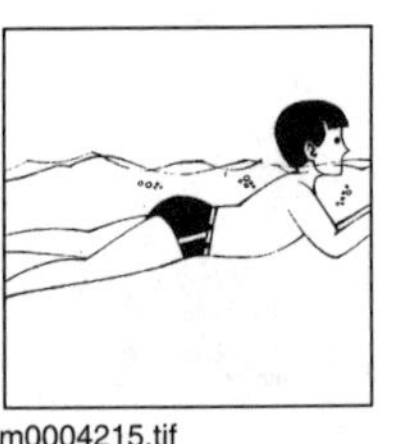
m0004215.tif

m0004216.tif

m0004217.tif

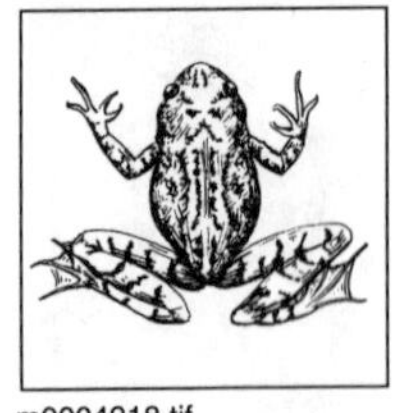
m0004218.tif

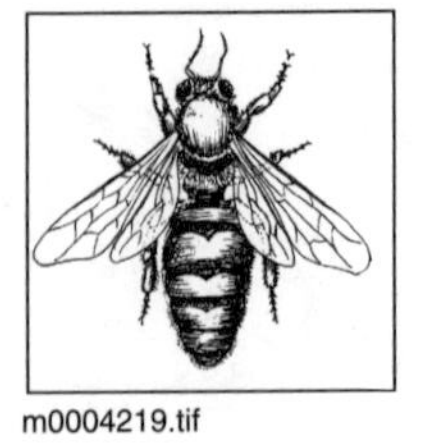
m0004219.tif

m0004220.tif

m0004221.tif

0004222.tif

m0004223.tif

m0004224.tif

m0004225.tif

0004226.tif

m0004227.tif

m0004228.tif

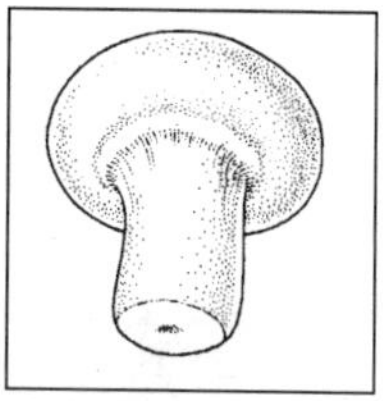

m0004229.tif

0004230.tif

m0004231.tif

m0004232.tif

m0004233.tif

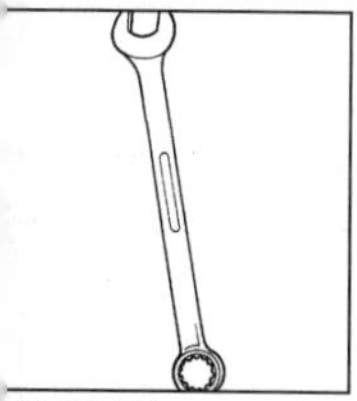

0004234.tif

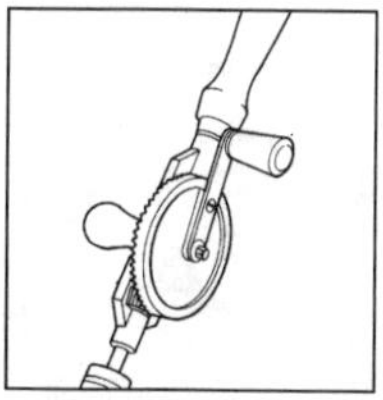

m0004235.tif

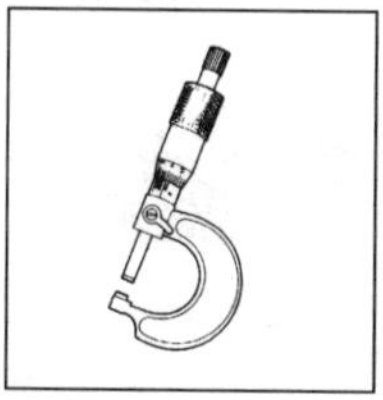

m0004236.tif

m0004237.tif

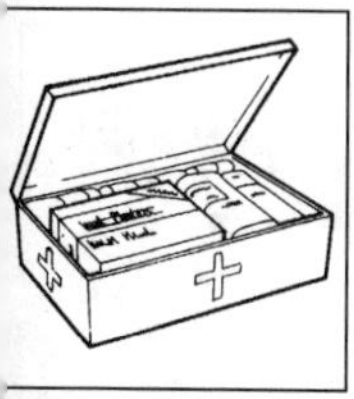

0004238.tif

m0004239.tif

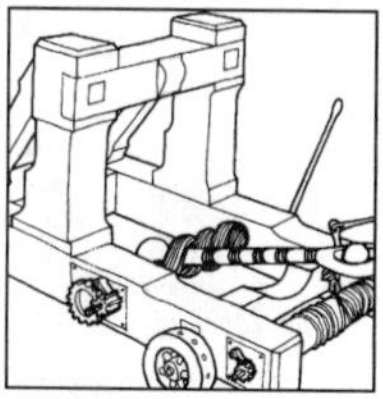

m0004240.tif

m0004241.tif

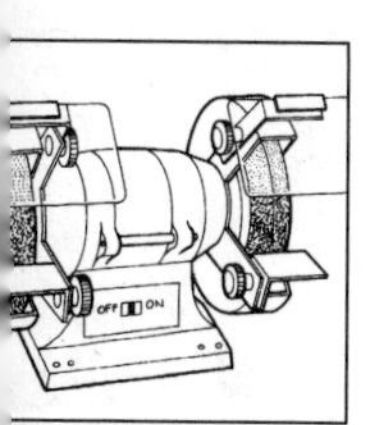

004242.tif

m0004243.tif

m0004244.tif

m0004245.tif

:\images\panth2

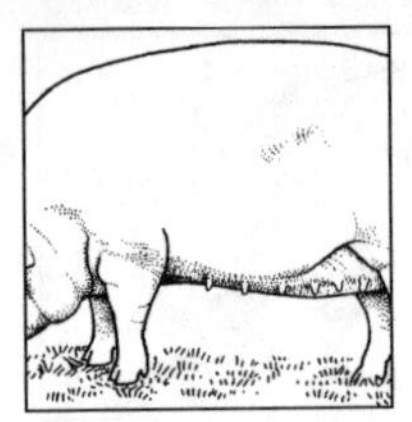
m0004246.tif

m0004247.tif

m0004248.tif

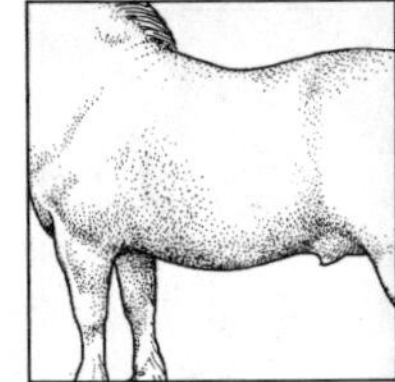
m0004249.tif

m0004250.tif

m0004251.tif

m0004252.tif

m0004253.tif

m0004254.tif

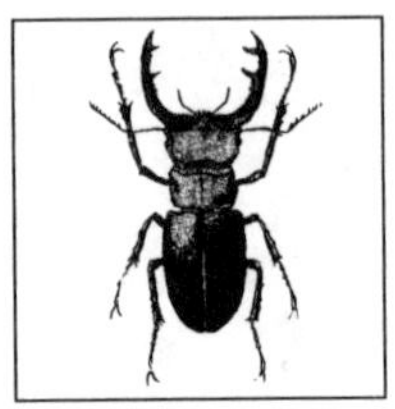
m0004255.tif

m0004256.tif

m0004257.tif

m0004258.tif

m0004259.tif

m0004260.tif

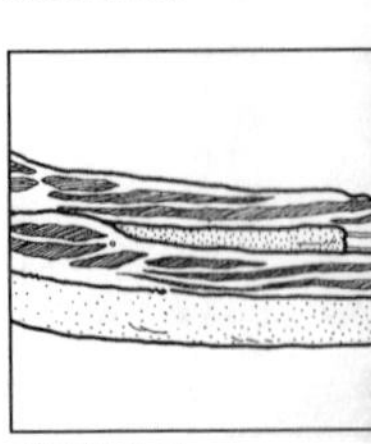
m0004261.tif

m0004262.tif

m0004263.tif

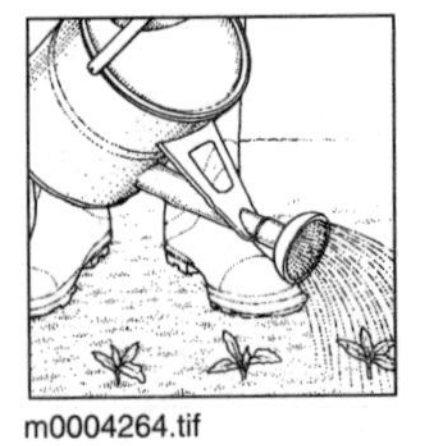
m0004264.tif

m0004265.tif

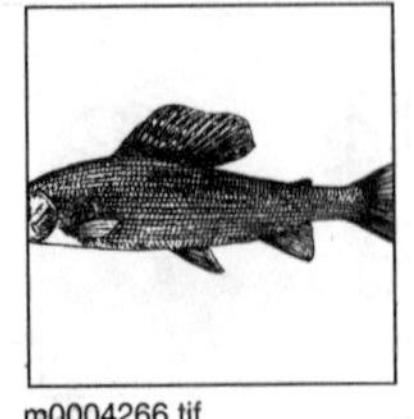
m0004266.tif

m0004267.tif

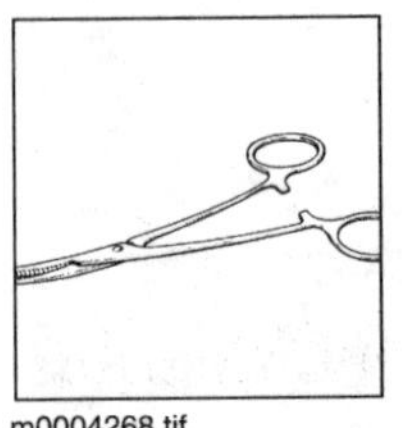
m0004268.tif

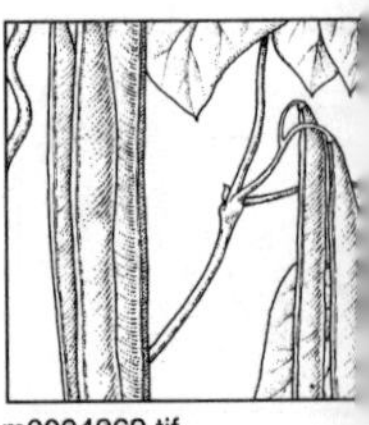
m0004269.tif

m0004270.tif

m0004271.tif

m0004272.tif

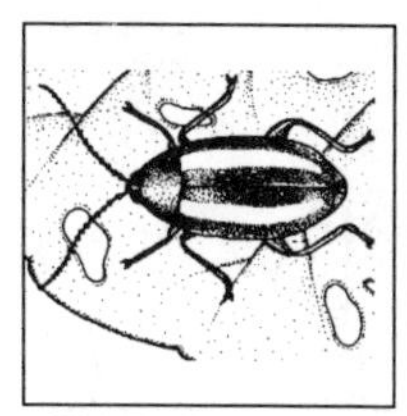

m0004273.tif

m0004274.tif

m0004275.tif

m0004276.tif

m0004277.tif

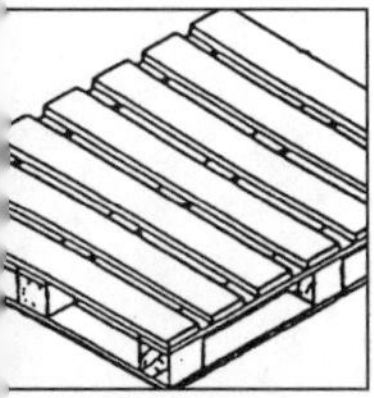

m0004278.tif

m0004279.tif

m0004280.tif

m0004281.tif

m0004282.tif

m0004283.tif

m0004284.tif

m0004285.tif

m0004286.tif

m0004287.tif

m0004288.tif

m0004289.tif

m0004290.tif

m0004291.tif

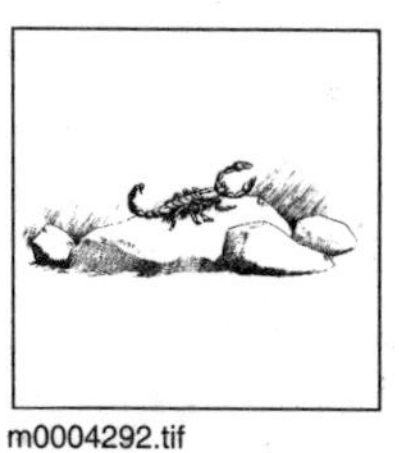

m0004292.tif

m0004293.tif

m0004294.tif

m0004295.tif

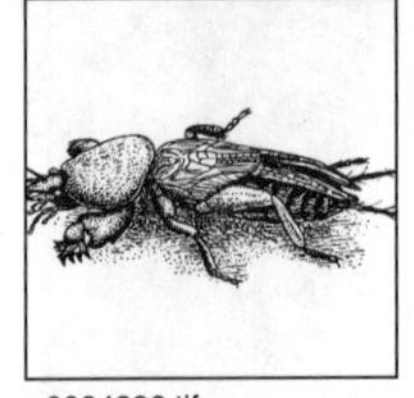
m0004296.tif

m0004297.tif

m0004298.tif

m0004303.tif

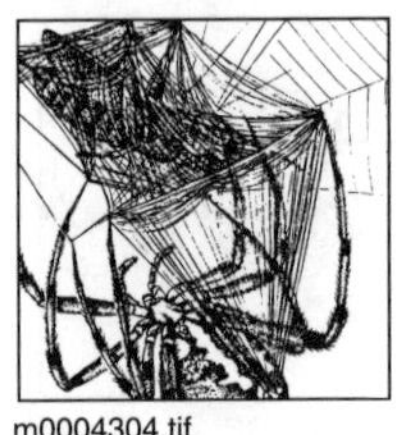
m0004304.tif

)004305.tif

c0004306.tif

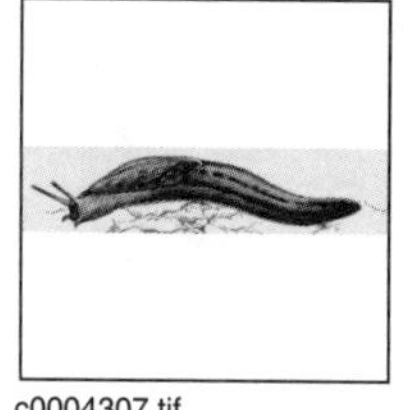
c0004307.tif

c0004308.tif

)004309.tif

c0004310.tif

c0004311.tif

c0004312.tif

)004313.tif

c0004314.tif

c0004315.tif

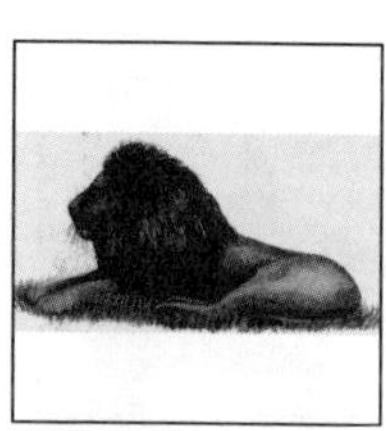
c0004316.tif

)004317.tif

c0004318.tif

c0004319.tif

c0004320.tif

)004321.tif

c0004322.tif

c0004323.tif

c0004324.tif

)04325.tif

c0004326.tif

c0004327.tif

c0004328.tif

:\images\panth3

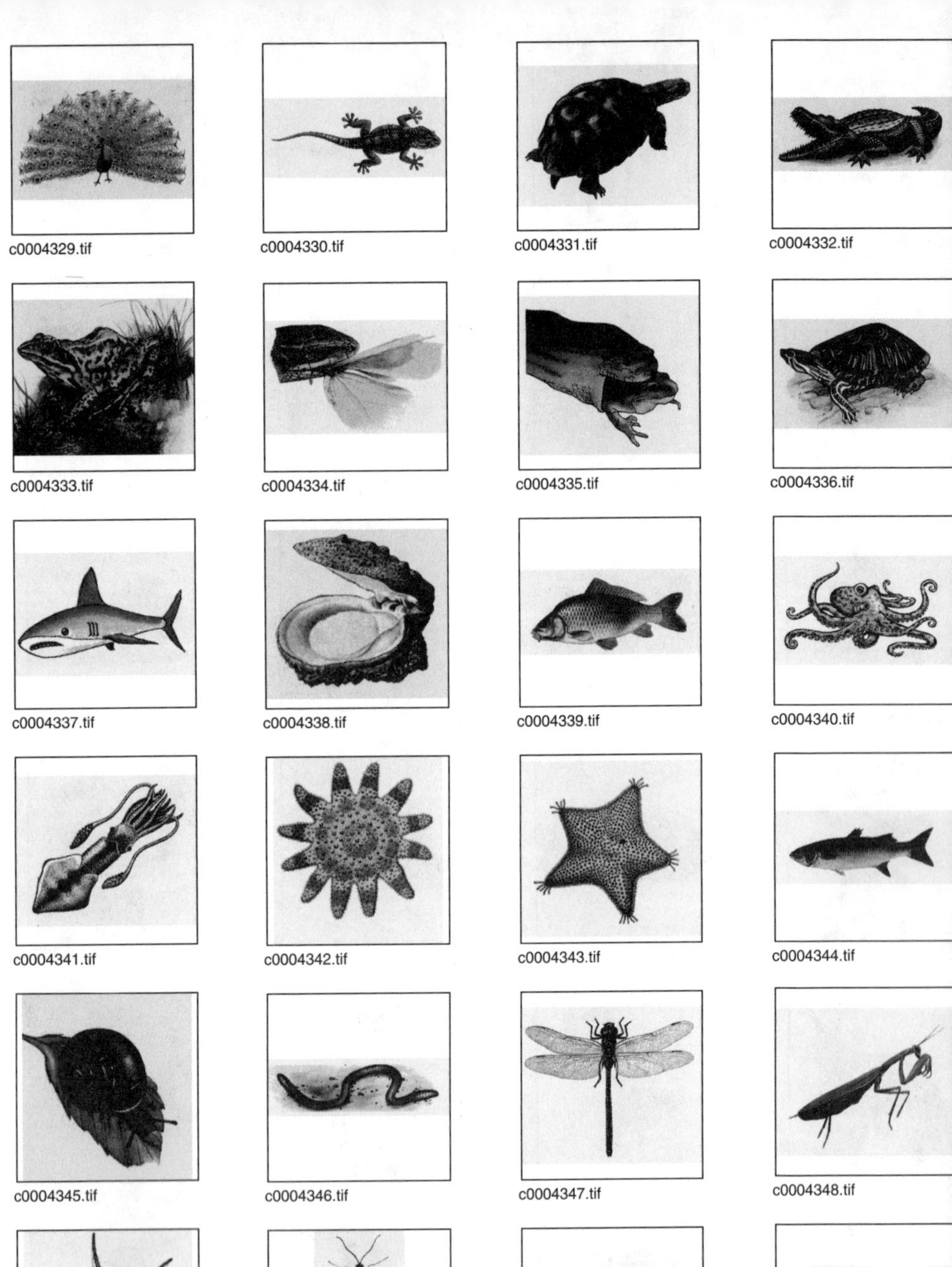

c0004329.tif c0004330.tif c0004331.tif c0004332.tif

c0004333.tif c0004334.tif c0004335.tif c0004336.tif

c0004337.tif c0004338.tif c0004339.tif c0004340.tif

c0004341.tif c0004342.tif c0004343.tif c0004344.tif

c0004345.tif c0004346.tif c0004347.tif c0004348.tif

c0004349.tif c0004350.tif c0004351.tif c0004352.tif

0004353.tif c0004354.tif c0004355.tif c0004356.tif

0004357.tif c0004358.tif c0004359.tif c0004360.tif

0004361.tif c0004362.tif c0004363.tif c0004364.tif

0004365.tif c0004366.tif c0004367.tif c0004368.tif

0004369.tif c0004370.tif c0004371.tif c0004372.tif

0004373.tif c0004374.tif c0004375.tif c0004376.tif

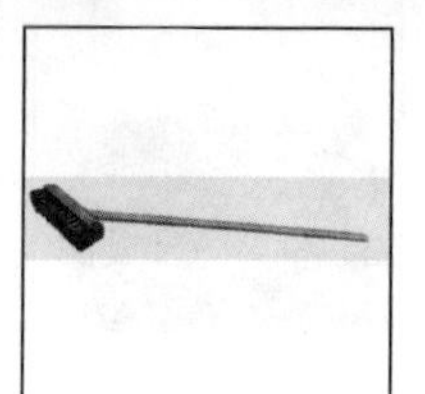
c0004377.tif

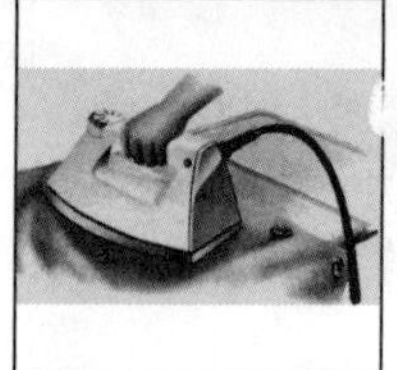
c0004378.tif

c0004379.tif

c0004380.tif

c0004381.tif

c0004382.tif

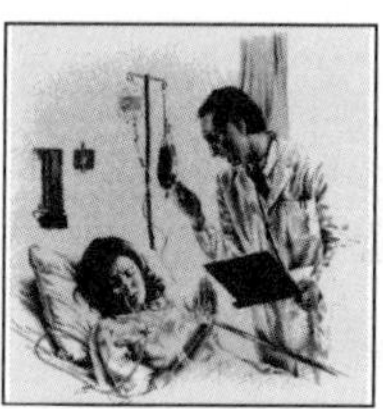
c0004383.tif

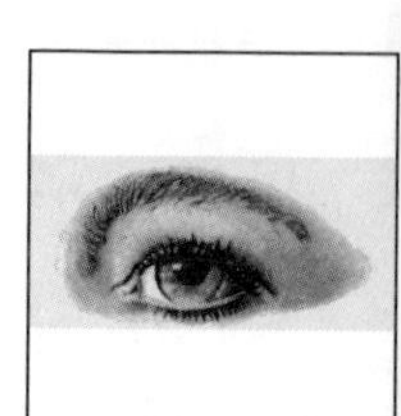
c0004384.tif

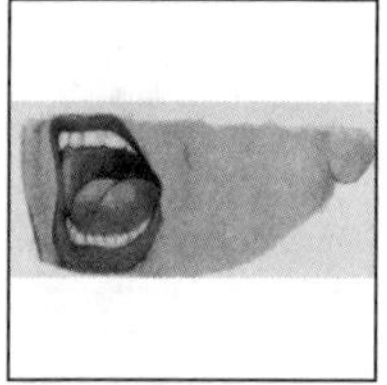
c0004385.tif

c0004386.tif

c0004387.tif

c0004388.tif

c0004389.tif

c0004390.tif

c0004391.tif

c0004392.tif

c0004393.tif

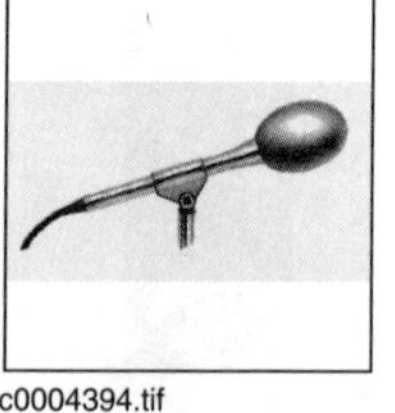
c0004394.tif

c0004395.tif

c0004396.tif

c0004397.tif

c0004398.tif

c0004399.tif

c0004400.tif

c0004401.tif

c0004402.tif

c0004403.tif

c0004404.tif

c0004405.tif

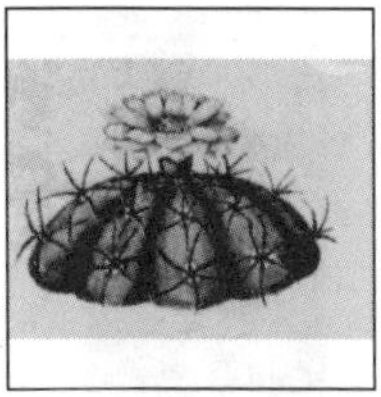

c0004406.tif

c0004407.tif

c0004408.tif

c0004409.tif

c0004410.tif

c0004411.tif

c0004412.tif

c0004413.tif

c0004414.tif

c0004415.tif

c0004416.tif

c0004417.tif

c0004418.tif

c0004419.tif

c0004420.tif

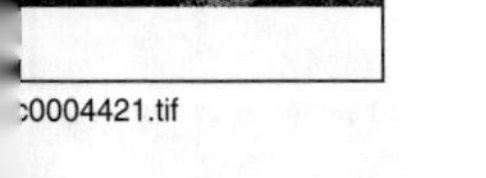

c0004421.tif

c0004422.tif

c0004423.tif

c0004424.tif

d:\images\panth3

c0004425.tif  c0004426.tif  c0004427.tif  c0004428.tif

c0004429.tif  c0004430.tif  c0004431.tif  c0004432.tif

c0004433.tif  c0004434.tif  c0004435.tif  c0004436.tif

c0004437.tif  c0004438.tif  c0004439.tif  c0004440.tif

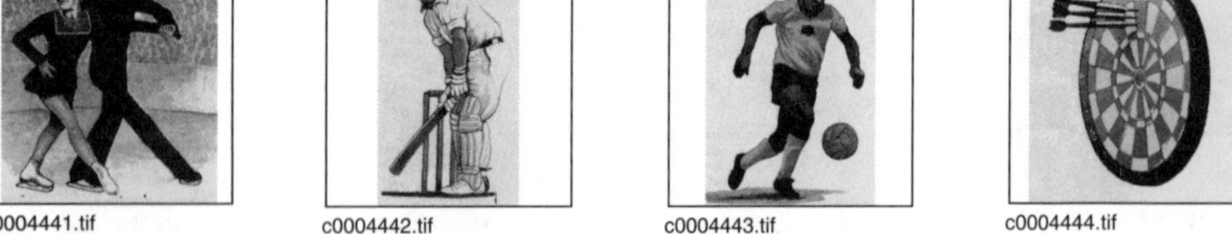

c0004441.tif c0004442.tif c0004443.tif c0004444.tif

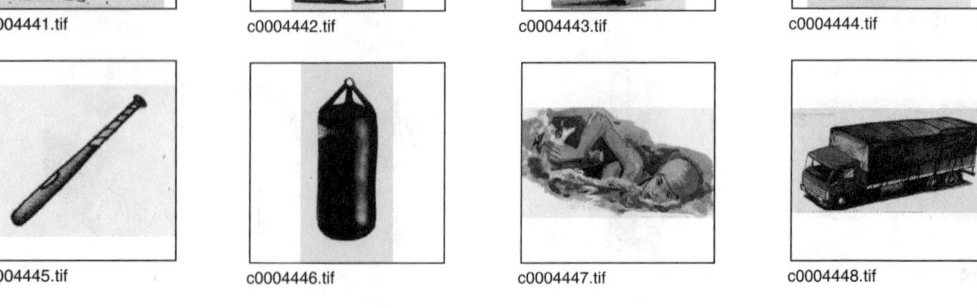

c0004445.tif c0004446.tif c0004447.tif c0004448.tif

d:\images\panth3

c0004449.tif

c0004450.tif

c0004451.tif

c0004452.tif

c0004453.tif

c0004454.tif

c0004455.tif

c0004456.tif

c0004457.tif

c0004483.tif

c0004484.tif

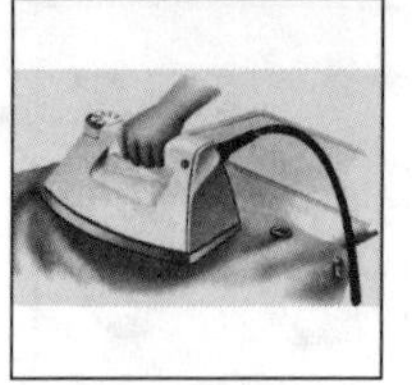
c0004485.tif

c0004486.tif

c0004554.tif

c0004555.tif

m0004458.tif

m0004461.tif

m0004462.tif

m0004463.tif

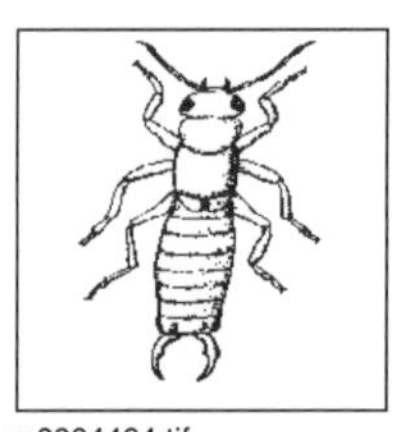
m0004464.tif

m0004465.tif

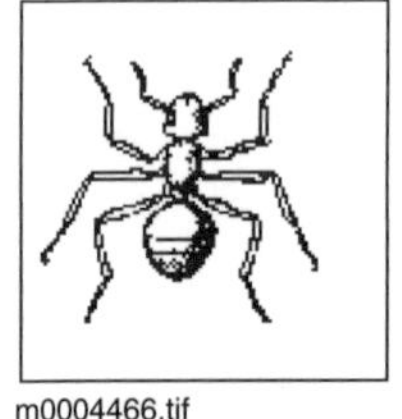
m0004466.tif

m0004468.tif

m0004469.tif

m0004470.tif

m0004471.tif

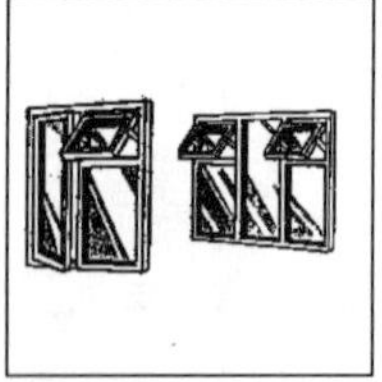
m0004472.tif

m0004474.tif

m0004476.tif

m0004480.tif

m0004481.tif

m0004482.tif

m0004487.tif

m0004488.tif

m0004489.tif

m0004490.tif

m0004491.tif

m0004492.tif

m0004493.tif

m0004494.tif

m0004496.tif

m0004497.tif

m0004498.tif

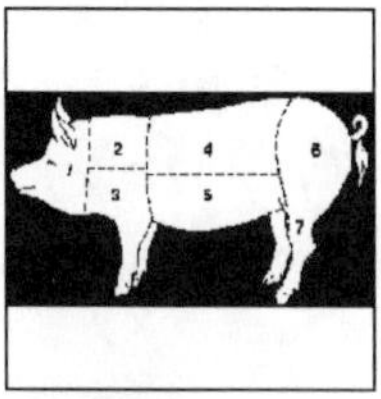

m0004499.tif

m0004500.tif

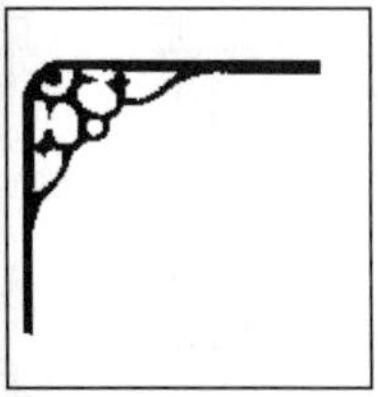

m0004501.tif

MERRY CHRISTMAS

m0004502.tif

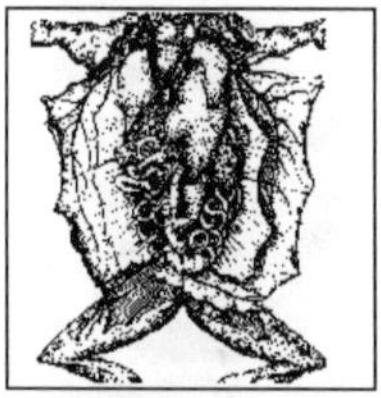

m0004505.tif

m0004506.tif

m0004508.tif

m0004509.tif

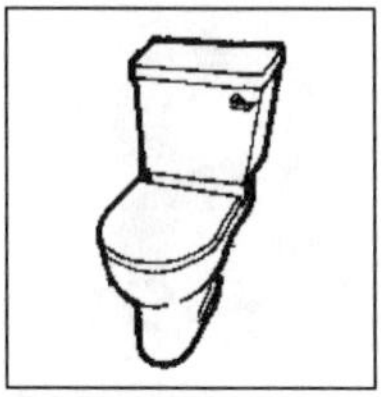

m0004510.tif

m0004511.tif

m0004512.tif

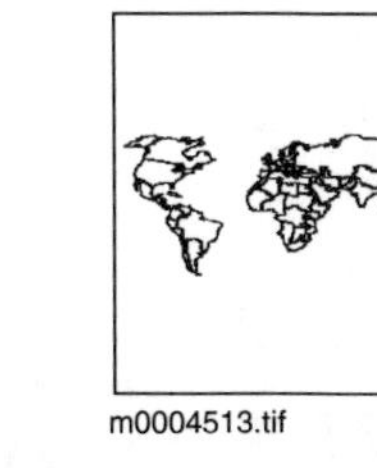

m0004513.tif

m0004514.tif

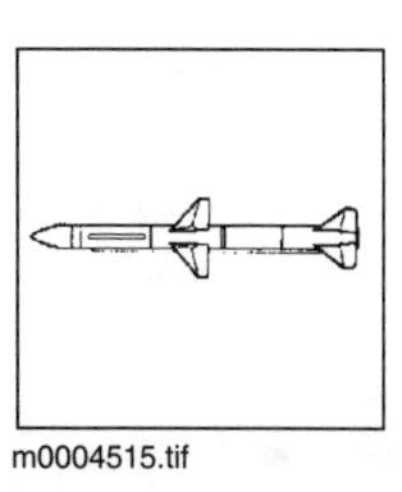

m0004515.tif

m0004517.tif

m0004518.tif

m0004519.tif

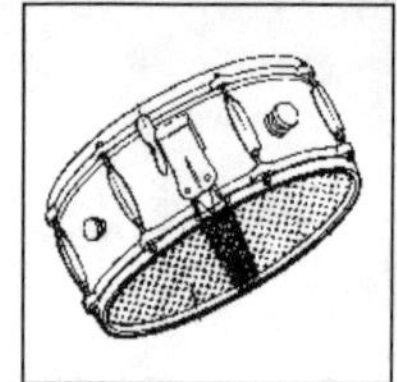
m0004520.tif

m0004521.tif

m0004522.tif

m0004523.tif

m0004525.tif

m0004527.tif

m0004528.tif

m0004529.tif

m0004532.tif

m0004534.tif

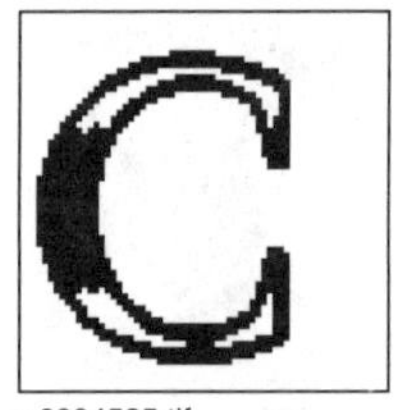
m0004535.tif

m0004537.tif

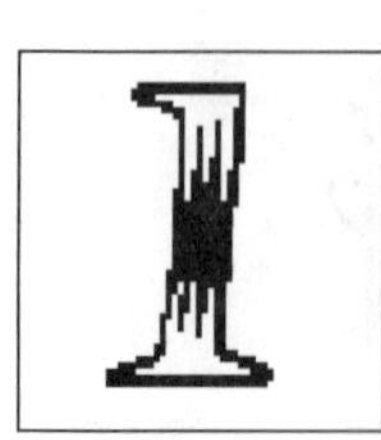
m0004538.tif

m0004539.tif

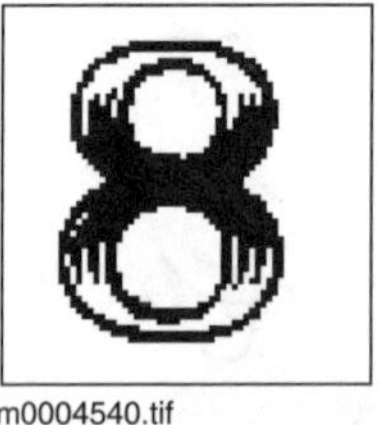
m0004540.tif

m0004543.tif

m0004544.tif

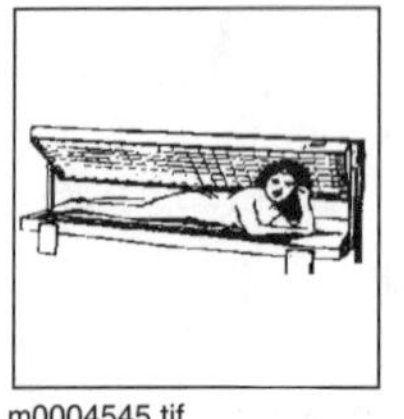
m0004545.tif

m0004547.tif

m0004548.tif

m0004549.tif

d:\images\panth4

m0004552.tif

m0004553.tif

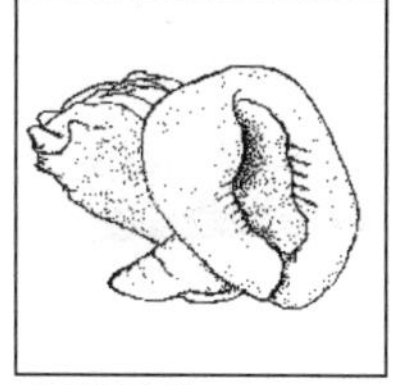
m0004556.tif

m0004557.tif

m0004558.tif

m0004559.tif

m0004560.tif

m0004561.tif

m0004562.tif

m0004563.tif

m0004564.tif

m0004565.tif

m0004566.tif

m0004567.tif

m0004568.tif

m0004569.tif

m0004570.tif

m0004571.tif

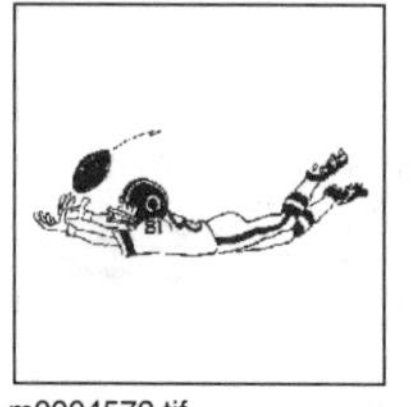
m0004572.tif

m0004573.tif

m0004574.tif

m0004575.tif

m0004576.tif

m0004577.tif

d:\images\panth4

m0004579.tif

m0004580.tif

m0004581.tif

m0004582.tif

m0004583.tif

m0004584.tif

m0004585.tif

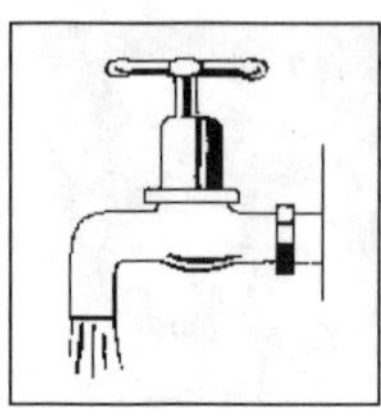
m0004586.tif

m0004587.tif

m0004588.tif

m0004589.tif

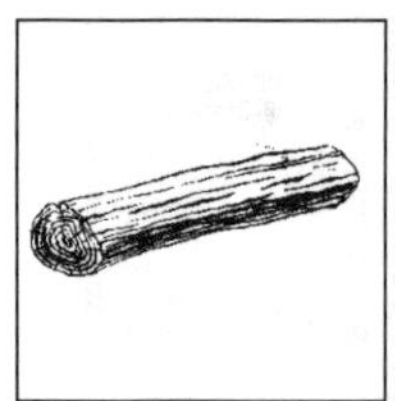
m0004590.tif

m0004591.tif

m0004592.tif

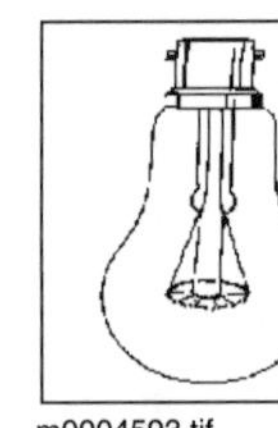
m0004593.tif

m0004594.tif

m0004595.tif

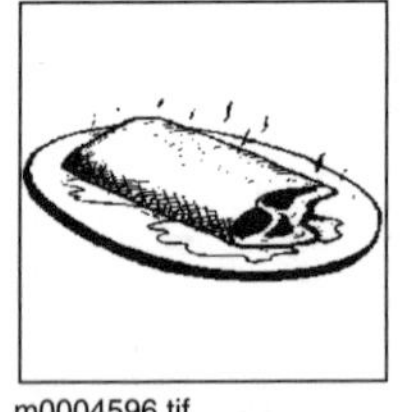
m0004596.tif

m0004597.tif

m0004598.tif

m0004599.tif

m0004600.tif

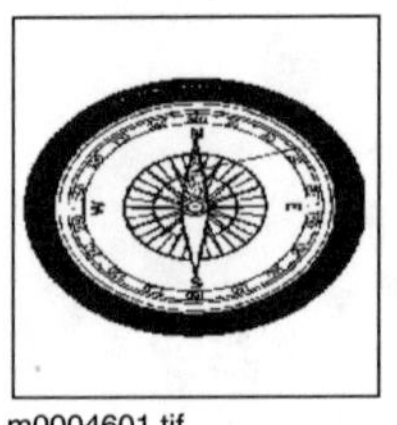
m0004601.tif

m0004602.tif

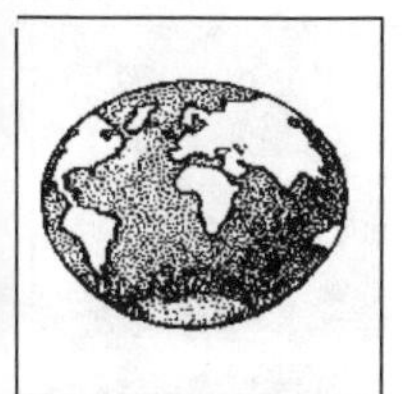
m0004603.tif

m0004604.tif

m0004605.tif

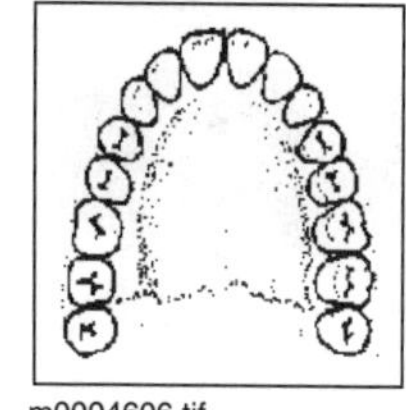
m0004606.tif

m0004607.tif

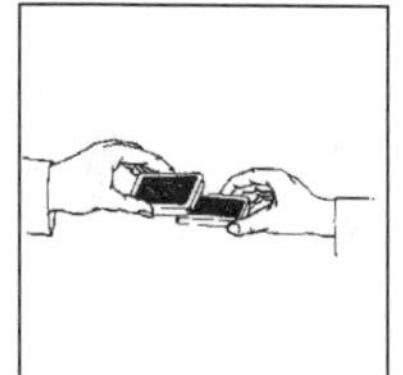
m0004608.tif

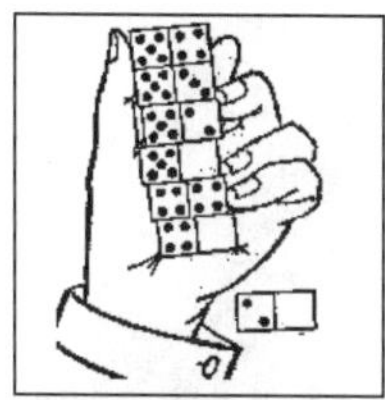
m0004609.tif

m0004610.tif

m0004611.tif

m0004612.tif

m0004613.tif

m0004614.tif

m0004615.tif

m0004616.tif

m0004617.tif

m0004618.tif

m0004619.tif

m0004620.tif

m0004621.tif

m0004623.tif

c0004694.tif

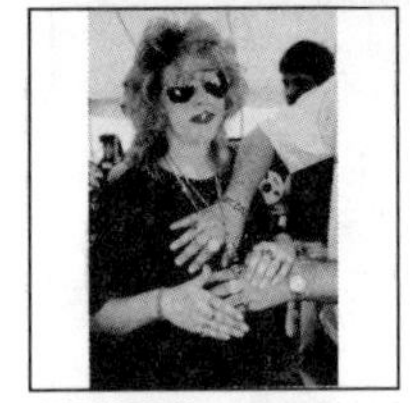
c0004696.tif

c0004701.tif

c0004703.tif

c0004719.tif

c0004739.tif

c0004740.tif

c0004741.tif

c0004742.tif

c0004810.tif

c0004811.tif

c0004812.tif

c0004814.tif

c0004816.tif

c0004818.tif

c0004819.tif

c0004820.tif

c0004821.tif

c0004822.tif

c0004823.tif

c0004836.tif

c0004837.tif

c0004838.tif

c0004841.tif

c0004842.tif

c0004843.tif

c0004844.tif

c0004845.tif

c0004846.tif

c0004847.tif

c0004848.tif

c0004849.tif

c0004850.tif

c0004851.tif

c0004852.tif

c0004853.tif

c0004854.tif

m0004624.tif

m0004625.tif

m0004626.tif

m0004627.tif

m0004628.tif

m0004629.tif

m0004630.tif

m0004631.tif

m0004633.tif

m0004634.tif

m0004635.tif

m0004636.tif

m0004637.tif

m0004638.tif

m0004639.tif

m0004640.tif

m0004642.tif

m0004643.tif

m0004644.tif

m0004645.tif

m0004646.tif

m0004647.tif

m0004648.tif

m0004649.tif

m0004650.tif

m0004651.tif

m0004652.tif

m0004653.tif

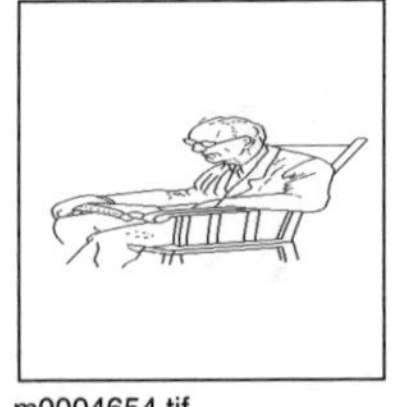
m0004654.tif

m0004655.tif

m0004656.tif

m0004657.tif

m0004658.tif

m0004659.tif

m0004660.tif

m0004661.tif

m0004662.tif

m0004663.tif

m0004664.tif

m0004665.tif

m0004666.tif

m0004667.tif

m0004668.tif

m0004669.tif

m0004670.tif

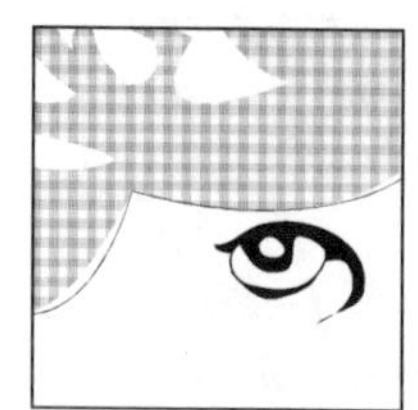
m0004671.tif

m0004672.tif

m0004673.tif

m0004675.tif

m0004676.tif

m0004677.tif

m0004678.tif

m0004679.tif

m0004680.tif

m0004681.tif

m0004682.tif

m0004683.tif

m0004684.tif

m0004685.tif

d:\images\people

m0004687.tif

m0004688.tif

m0004689.tif

m0004690.tif

m0004691.tif

m0004692.tif

m0004693.tif

m0004695.tif

m0004697.tif

m0004698.tif

m0004699.tif

m0004700.tif

m0004702.tif

m0004704.tif

m0004705.tif

m0004706.tif

m0004707.tif

m0004708.tif

m0004709.tif

m0004710.tif

m0004711.tif

m0004712.tif

m0004713.tif

m0004714.tif

m0004715.tif

m0004716.tif

m0004717.tif

m0004718.tif

m0004720.tif

m0004721.tif

m0004722.tif

m0004723.tif

m0004724.tif

m0004725.tif

m0004726.tif

m0004727.tif

m0004728.tif

m0004729.tif

m0004730.tif

m0004731.tif

m0004732.tif

m0004733.tif

m0004734.tif

m0004735.tif

m0004736.tif

m0004737.tif

m0004738.tif

m0004743.tif

m0004744.tif

m0004745.tif

m0004746.tif

m0004747.tif

m0004748.tif

m0004749.tif

m0004750.tif

m0004751.tif

m0004752.tif

m0004753.tif

m0004754.tif

m0004755.tif

m0004756.tif

m0004757.tif

m0004758.tif

m0004759.tif

m0004760.tif

m0004761.tif

m0004762.tif

m0004763.tif

m0004764.tif

m0004765.tif

m0004766.tif

m0004767.tif

m0004768.tif

m0004769.tif

m0004770.tif

m0004771.tif

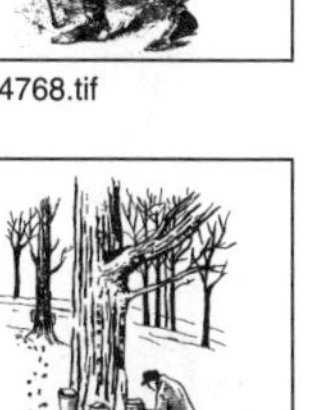

m0004772.tif

m0004773.tif

m0004774.tif

m0004775.tif

m0004776.tif

m0004777.tif

m0004778.tif

m0004779.tif

m0004780.tif

m0004781.tif

m0004782.tif

m0004783.tif

m0004784.tif

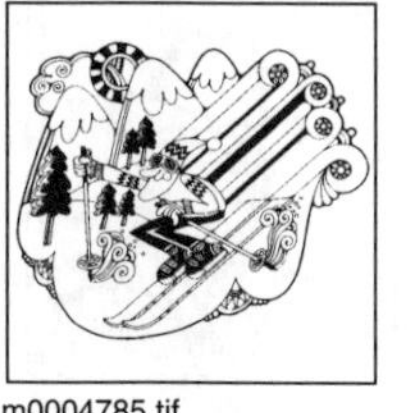

m0004785.tif

m0004786.tif

m0004787.tif

m0004788.tif

m0004789.tif

m0004790.tif

m0004791.tif

m0004792.tif

m0004793.tif

m0004794.tif

m0004795.tif

m0004796.tif

m0004797.tif

m0004798.tif

m0004799.tif

m0004800.tif

m0004801.tif

m0004802.tif

m0004803.tif

m0004804.tif

m0004805.tif

m0004806.tif

m0004807.tif

m0004808.tif

m0004809.tif

m0004813.tif

m0004817.tif

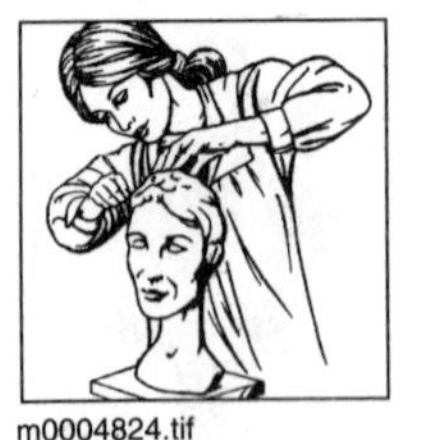
m0004824.tif

m0004825.tif

m0004826.tif

m0004827.tif

m0004828.tif

m0004829.tif

m0004830.tif

m0004831.tif

m0004832.tif

m0004833.tif

m0004834.tif

m0004835.tif

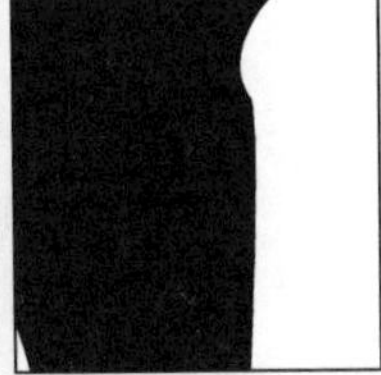
m0004839.tif

m0004840.tif

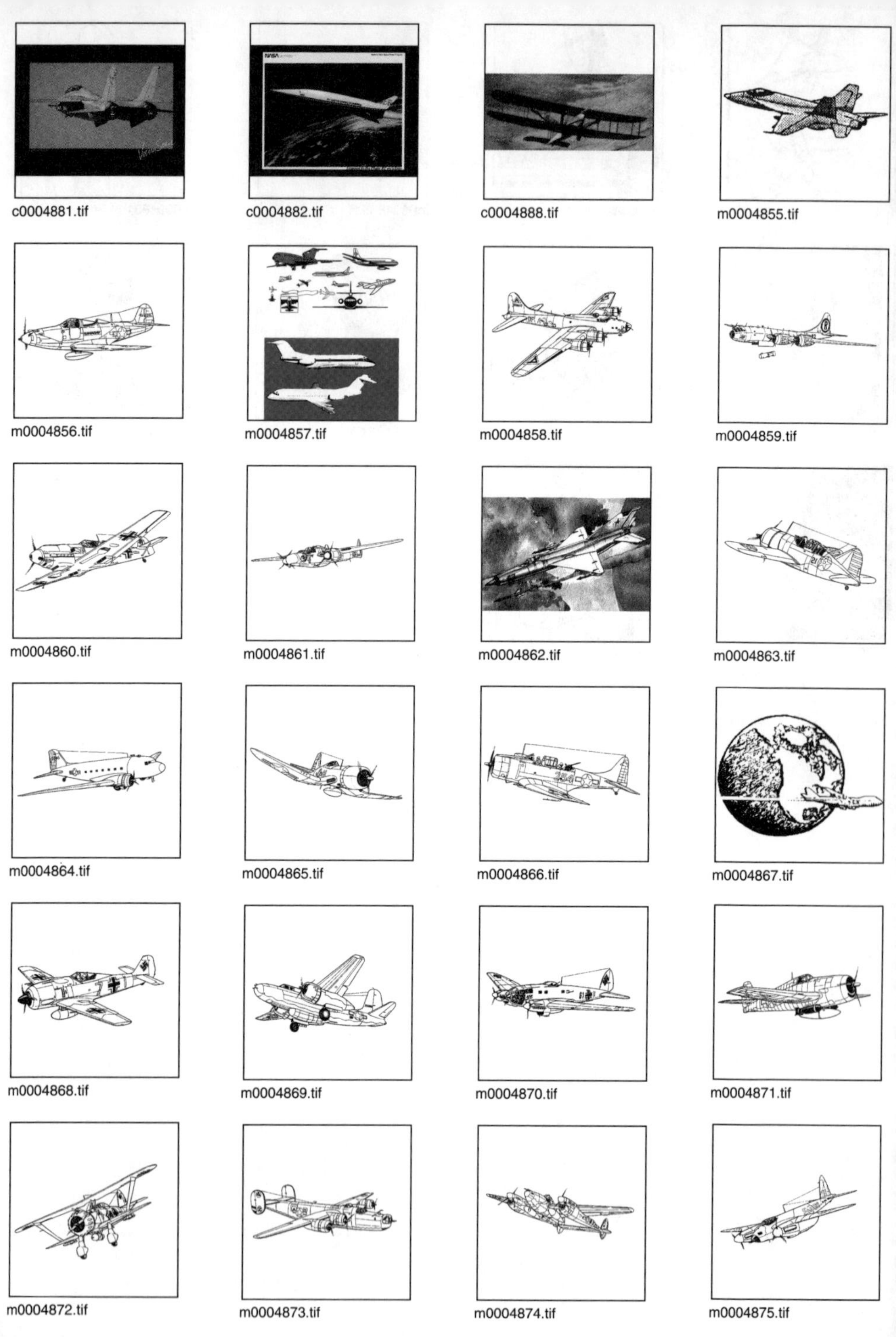

d:\images\plane

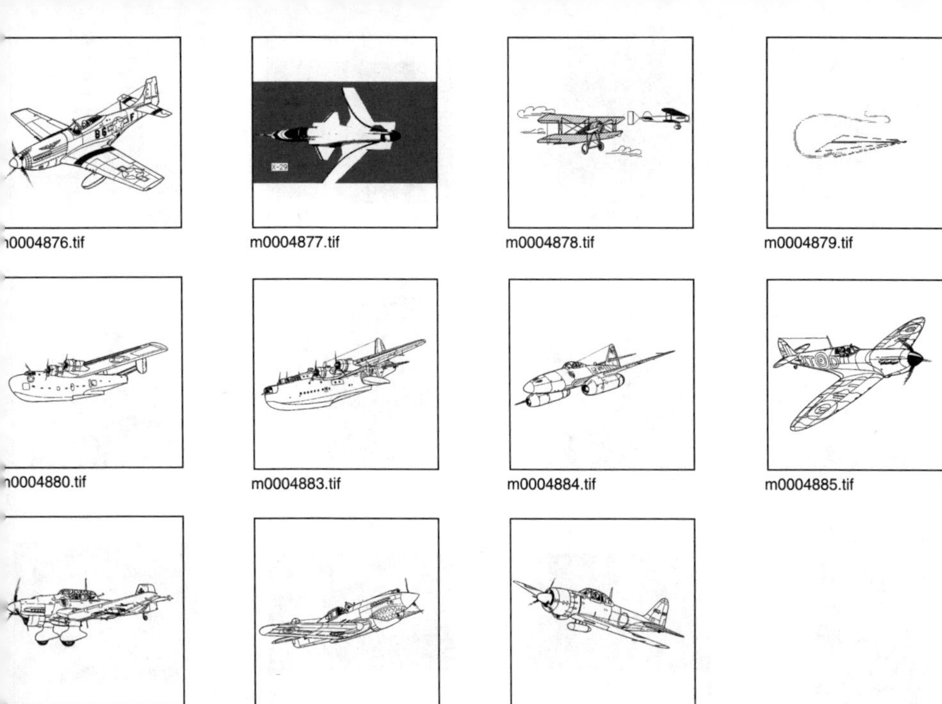

ı0004876.tif m0004877.tif m0004878.tif m0004879.tif

ı0004880.tif m0004883.tif m0004884.tif m0004885.tif

ı0004886.tif m0004887.tif m0004889.tif

c0004890.tif c0004891.tif c0004892.tif c0004893.tif

c0004894.tif c0004901.tif c0004902.tif c0004903.tif

c0004904.tif c0004913.tif c0004915.tif c0004917.tif

c0004919.tif c0004920.tif c0004921.tif c0004922.tif

c0004923.tif c0004924.tif c0004925.tif c0004926.tif

c0004928.tif c0004929.tif c0004930.tif c0004931.tif

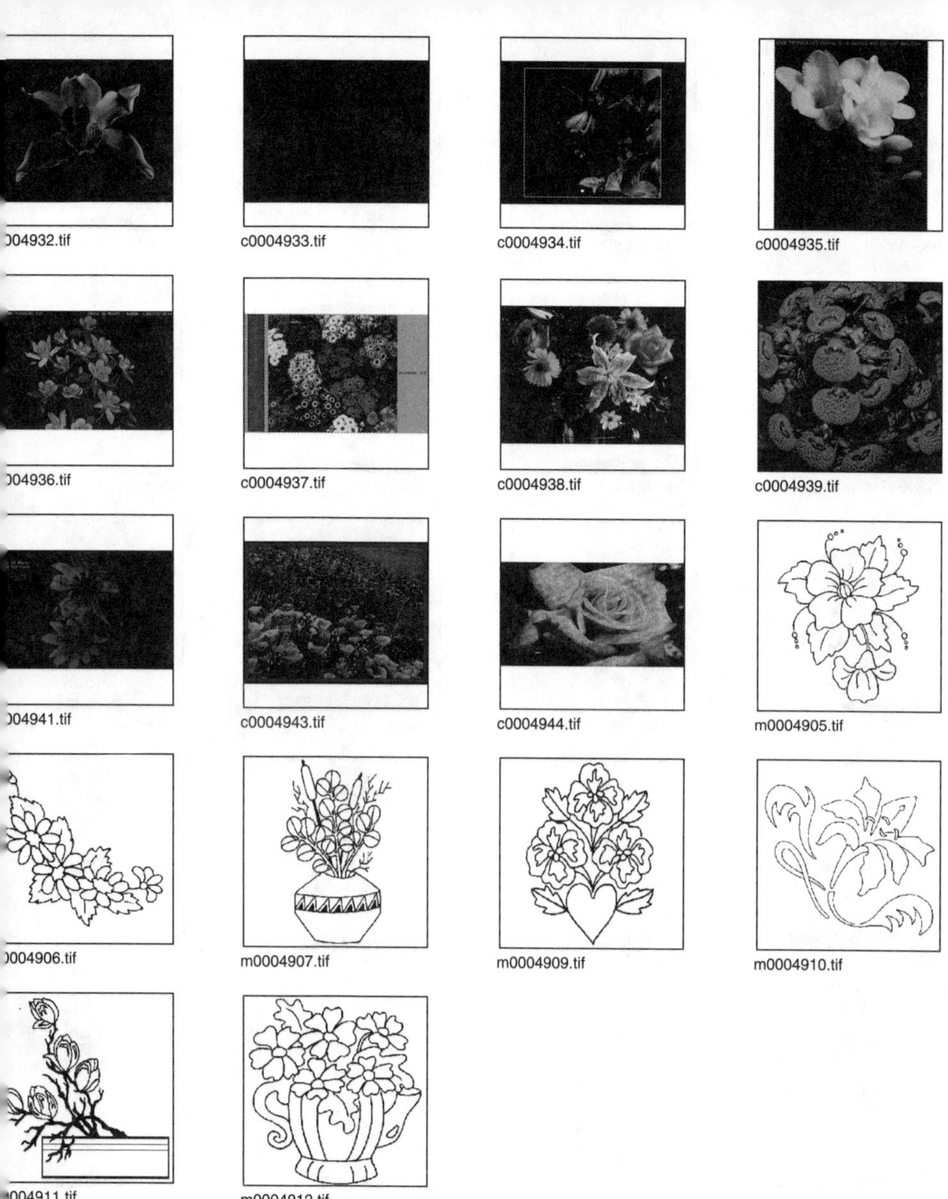

004932.tif c0004933.tif c0004934.tif c0004935.tif

004936.tif c0004937.tif c0004938.tif c0004939.tif

004941.tif c0004943.tif c0004944.tif m0004905.tif

004906.tif m0004907.tif m0004909.tif m0004910.tif

004911.tif m0004912.tif

d:\images\punc

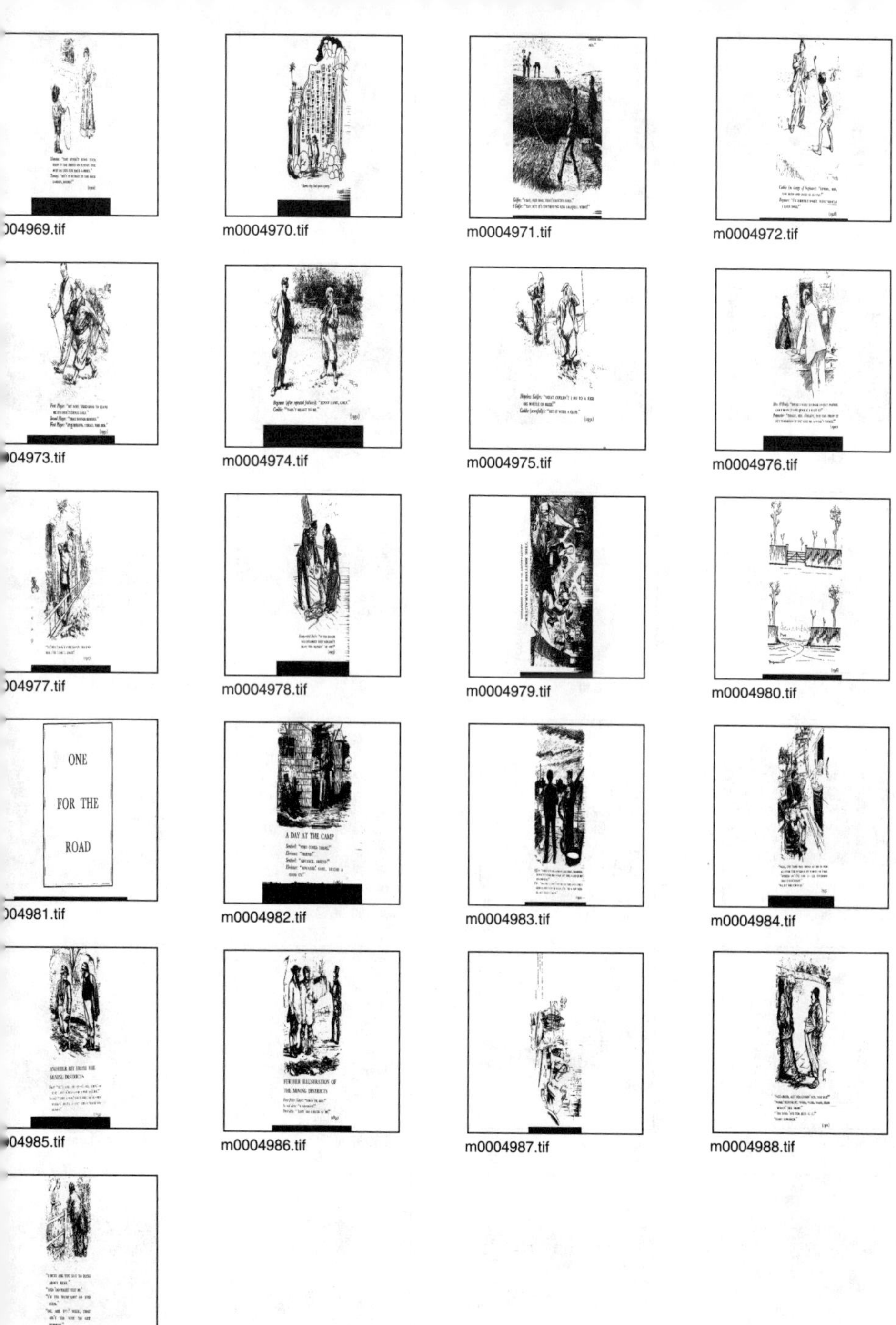

04989.tif

images\punch

d:\images\relig

0005043.tif c0005044.tif c0005045.tif m0004990.tif

m0004991.tif m0004992.tif m0004993.tif m0004994.tif

m0004995.tif m0004996.tif m0004997.tif m0004998.tif

m0004999.tif m0005000.tif m0005001.tif m0005002.tif

m0005003.tif m0005004.tif m0005005.tif m0005006.tif

m0005007.tif m0005008.tif m0005009.tif m0005010.tif

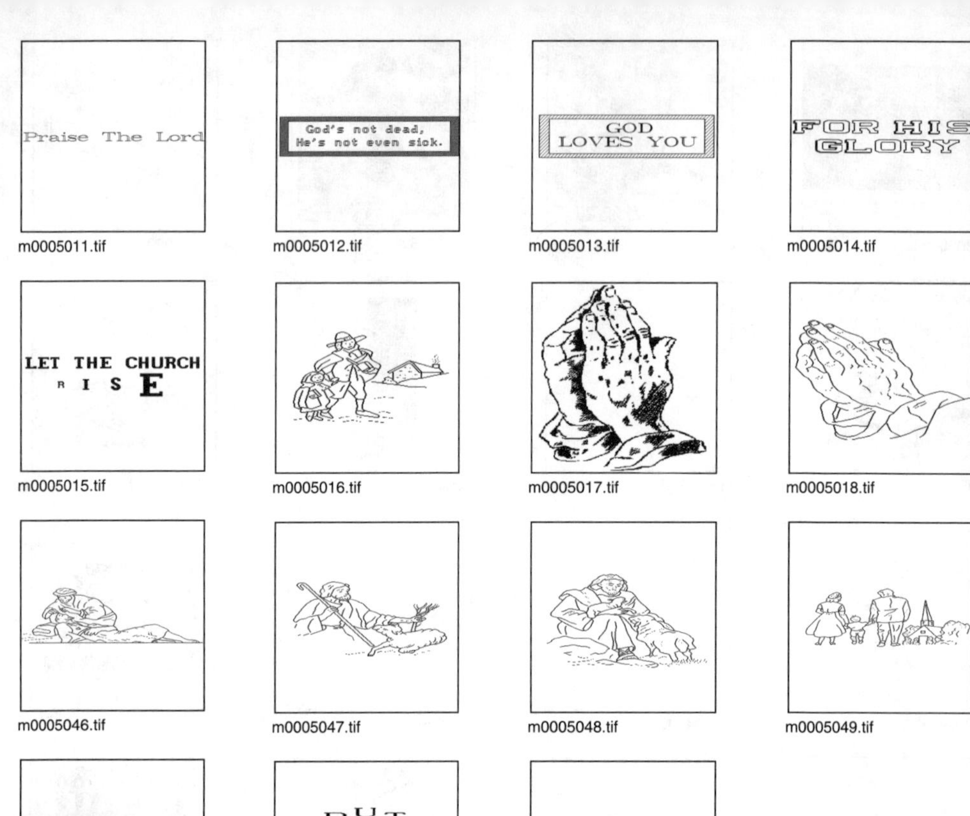

m0005011.tif m0005012.tif m0005013.tif m0005014.tif

m0005015.tif m0005016.tif m0005017.tif m0005018.tif

m0005046.tif m0005047.tif m0005048.tif m0005049.tif

m0005050.tif m0005051.tif m0005052.tif

0005053.tif	 c0005054.tif	 c0005055.tif	 c0005058.tif
 0005060.tif	 c0005061.tif	 c0005062.tif	 c0005064.tif
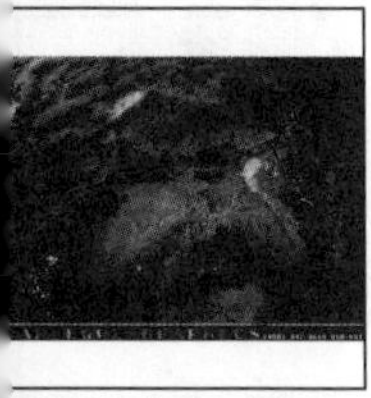 0005065.tif	 c0005066.tif	 c0005069.tif	 c0005070.tif
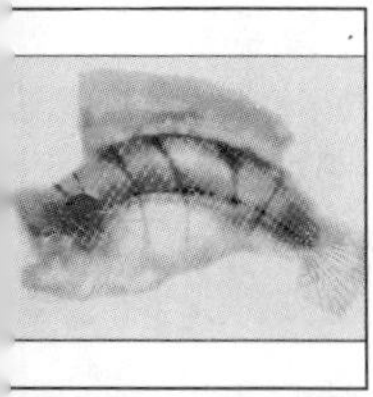 0005071.tif	 c0005073.tif	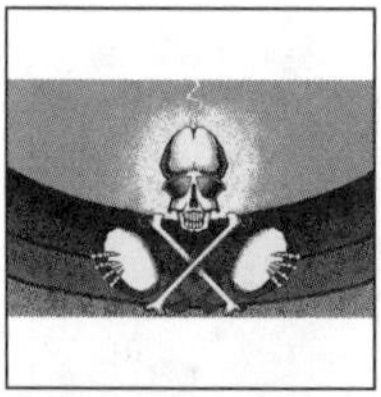 c0005074.tif	 c0005075.tif
 0005076.tif	 c0005077.tif	 c0005078.tif	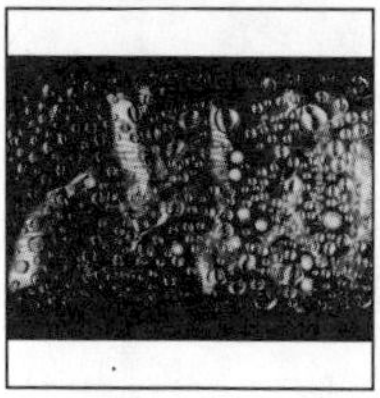 c0005079.tif
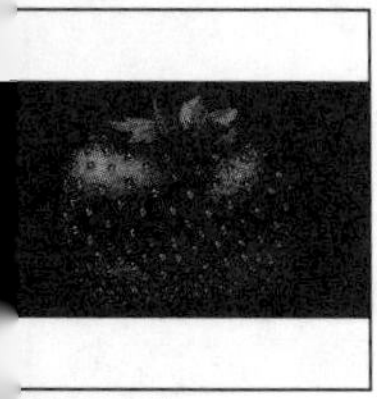 0005080.tif	 c0005081.tif	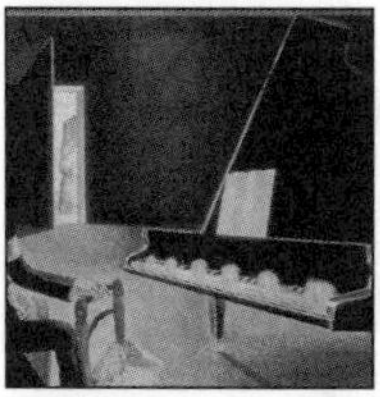 c0005083.tif	 c0005085.tif

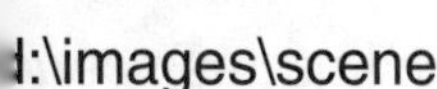
:\images\scene

c0005086.tif c0005087.tif c0005088.tif c0005089.tif

c0005092.tif c0005094.tif c0005096.tif c0005097.tif

c0005098.tif c0005099.tif c0005101.tif c0005102.tif

c0005103.tif c0005104.tif c0005105.tif c0005106.tif

c0005107.tif c0005109.tif c0005110.tif c0005111.tif

c0005113.tif c0005114.tif c0005115.tif c0005116.tif

d:\images\scene

0005117.tif
c0005118.tif
c0005119.tif
c0005121.tif
0005122.tif
c0005123.tif
c0005124.tif
c0005125.tif
0005126.tif
c0005127.tif
c0005128.tif
c0005129.tif
c0005130.tif
c0005131.tif
c0005132.tif
c0005133.tif
0005134.tif
c0005135.tif
c0005136.tif
c0005137.tif
0005138.tif
c0005139.tif
c0005140.tif
c0005141.tif

c0005142.tif c0005143.tif c0005144.tif c0005145.tif
c0005146.tif c0005147.tif c0005148.tif c0005149.tif
c0005150.tif c0005151.tif c0005152.tif c0005153.tif
c0005154.tif c0005155.tif c0005156.tif c0005157.tif
c0005158.tif c0005159.tif c0005160.tif c0005161.tif
c0005162.tif c0005163.tif c0005164.tif c0005165.tif

c0005166.tif

c0005167.tif

c0005168.tif

c0005169.tif

c0005170.tif

m0005056.tif

m0005059.tif

m0005090.tif

m0005091.tif

m0005095.tif

d:\images\scene

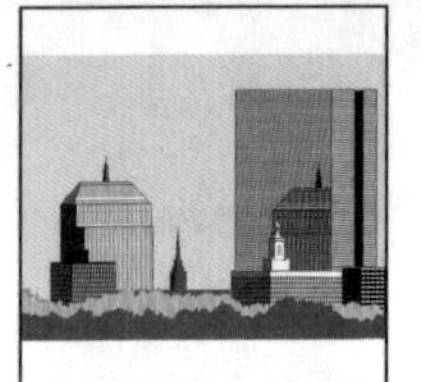
m0005172.tif

m0005173.tif

m0005174.tif

m0005175.tif

m0005176.tif

m0005177.tif

m0005178.tif

m0005179.tif

m0005180.tif

m0005181.tif

m0005182.tif

m0005183.tif

m0005184.tif

m0005185.tif

m0005186.tif

m0005187.tif

m0005188.tif

m0005189.tif

m0005190.tif

m0005191.tif

m0005192.tif

m0005193.tif

m0005194.tif

m0005195.tif

d:\images\softscen

005196.tif

m0005197.tif

m0005198.tif

m0005199.tif

005200.tif

c0005225.tif

c0005231.tif

c0005232.tif

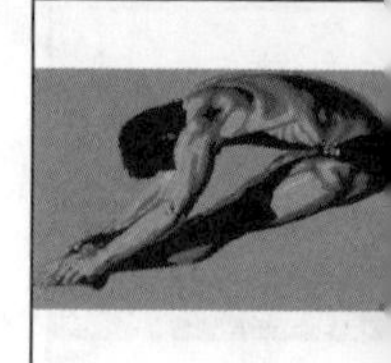
c0005236.tif

c0005237.tif

c0005240.tif

c0005250.tif

m0005222.tif

m0005223.tif

m0005224.tif

m0005226.tif

m0005227.tif

m0005228.tif

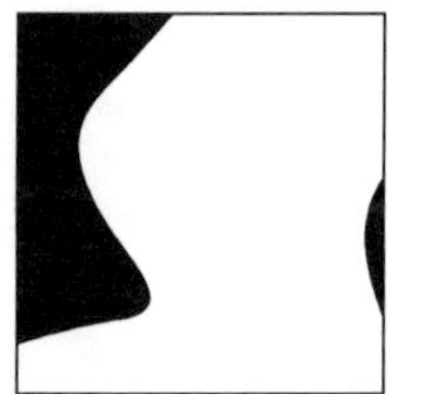
m0005229.tif

m0005230.tif

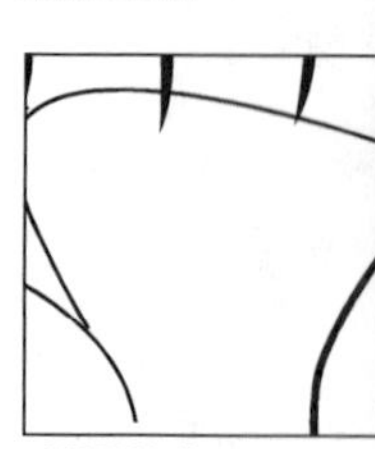
m0005233.tif

m0005234.tif

m0005235.tif

m0005238.tif

m0005239.tif

m0005241.tif

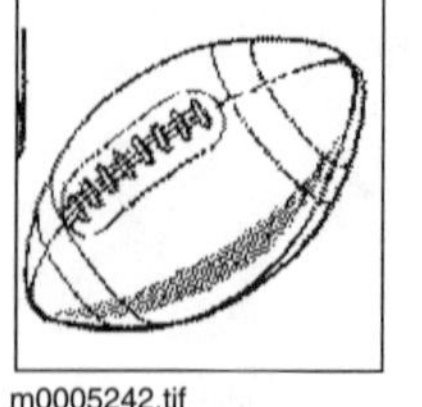
m0005242.tif

m0005243.tif

m0005244.tif

0005245.tif

m0005246.tif

m0005247.tif

m0005248.tif

0005249.tif

m0005251.tif

m0005252.tif

c0005268.tif

c0005313.tif

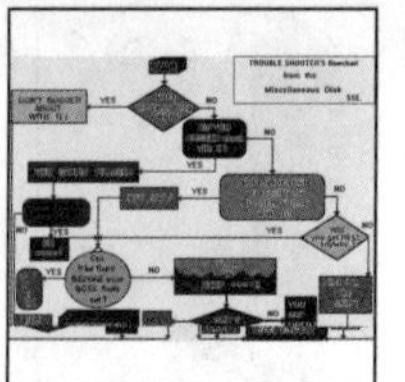

c0005330.tif

m0005253.tif

m0005254.tif

m0005255.tif

m0005256.tif

m0005257.tif

m0005258.tif

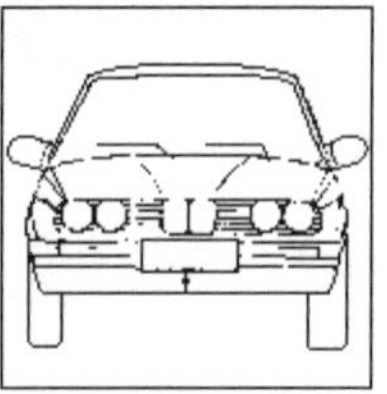

m0005259.tif

m0005260.tif

m0005261.tif

m0005262.tif

m0005263.tif

m0005264.tif

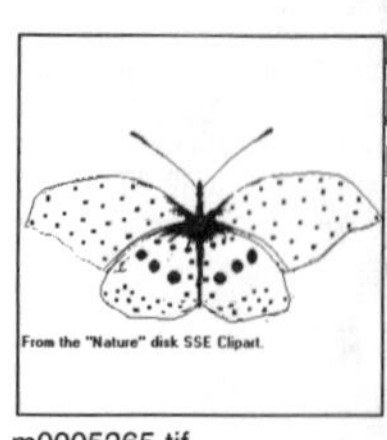

m0005265.tif

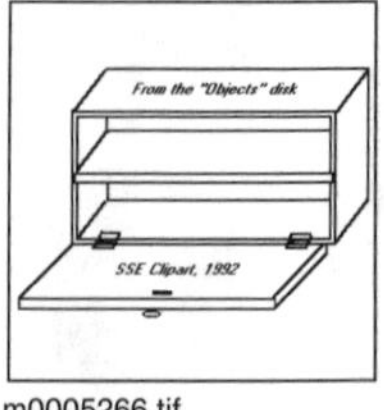

m0005266.tif

m0005267.tif

m0005270.tif

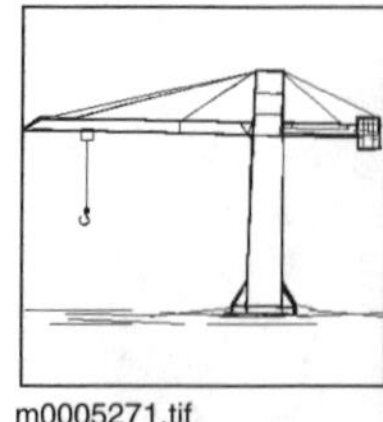

m0005271.tif

m0005272.tif

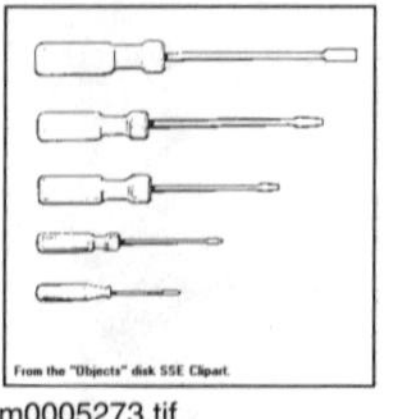

m0005273.tif

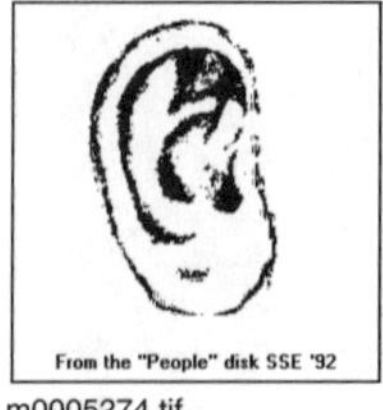

m0005274.tif

m0005275.tif

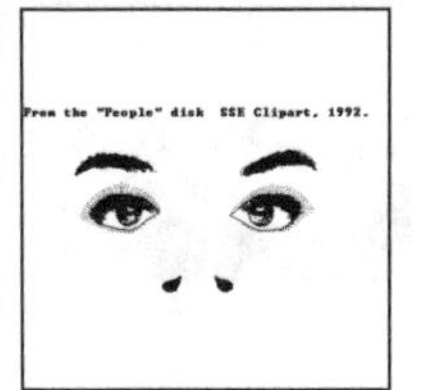

m0005276.tif

m0005277.tif

m0005278.tif

m0005283.tif

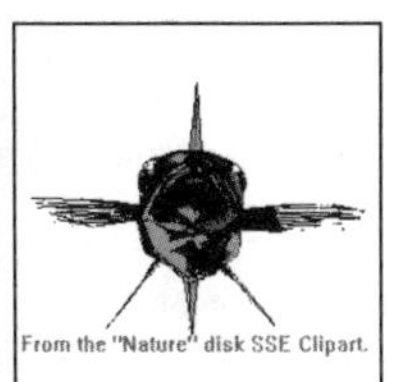

m0005290.tif

m0005291.tif

m0005292.tif

m0005293.tif

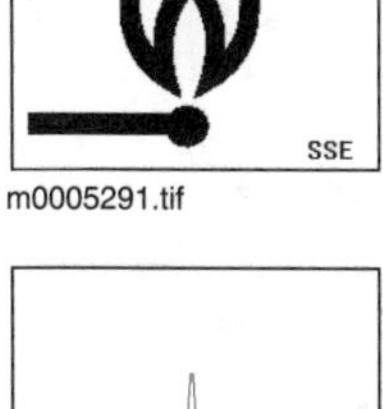

m0005295.tif

m0005296.tif

m0005297.tif

m0005299.tif

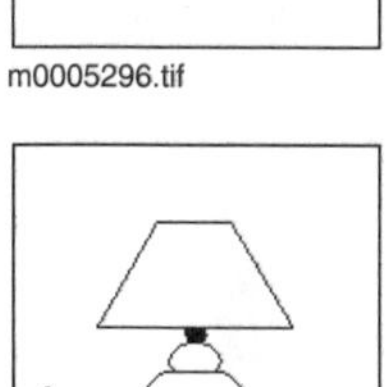

m0005300.tif

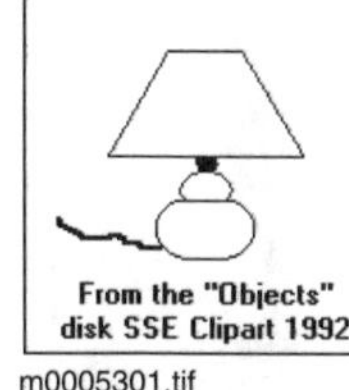

m0005301.tif

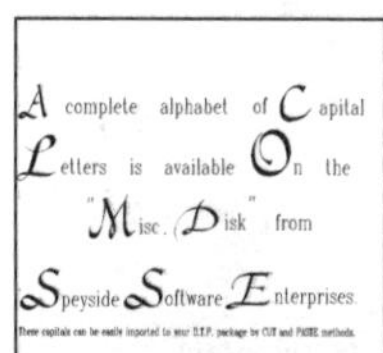

m0005302.tif

m0005303.tif

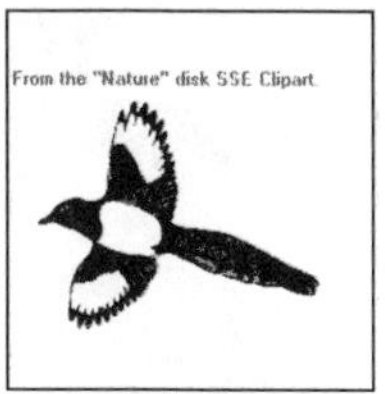

m0005304.tif

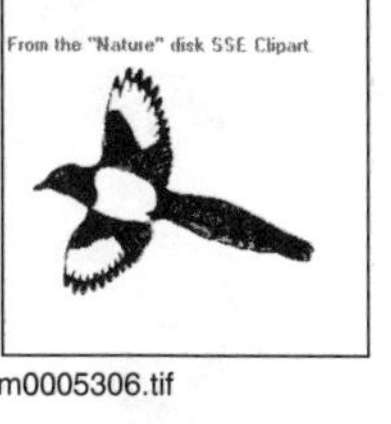

m0005306.tif

m0005307.tif

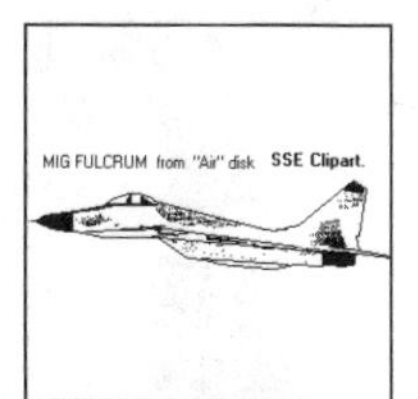

m0005308.tif

m0005309.tif

m0005310.tif

m0005311.tif

m0005312.tif

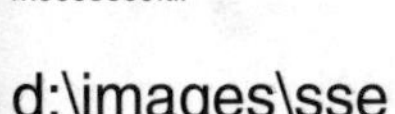

d:\images\sse

m0005314.tif

m0005315.tif

m0005316.tif

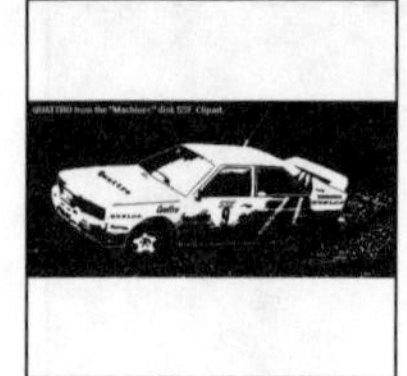

m0005317.tif

m0005318.tif

m0005319.tif

m0005320.tif

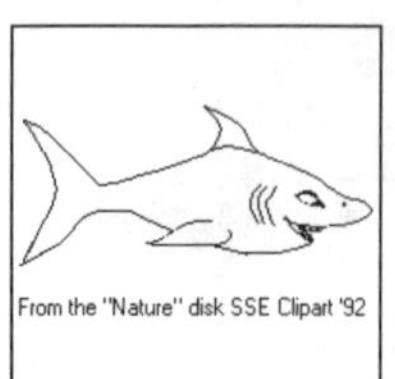

m0005321.tif

m0005322.tif

m0005323.tif

m0005324.tif

m0005325.tif

m0005327.tif

m0005328.tif

m0005329.tif

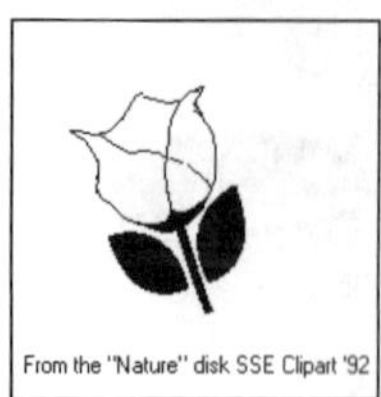

m0005331.tif

m0005332.tif

m0005334.tif

m0005335.tif

m0005336.tif

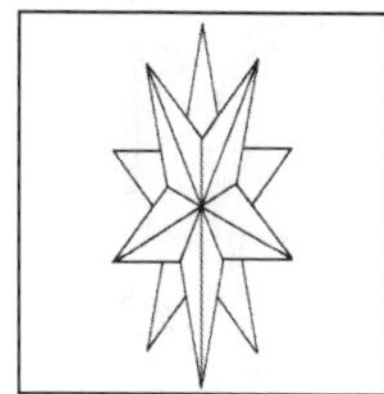
m0005337.tif

m0005338.tif

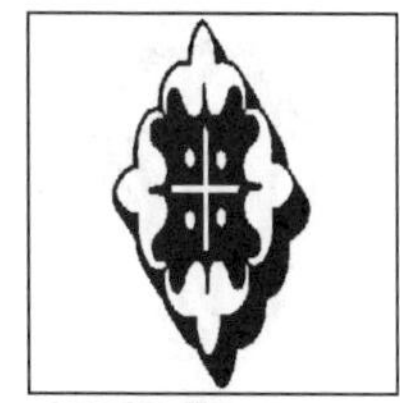
m0005339.tif

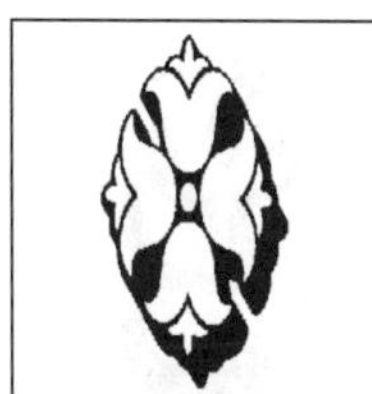
m0005340.tif

m0005341.tif

m0005342.tif

m0005343.tif

m0005344.tif

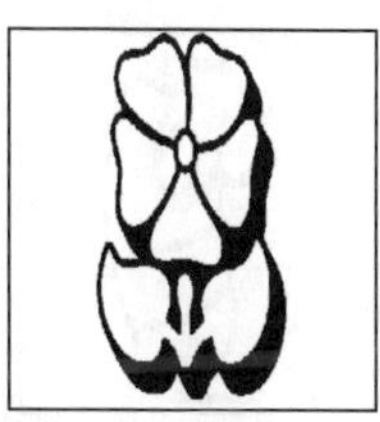
m0005345.tif

m0005346.tif

m0005347.tif

m0005348.tif

m0005349.tif

m0005350.tif

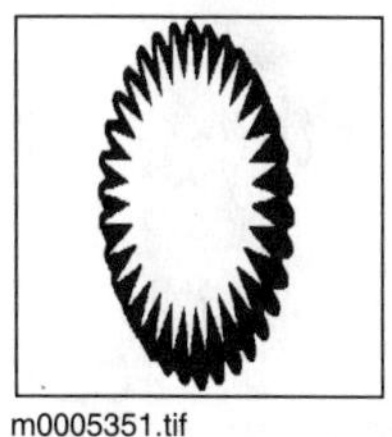
m0005351.tif

m0005352.tif

m0005353.tif

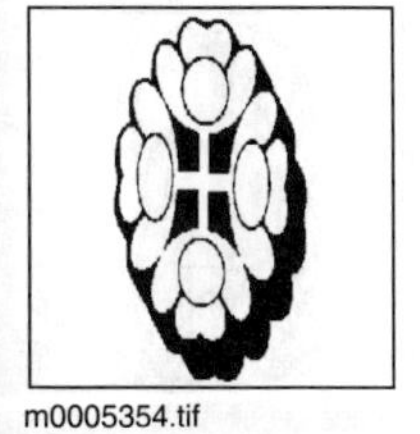
m0005354.tif

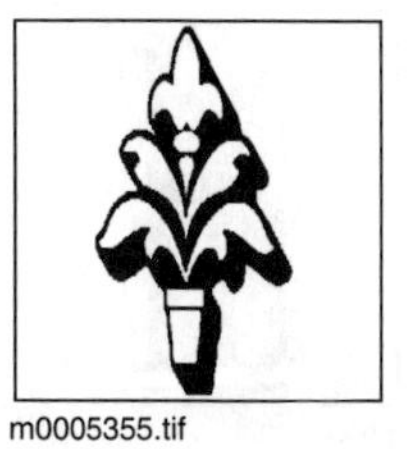
m0005355.tif

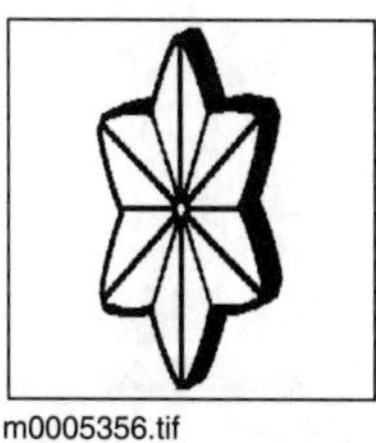
m0005356.tif

m0005357.tif

d:\images\st

m0005358.tif

m0005359.tif

m0005360.tif

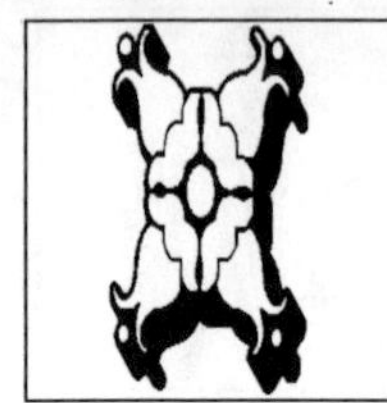
m0005361.tif

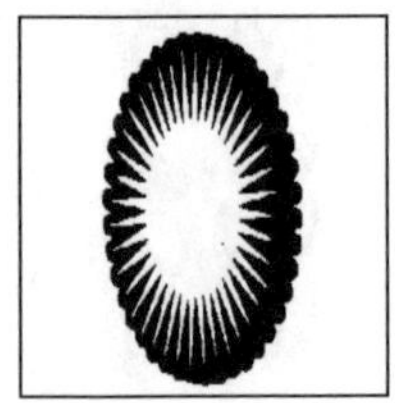
m0005362.tif

m0005363.tif

m0005364.tif

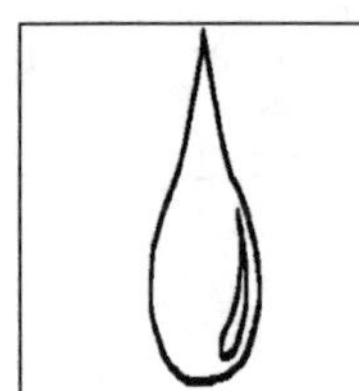
m0005365.tif

m0005366.tif

m0005367.tif

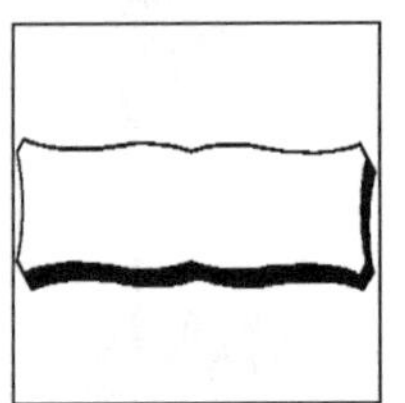
m0005368.tif

m0005369.tif

m0005370.tif

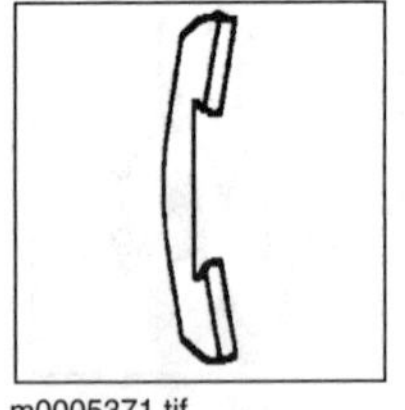
m0005371.tif

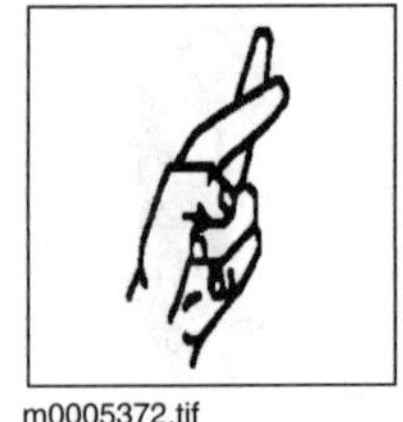
m0005372.tif

m0005373.tif

m0005374.tif

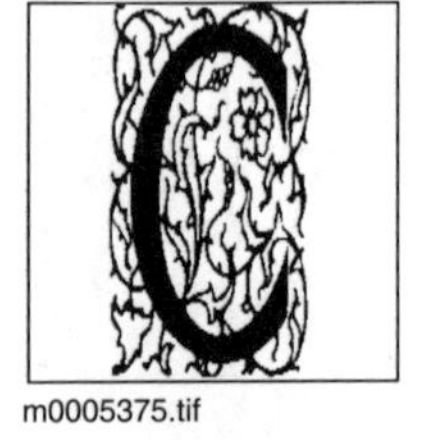

m0005375.tif

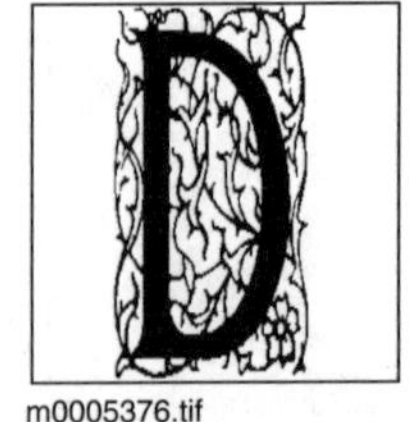

m0005376.tif

m0005377.tif

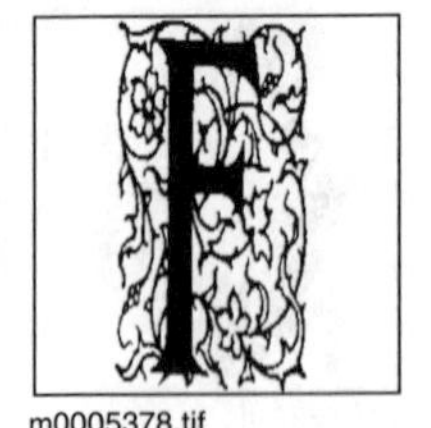

m0005378.tif

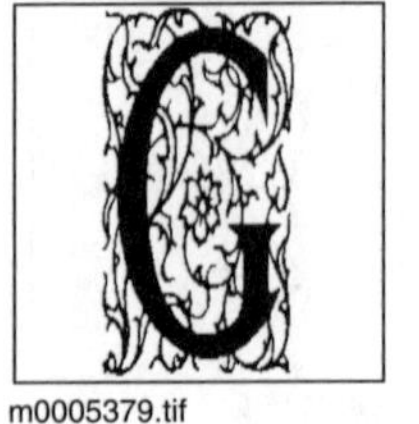

m0005379.tif

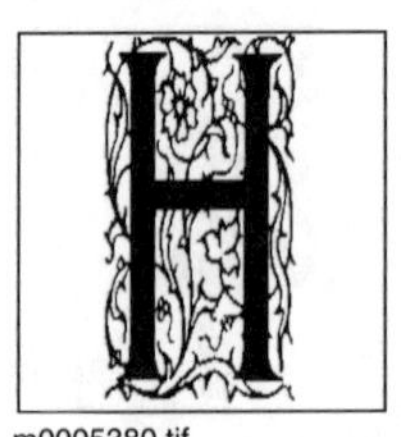

m0005380.tif

m0005381.tif

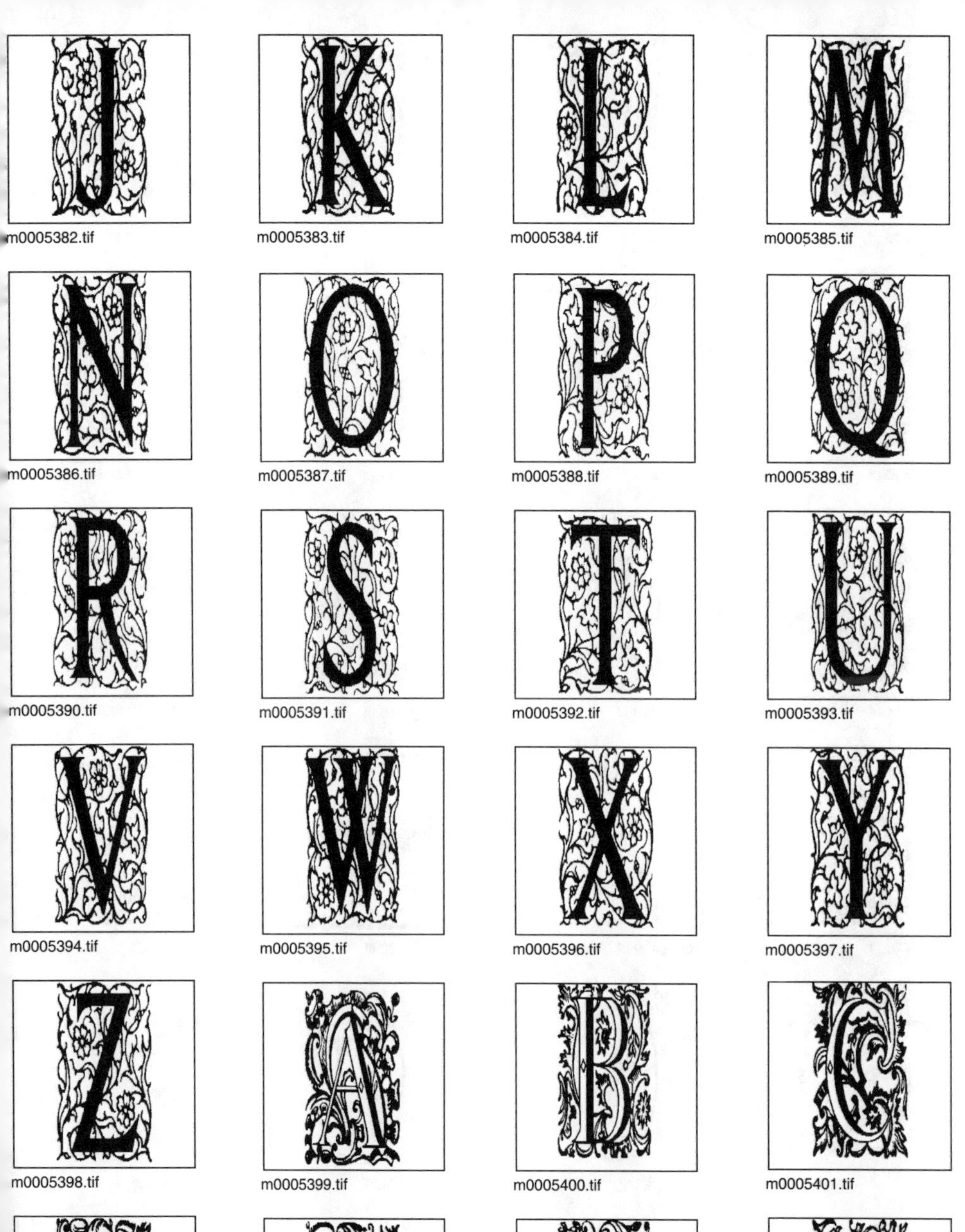

m0005382.tif m0005383.tif m0005384.tif m0005385.tif

m0005386.tif m0005387.tif m0005388.tif m0005389.tif

m0005390.tif m0005391.tif m0005392.tif m0005393.tif

m0005394.tif m0005395.tif m0005396.tif m0005397.tif

m0005398.tif m0005399.tif m0005400.tif m0005401.tif

m0005402.tif m0005403.tif m0005404.tif m0005405.tif

d:\images\st

m0005406.tif

m0005407.tif

m0005408.tif

m0005409.tif

m0005410.tif

m0005411.tif

m0005412.tif

m0005413.tif

m0005414.tif

m0005415.tif

m0005416.tif

m0005417.tif

m0005418.tif

m0005419.tif

m0005420.tif

m0005421.tif

m0005422.tif

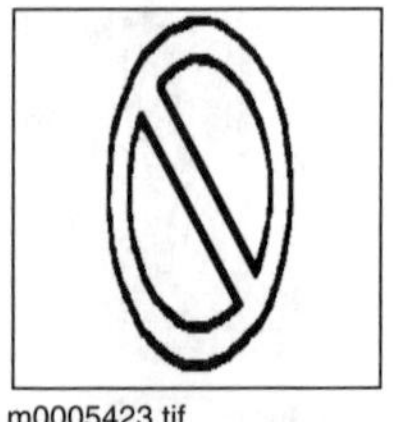
m0005423.tif

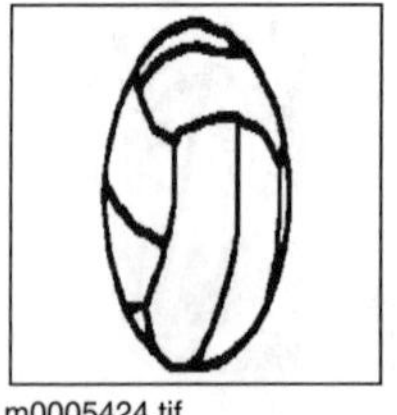
m0005424.tif

m0005425.tif

m0005426.tif

m0005427.tif

m0005428.tif

m0005429.tif

m0005430.tif

m0005431.tif

m0005432.tif

m0005433.tif

m0005434.tif

m0005435.tif

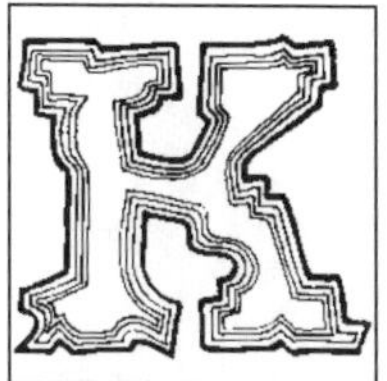
m0005436.tif

m0005437.tif

m0005438.tif

m0005439.tif

m0005440.tif

m0005441.tif

m0005442.tif

m0005443.tif

m0005444.tif

m0005445.tif

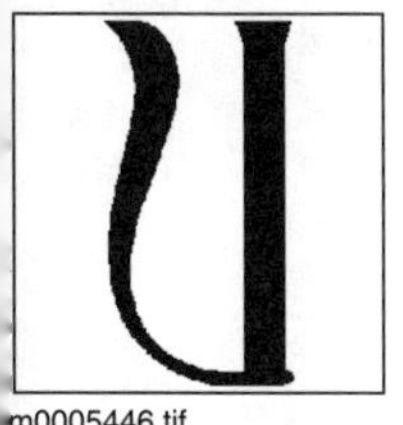
m0005446.tif

m0005447.tif

m0005448.tif

m0005449.tif

m0005450.tif

m0005451.tif

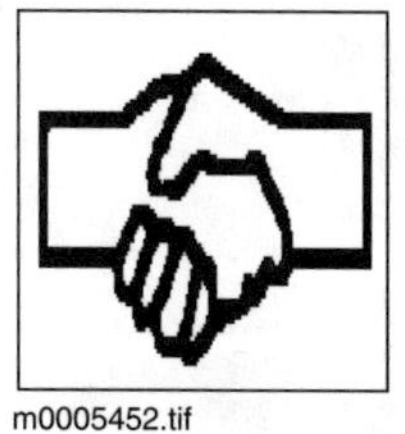
m0005452.tif

m0005453.tif

d:\images\st

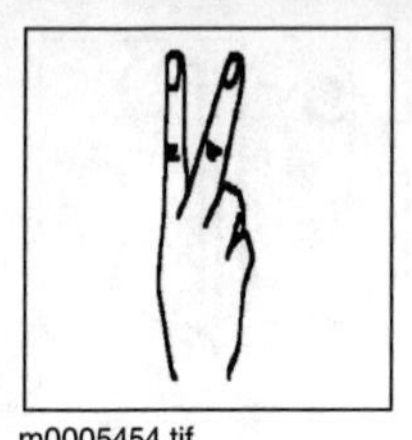
m0005454.tif

m0005455.tif

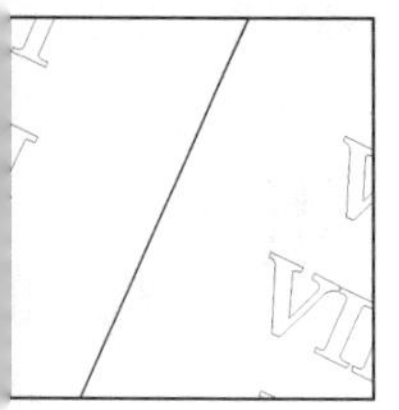
m0005456.tif

m0005457.tif

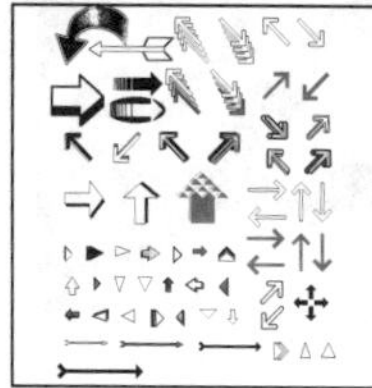
m0005458.tif

m0005459.tif

m0005460.tif

m0005461.tif

m0005462.tif

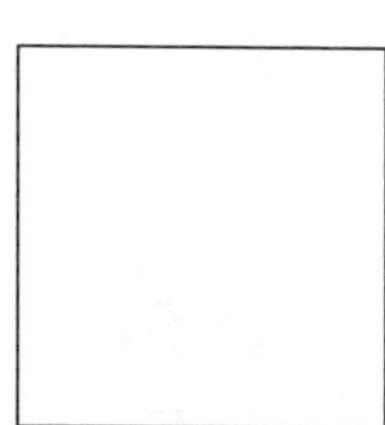
m0005463.tif

m0005464.tif

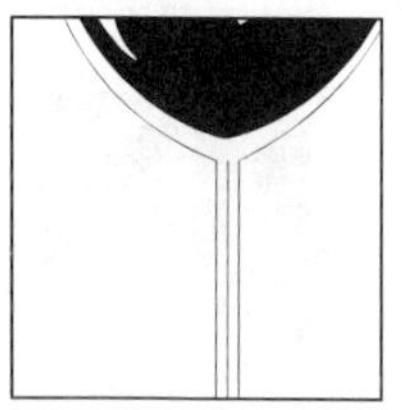
m0005465.tif

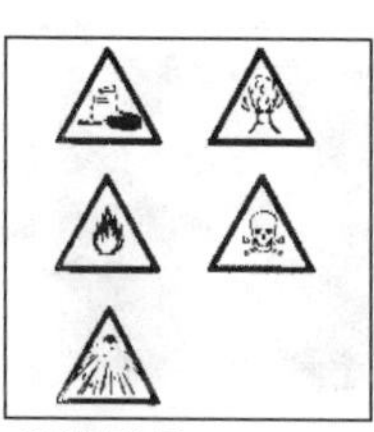
m0005466.tif

m0005467.tif

m0005468.tif

m0005469.tif

m0005470.tif

m0005472.tif

m0005473.tif

m0005474.tif

m0005475.tif

m0005476.tif

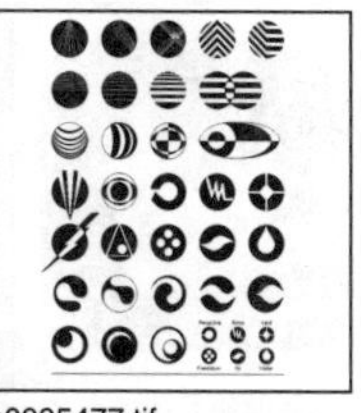
m0005477.tif

m0005478.tif

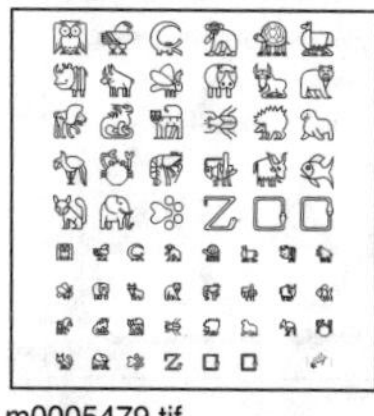
m0005479.tif

m0005480.tif

m0005481.tif

m0005482.tif

m0005483.tif

m0005484.tif

m0005485.tif

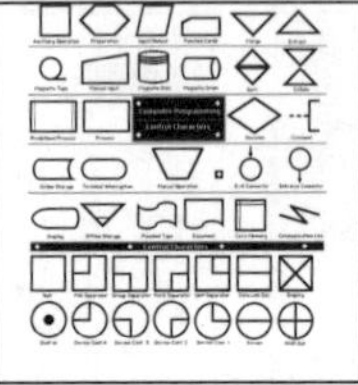
m0005486.tif

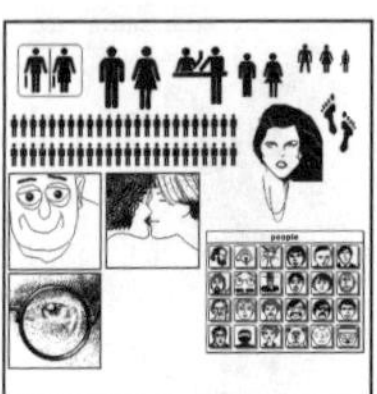
m0005487.tif

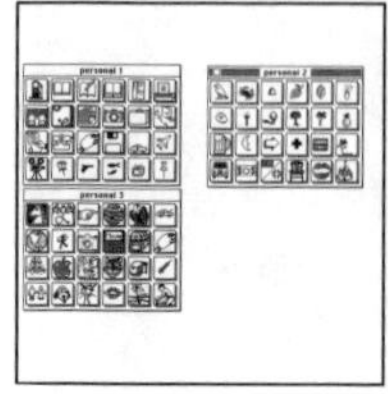
m0005488.tif

m0005489.tif

m0005490.tif

m0005491.tif

m0005492.tif

m0005493.tif

m0005494.tif

m0005495.tif

m0005496.tif

m0005497.tif

m0005498.tif

m0005499.tif

m0005500.tif

m0005501.tif

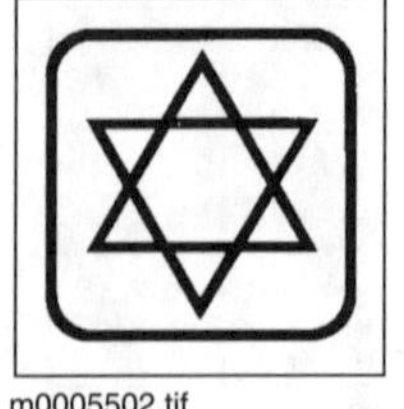
m0005502.tif

m0005503.tif

m0005504.tif

0005505.tif

m0005506.tif

m0005507.tif

m0005508.tif

0005509.tif

m0005510.tif

m0005511.tif

m0005512.tif

0005513.tif

m0005514.tif

m0005515.tif

m0005516.tif

0005517.tif

:\images\symbol

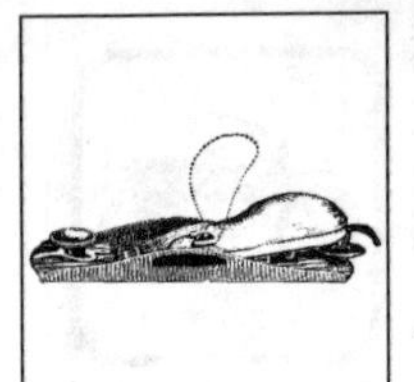
m0005518.tif

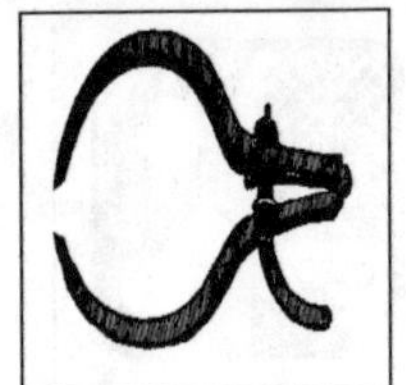
m0005519.tif

m0005520.tif

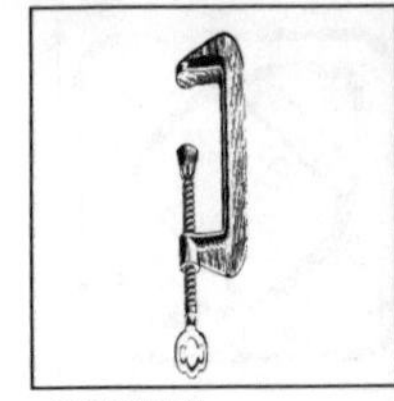
m0005521.tif

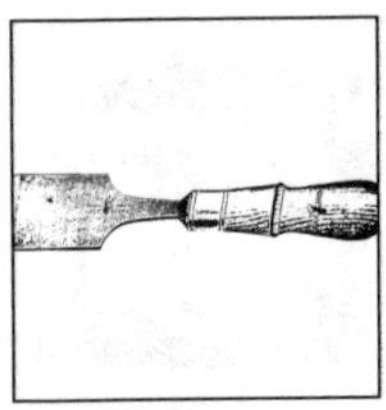
m0005522.tif

m0005523.tif

m0005524.tif

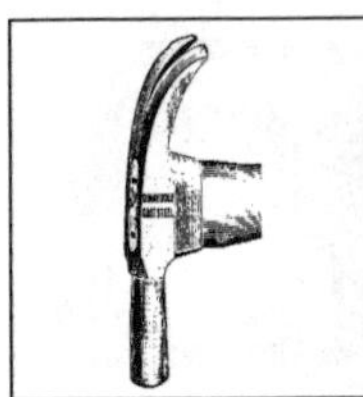
m0005525.tif

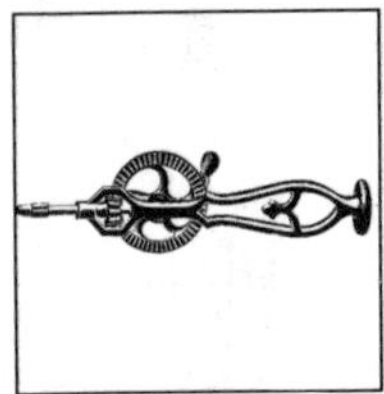
m0005526.tif

m0005527.tif

m0005528.tif

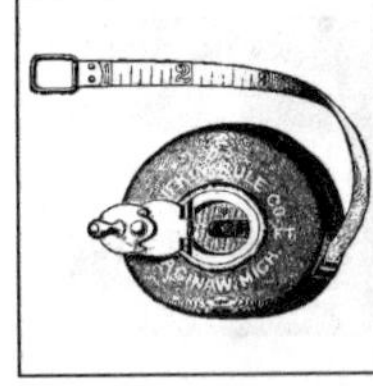
m0005529.tif

m0005530.tif

m0005531.tif

m0005532.tif

m0005533.tif

m0005534.tif

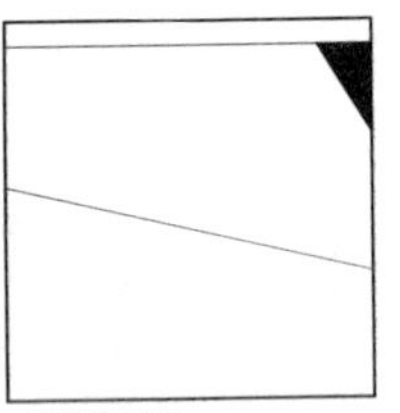
m0005535.tif

m0005536.tif

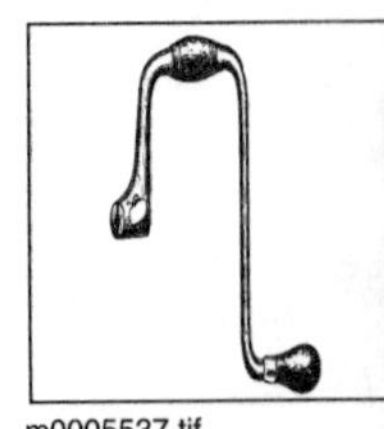
m0005537.tif

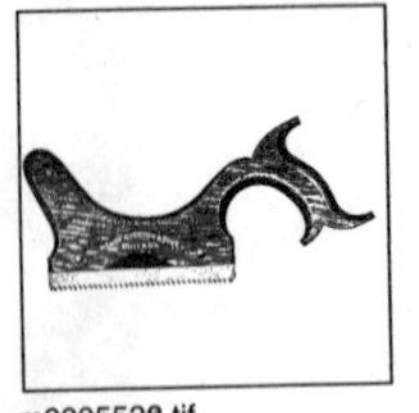
m0005538.tif

m0005539.tif

m0005540.tif

m0005541.tif

d:\images\to

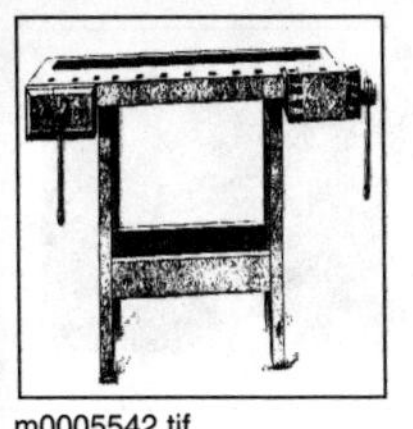
m0005542.tif

m0005543.tif

d:\images\tool

c0005544.tif

c0005545.tif

c0005689.tif

c0005690.tif

c0005694.tif

c0005697.tif

c0005698.tif

c0005702.tif

c0005753.tif

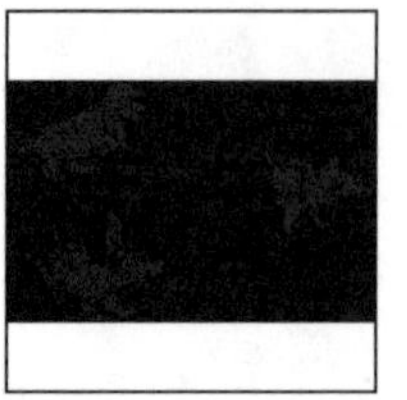
c0005756.tif

c0005757.tif

m0005546.tif

m0005547.tif

m0005548.tif

m0005549.tif

m0005550.tif

m0005551.tif

m0005552.tif

m0005553.tif

m0005554.tif

m0005555.tif

m0005556.tif

m0005557.tif

m0005558.tif

m0005559.tif

m0005560.tif

m0005561.tif

m0005562.tif

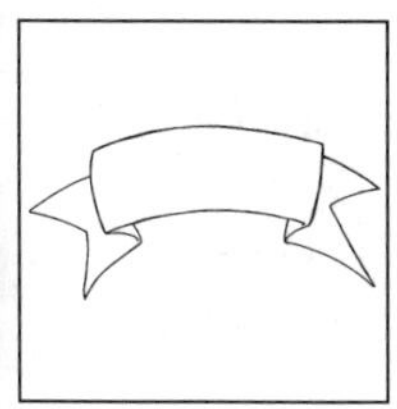

m0005563.tif

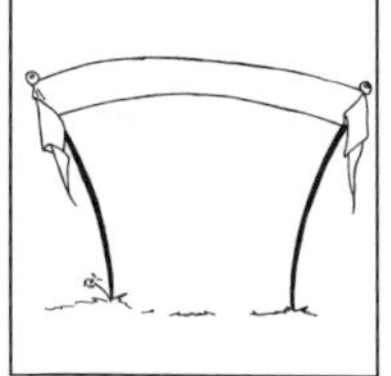

m0005564.tif

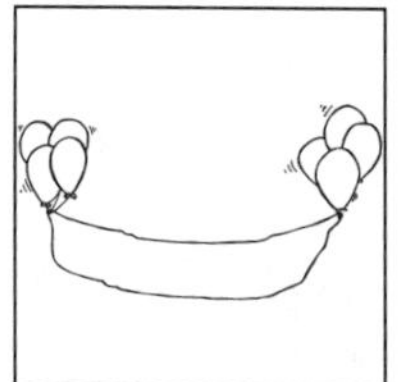

m0005565.tif

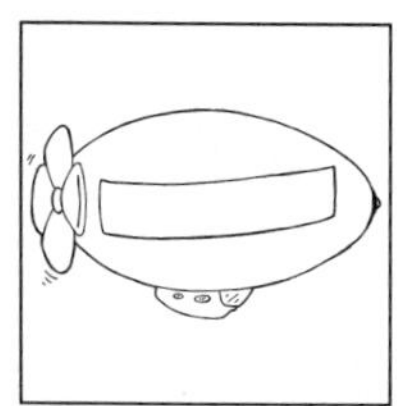

m0005566.tif

m0005567.tif

m0005568.tif

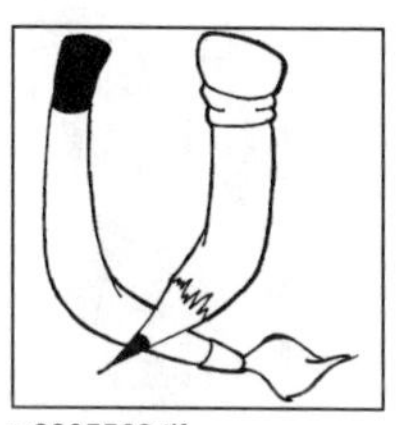

m0005569.tif

m0005570.tif

m0005571.tif

m0005572.tif

m0005573.tif

m0005574.tif

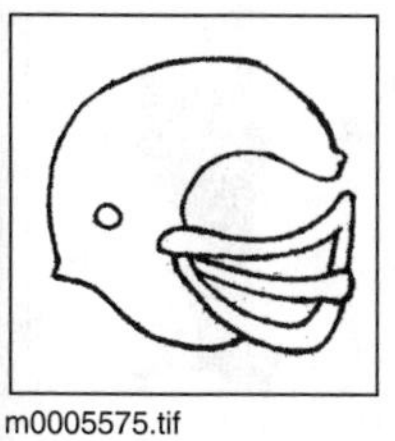

m0005575.tif

m0005576.tif

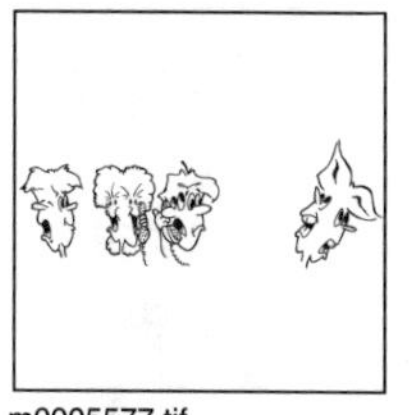

m0005577.tif

m0005578.tif

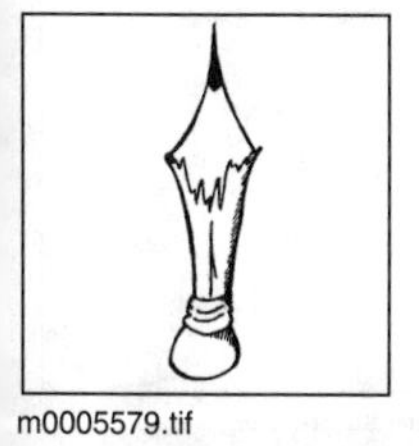

m0005579.tif

m0005580.tif

m0005581.tif

m0005582.tif

d:\images\toon

m0005583.tif m0005584.tif m0005585.tif m0005586.tif

m0005587.tif m0005588.tif m0005589.tif m0005590.tif

m0005591.tif m0005592.tif m0005593.tif m0005594.tif

m0005595.tif m0005596.tif m0005597.tif m0005598.tif

m0005599.tif m0005600.tif m0005601.tif m0005602.tif

m0005603.tif m0005604.tif m0005605.tif m0005606.tif

0005607.tif m0005608.tif m0005609.tif m0005610.tif

0005611.tif m0005612.tif m0005613.tif m0005614.tif

0005615.tif m0005616.tif m0005617.tif m0005618.tif

0005619.tif m0005620.tif m0005621.tif m0005622.tif

0005623.tif m0005624.tif m0005625.tif m0005626.tif

0005627.tif m0005628.tif m0005629.tif m0005630.tif

d:\images\toon

m0005632.tif

m0005634.tif

m0005635.tif

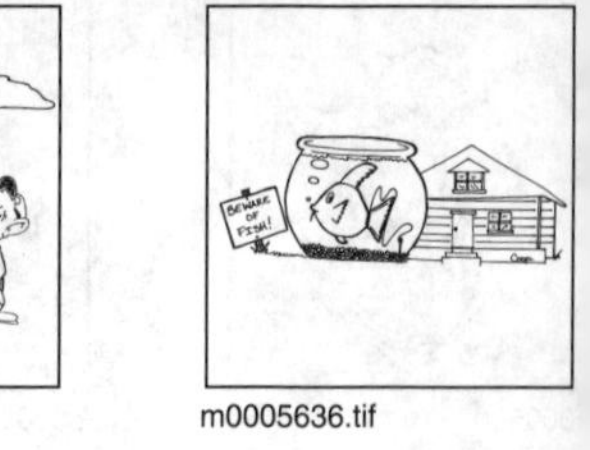

m0005636.tif

m0005637.tif

m0005638.tif

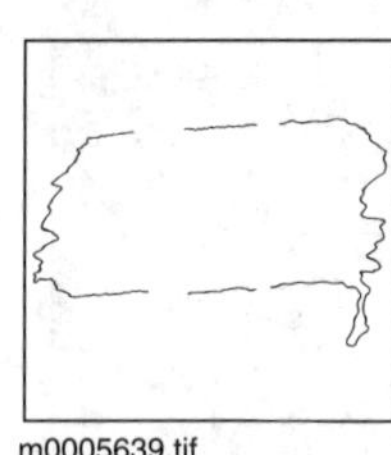

m0005639.tif

m0005640.tif

m0005641.tif

m0005642.tif

m0005643.tif

m0005644.tif

m0005645.tif

m0005646.tif

m0005647.tif

m0005648.tif

m0005649.tif

m0005650.tif

m0005651.tif

m0005652.tif

m0005653.tif

m0005654.tif

m0005656.tif

m0005657.tif

0005658.tif  | m0005659.tif  | m0005660.tif  | m0005661.tif

0005662.tif  | m0005663.tif  | m0005664.tif  | m0005665.tif

0005666.tif  | m0005667.tif  | m0005668.tif  | m0005669.tif

0005670.tif  | m0005671.tif  | m0005672.tif  | m0005673.tif

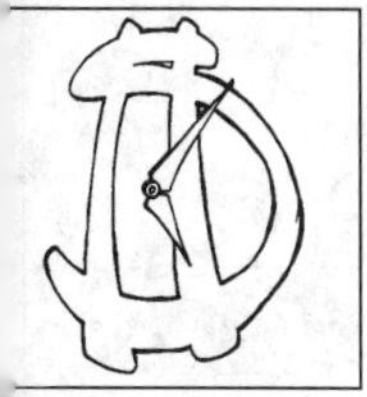

0005674.tif  | m0005675.tif 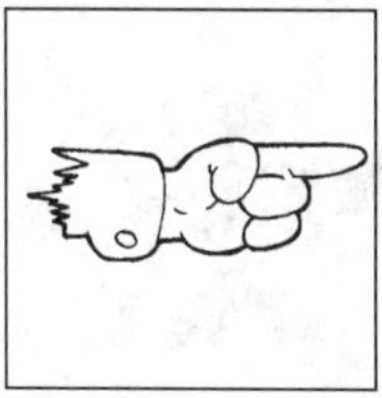 | m0005676.tif  | m0005677.tif

0005678.tif  | m0005679.tif  | m0005680.tif  | m0005681.tif

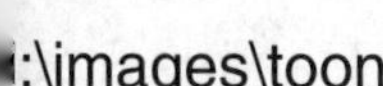

:\images\toon

m0005682.tif

m0005683.tif

m0005684.tif

m0005685.tif

m0005686.tif

m0005687.tif

m0005688.tif

m0005695.tif

m0005696.tif

m0005699.tif

m0005700.tif

m0005701.tif

m0005703.tif

m0005704.tif

m0005705.tif

m0005706.tif

m0005707.tif

m0005708.tif

m0005709.tif

m0005710.tif

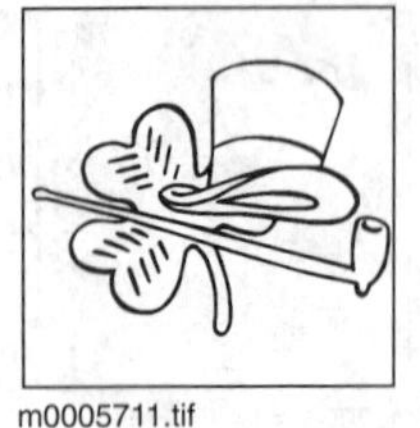
m0005711.tif

m0005712.tif

m0005713.tif

m0005714.tif

m0005715.tif

m0005716.tif

m0005717.tif

m0005718.tif

m0005719.tif

m0005720.tif

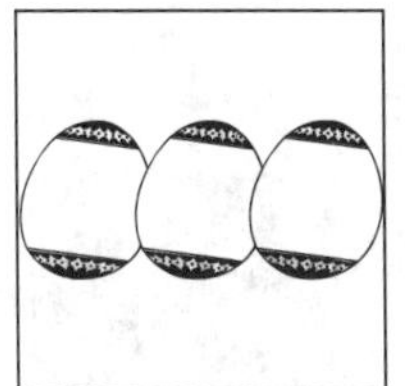
m0005721.tif

m0005722.tif

m0005723.tif

m0005724.tif

m0005725.tif

m0005726.tif

m0005727.tif

m0005728.tif

m0005730.tif

m0005731.tif

m0005732.tif

m0005733.tif

m0005734.tif

m0005735.tif

m0005736.tif

m0005737.tif

m0005738.tif

m0005739.tif

d:\images\toon

m0005740.tif

m0005741.tif

m0005742.tif

m0005743.tif

m0005744.tif

m0005746.tif

m0005748.tif

m0005749.tif

m0005755.tif

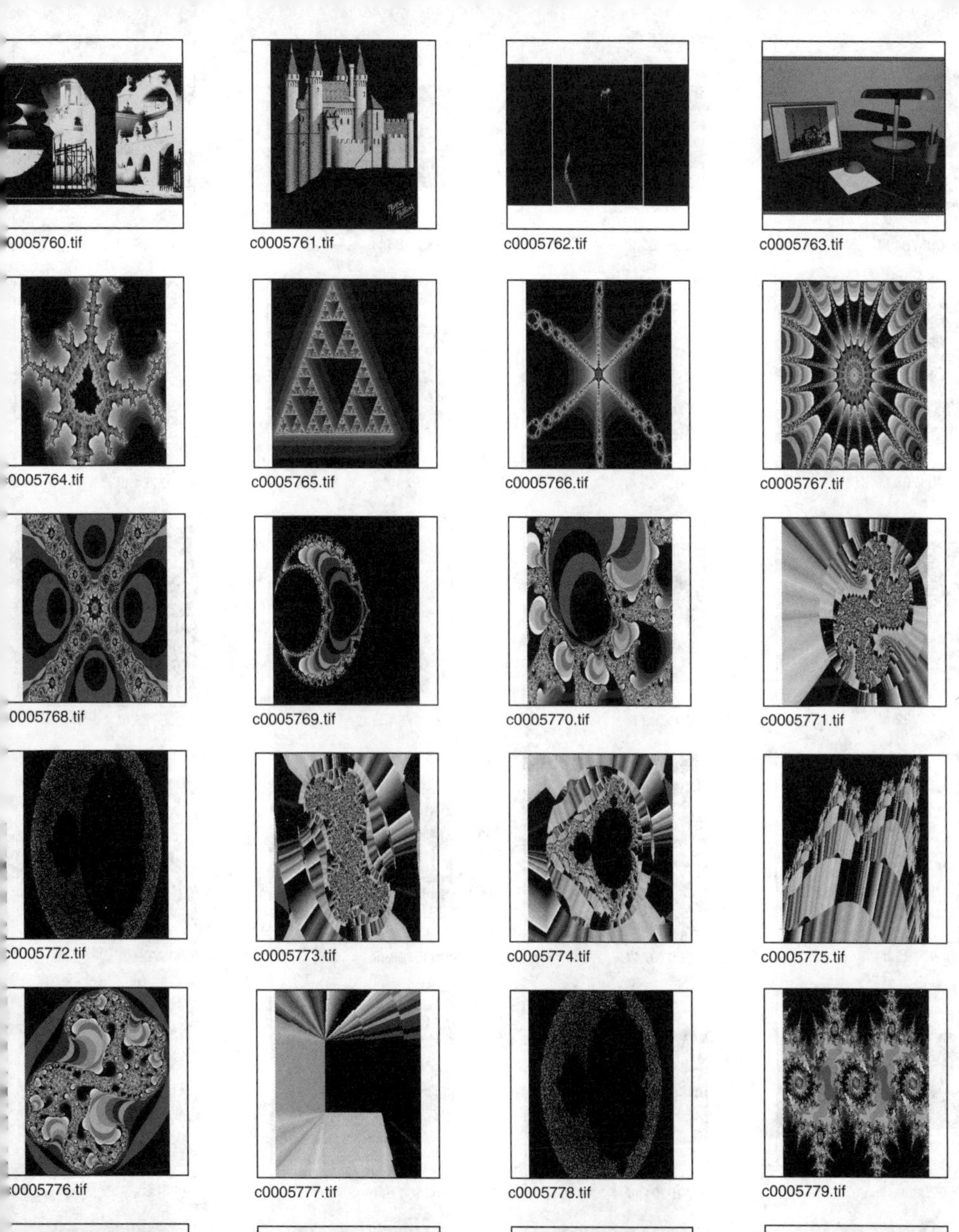

0005760.tif c0005761.tif c0005762.tif c0005763.tif

0005764.tif c0005765.tif c0005766.tif c0005767.tif

0005768.tif c0005769.tif c0005770.tif c0005771.tif

c0005772.tif c0005773.tif c0005774.tif c0005775.tif

c0005776.tif c0005777.tif c0005778.tif c0005779.tif

c0005780.tif c0005781.tif c0005782.tif c0005783.tif

d:\images\trace

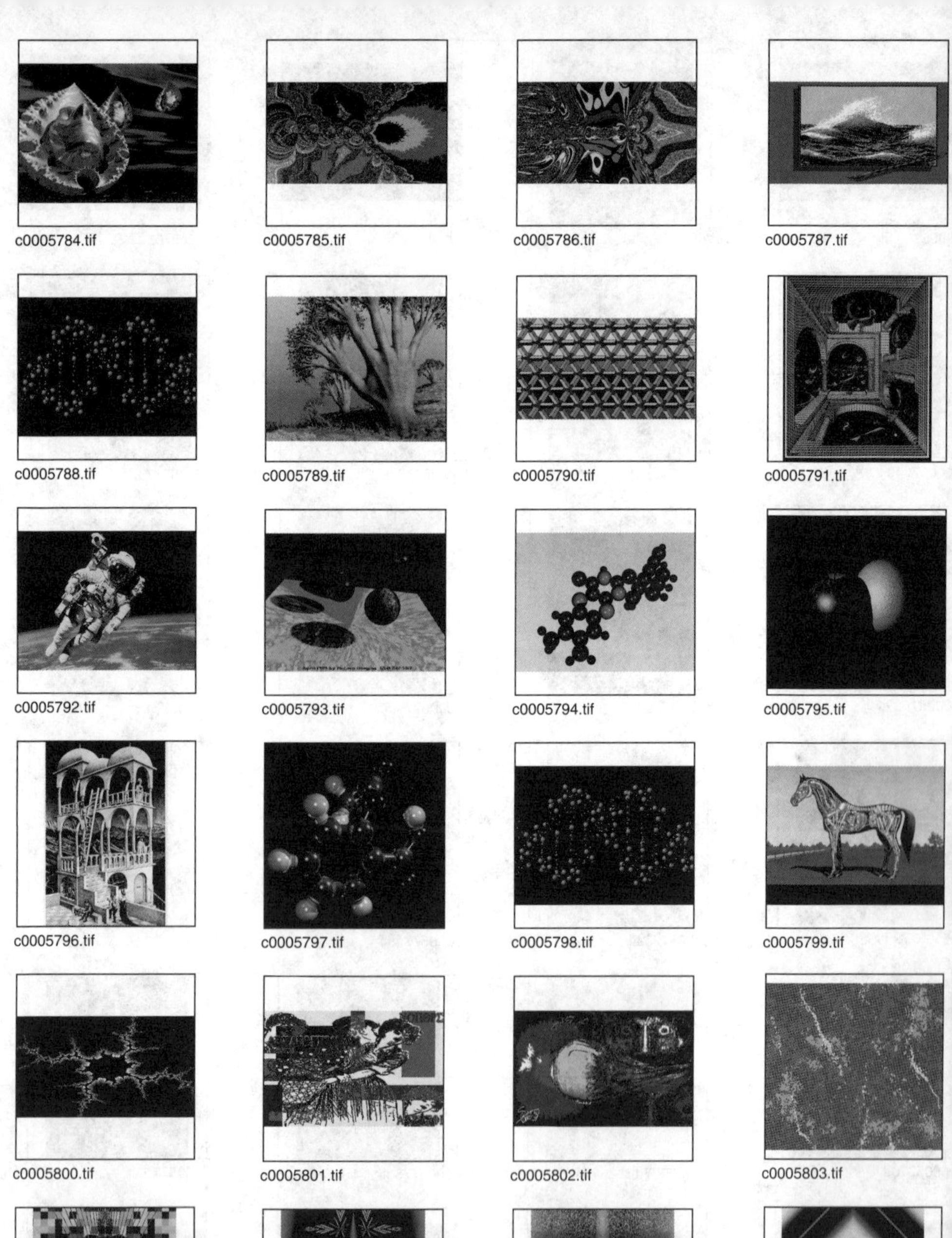

c0005784.tif c0005785.tif c0005786.tif c0005787.tif

c0005788.tif c0005789.tif c0005790.tif c0005791.tif

c0005792.tif c0005793.tif c0005794.tif c0005795.tif

c0005796.tif c0005797.tif c0005798.tif c0005799.tif

c0005800.tif c0005801.tif c0005802.tif c0005803.tif

c0005804.tif c0005805.tif c0005806.tif c0005807.tif

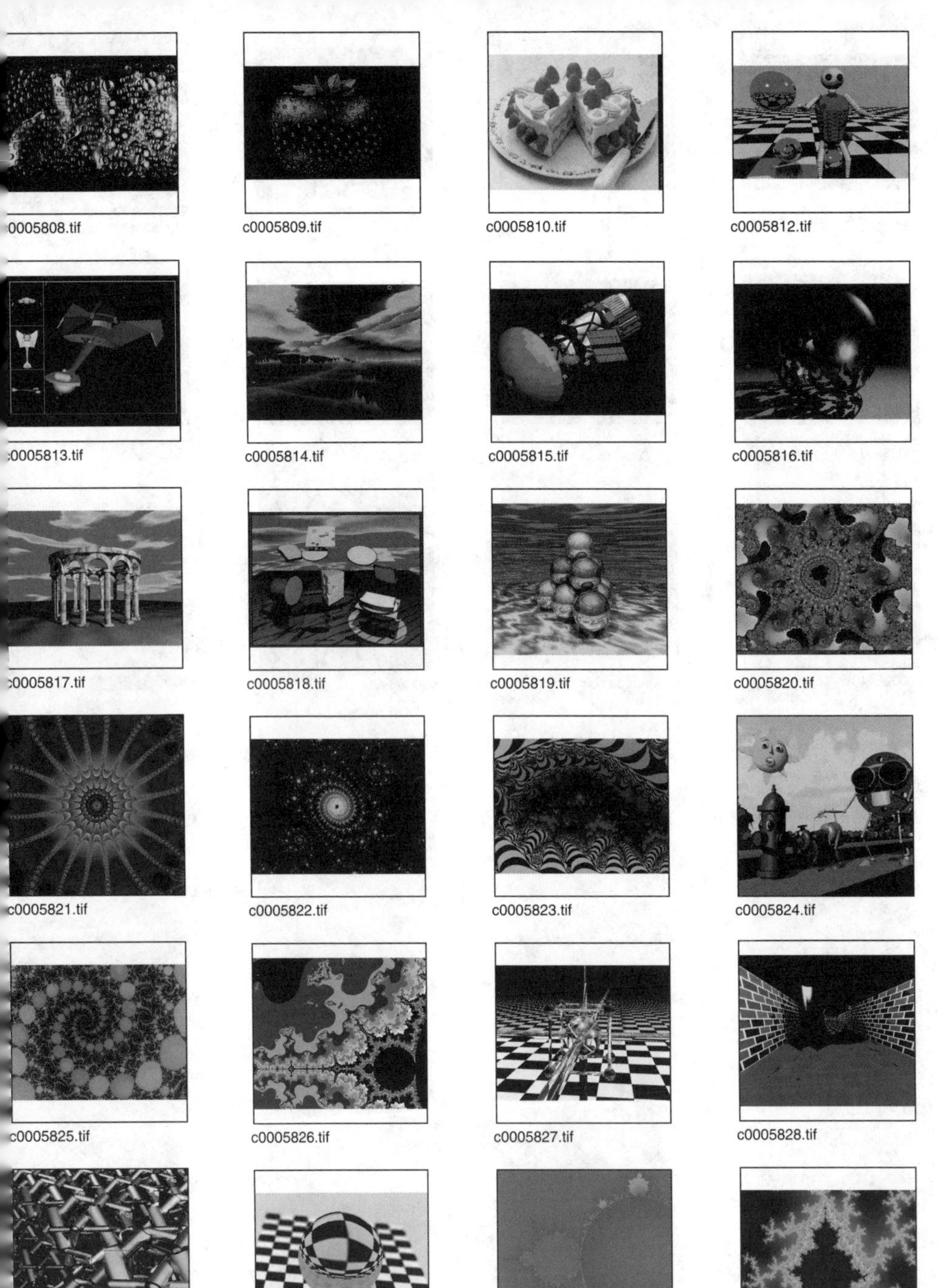

c0005808.tif c0005809.tif c0005810.tif c0005812.tif

c0005813.tif c0005814.tif c0005815.tif c0005816.tif

c0005817.tif c0005818.tif c0005819.tif c0005820.tif

c0005821.tif c0005822.tif c0005823.tif c0005824.tif

c0005825.tif c0005826.tif c0005827.tif c0005828.tif

c0005829.tif c0005830.tif c0005831.tif c0005832.tif

d:\images\trace

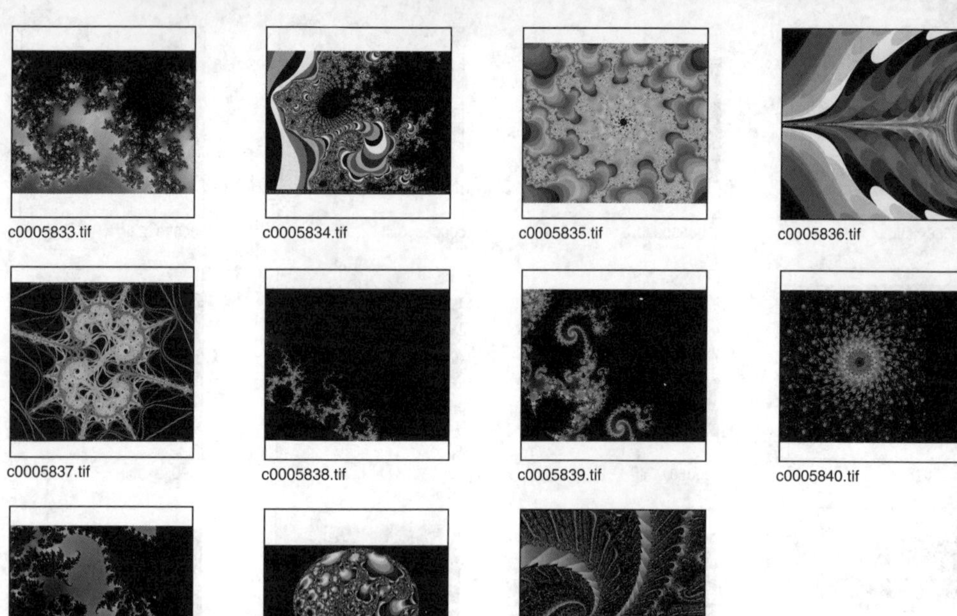

c0005833.tif c0005834.tif c0005835.tif c0005836.tif

c0005837.tif c0005838.tif c0005839.tif c0005840.tif

c0005841.tif c0005842.tif c0005843.tif

c0005844.tif

c0005845.tif

c0005847.tif

c0005867.tif

c0005870.tif

c0005874.tif

c0005875.tif

c0005876.tif

c0005877.tif

c0005878.tif

c0005885.tif

c0005894.tif

c0005895.tif

c0005896.tif

c0005897.tif

c0005898.tif

c0005899.tif

c0005900.tif

c0005901.tif

c0005902.tif

c0005903.tif

c0005904.tif

c0005905.tif

c0005908.tif

d:\images\travel

c0005924.tif

c0005925.tif

c0005926.tif

c0005927.tif

c0005928.tif

c0005929.tif

c0005936.tif

c0005940.tif

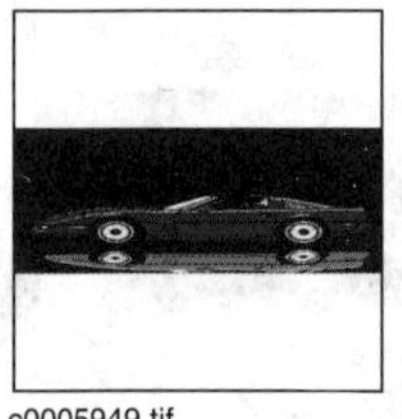
c0005949.tif

m0005846.tif

m0005848.tif

m0005849.tif

m0005850.tif

m0005851.tif

m0005852.tif

m0005853.tif

m0005854.tif

m0005855.tif

m0005856.tif

m0005857.tif

m0005858.tif

m0005859.tif

m0005860.tif

m0005861.tif

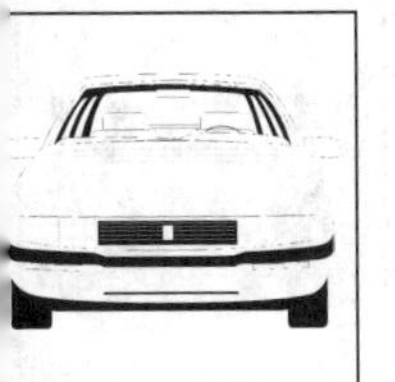
0005862.tif

m0005863.tif

m0005864.tif

m0005865.tif

0005866.tif

m0005868.tif

m0005869.tif

m0005871.tif

0005872.tif

m0005873.tif

m0005879.tif

m0005880.tif

0005881.tif

m0005882.tif

m0005883.tif

m0005884.tif

0005886.tif

m0005887.tif

m0005888.tif

m0005889.tif

0005890.tif

m0005891.tif

m0005892.tif

m0005893.tif

d:\images\travel

m0005906.tif

m0005907.tif

m0005909.tif

m0005910.tif

m0005911.tif

m0005912.tif

m0005913.tif

m0005914.tif

m0005915.tif

m0005916.tif

m0005917.tif

m0005918.tif

m0005919.tif

m0005920.tif

m0005921.tif

m0005922.tif

m0005923.tif

m0005930.tif

m0005931.tif

m0005932.tif

m0005933.tif

m0005934.tif

m0005935.tif

m0005937.tif

m0005938.tif

m0005939.tif

m0005941.tif

m0005942.tif

m0005943.tif

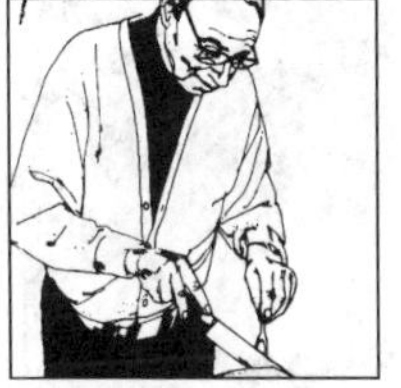
m0005944.tif

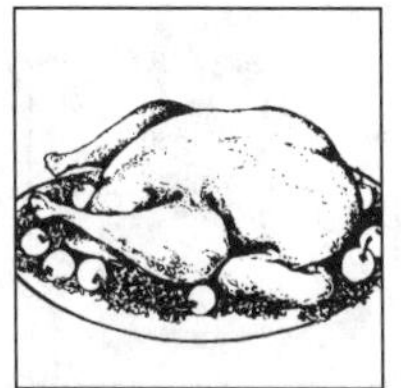
m0005945.tif

m0005946.tif

m0005947.tif

m0005948.tif

m0005950.tif

m0005951.tif

m0005952.tif

m0005953.tif m0005954.tif m0005955.tif m0005956.tif

m0005957.tif m0005958.tif m0005959.tif m0005960.tif

m0005961.tif m0005962.tif m0005963.tif m0005964.tif

m0005965.tif m0005966.tif m0005967.tif m0005968.tif

m0005969.tif m0005970.tif m0005971.tif m0005972.tif

m0005973.tif m0005974.tif m0005975.tif m0005976.tif

m0005977.tif

m0005978.tif

m0005979.tif

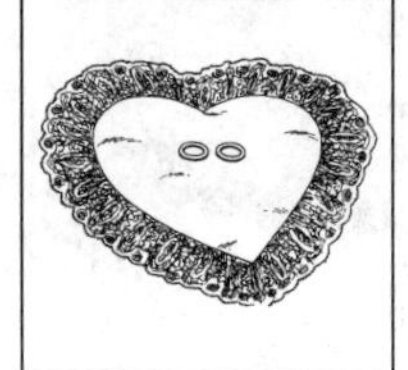
m0005980.tif

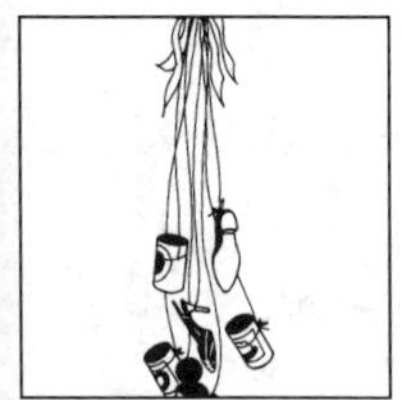
m0005981.tif

m0005982.tif

m0005983.tif

m0005984.tif

m0005985.tif

m0005986.tif

m0005987.tif

m0005988.tif

m0005989.tif

m0005990.tif

m0005991.tif

m0005992.tif

m0005994.tif

m0005995.tif

m0005996.tif

m0005997.tif

m0005998.tif

m0005999.tif

m0006000.tif

m0006001.tif

m0006002.tif

m0006003.tif

m0006004.tif

m0006008.tif

m0006009.tif

m0006010.tif

m0006011.tif

m0006013.tif

m0006014.tif

m0006015.tif

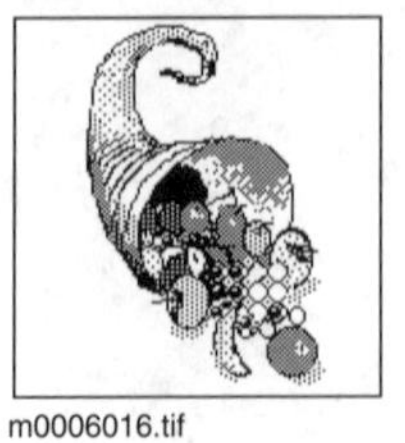
m0006016.tif

m0006017.tif

m0006018.tif

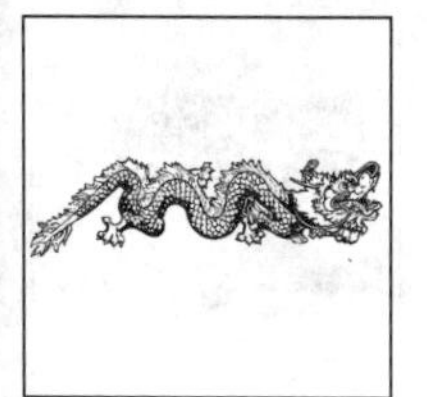
m0006020.tif

m0006021.tif

m0006022.tif

m0006023.tif

m0006024.tif

m0006025.tif

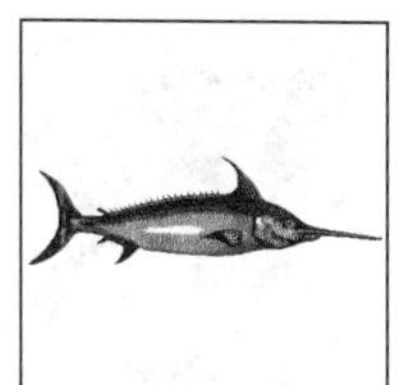
m0006026.tif

m0006027.tif

m0006028.tif

m0006029.tif

m0006031.tif

m0006032.tif

m0006033.tif

m0006034.tif

m0006036.tif

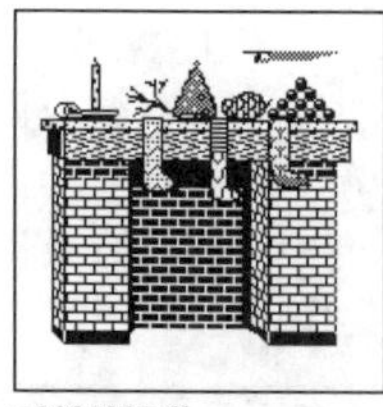
m0006037.tif

m0006038.tif

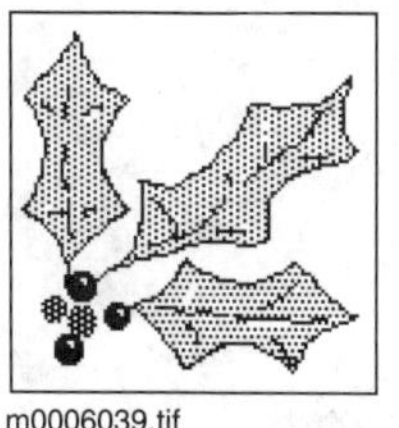
m0006039.tif

m0006040.tif

m0006041.tif

m0006042.tif

m0006043.tif

m0006044.tif

m0006045.tif

d:\images\wpgpcx

m0006046.tif

m0006047.tif

m0006048.tif

m0006049.tif

m0006050.tif

m0006051.tif

m0006053.tif

m0006054.tif

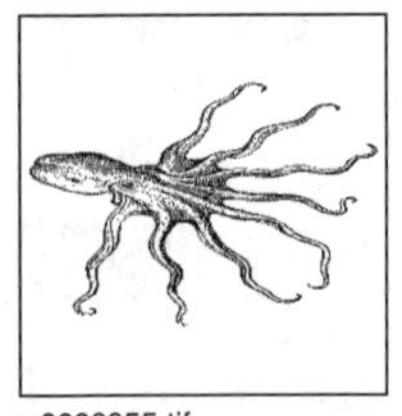
m0006055.tif

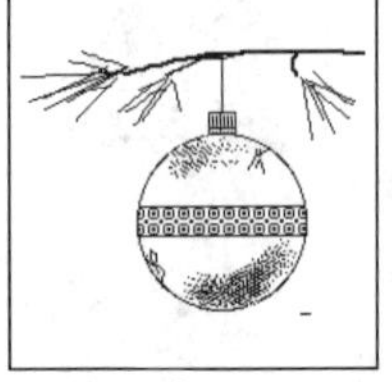
m0006056.tif

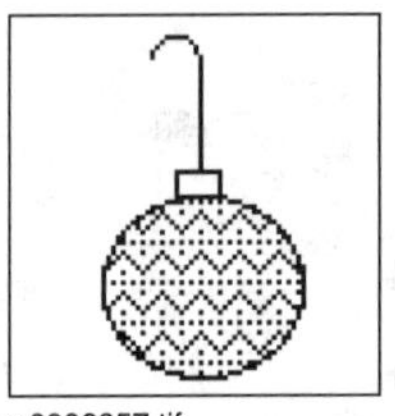
m0006057.tif

m0006058.tif

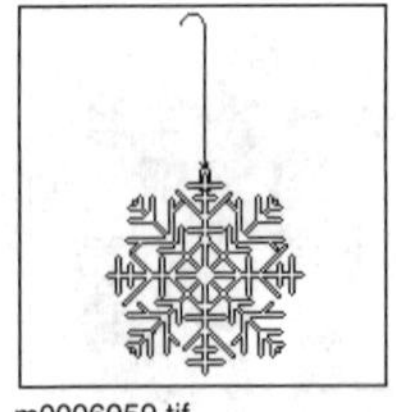
m0006059.tif

m0006060.tif

m0006061.tif

m0006062.tif

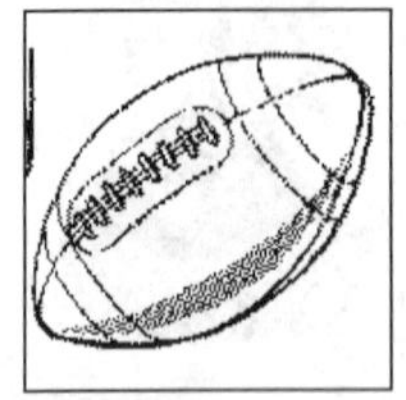
m0006063.tif

m0006064.tif

m0006065.tif

m0006066.tif

m0006067.tif

m0006068.tif

m0006070.tif

m0006071.tif

d:\images\wpgpcx

n0006072.tif

m0006073.tif

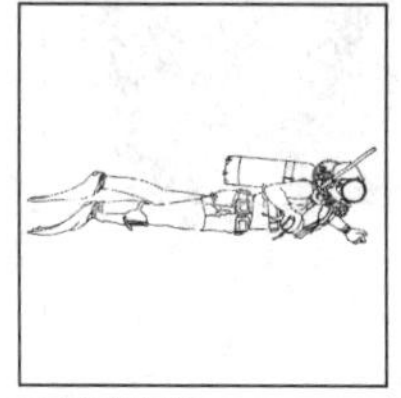
m0006074.tif

m0006075.tif

n0006076.tif

m0006077.tif

m0006078.tif

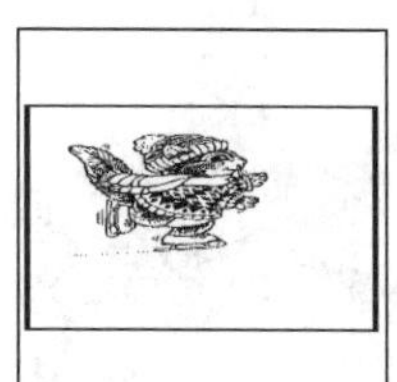
m0006079.tif

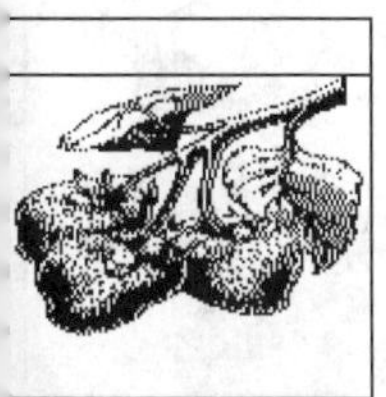
n0006080.tif

m0006081.tif

m0006082.tif

m0006083.tif

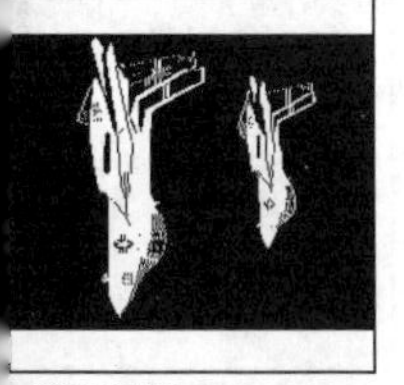
n0006084.tif

m0006085.tif

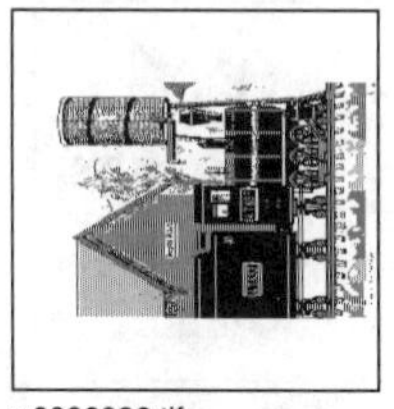
m0006086.tif

m0006087.tif

n0006088.tif

m0006089.tif

m0006090.tif

m0006091.tif

n0006092.tif

m0006093.tif

m0006094.tif

m0006095.tif

m0006096.tif

m0006097.tif

m0006098.tif

m0006099.tif

m0006100.tif

m0006101.tif

m0006102.tif

m0006103.tif

m0006104.tif

m0006105.tif

m0006106.tif

m0006107.tif

m0006108.tif

m0006109.tif

m0006110.tif

m0006111.tif

m0006112.tif

m0006113.tif

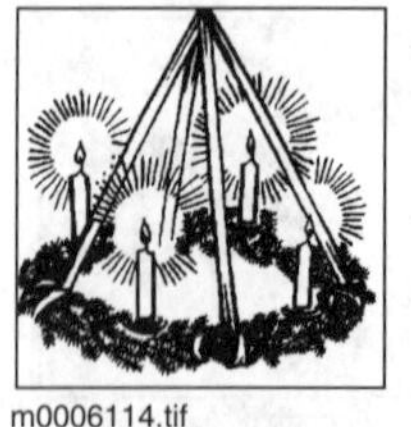
m0006114.tif

m0006115.tif

m0006116.tif

m0006117.tif

m0006118.tif

m0006119.tif

m0006120.tif

m0006121.tif

m0006122.tif

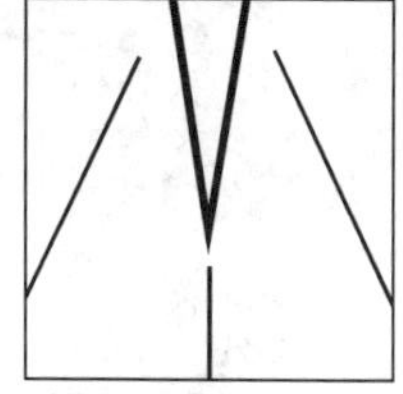
m0006123.tif

m0006124.tif

m0006125.tif

m0006126.tif

m0006127.tif

m0006128.tif

m0006129.tif

m0006130.tif

m0006131.tif

m0006132.tif

m0006133.tif

m0006134.tif

m0006135.tif

m0006136.tif

m0006137.tif

m0006138.tif

m0006139.tif

m0006140.tif

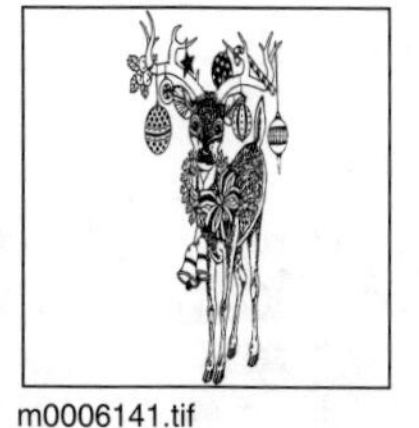
m0006141.tif

m0006142.tif

m0006143.tif

d:\images\xmas

m0006144.tif

m0006145.tif

m0006146.tif

m0006147.tif

m0006148.tif

m0006149.tif

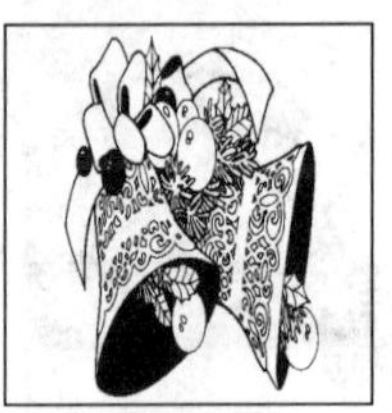
m0006150.tif

m0006151.tif

m0006152.tif

m0006153.tif

m0006154.tif

m0006155.tif

m0006156.tif

m0006157.tif

m0006158.tif

m0006159.tif

m0006160.tif

m0006161.tif

m0006162.tif

m0006163.tif

m0006164.tif

m0006165.tif